Loving God and Neighbor

Loving God and Neighbor

A Guide to Reading, Teaching, and Preaching Deuteronomy

By **George Van Pelt Campbell**
and **Derek Van Pelt Campbell**

foreword by **Will Ross**

WIPF & STOCK · Eugene, Oregon

LOVING GOD AND NEIGHBOR
A Guide to Reading, Teaching, and Preaching Deuteronomy

Copyright © 2024 George Van Pelt Campbell and Derek Van Pelt Campbell. All rights reserved. Except for brief quotations in critical publications or reviews, no part of this book may be reproduced in any manner without prior written permission from the publisher. Write: Permissions, Wipf and Stock Publishers, 199 W. 8th Ave., Suite 3, Eugene, OR 97401.

Wipf & Stock
An Imprint of Wipf and Stock Publishers
199 W. 8th Ave., Suite 3
Eugene, OR 97401

www.wipfandstock.com

PAPERBACK ISBN: 979-8-3852-2372-5
HARDCOVER ISBN: 979-8-3852-2373-2
EBOOK ISBN: 979-8-3852-2374-9

09/04/24

Unless otherwise noted, "Scripture quotations are from The ESV® Bible (The Holy Bible, English Standard Version®), © 2001 by Crossway, a publishing ministry of Good News Publishers. Used by permission. All rights reserved."

Unless otherwise specified, all Scripture quotations in chapter 1 are from the NKJV: Scripture taken from the New King James Version®. Copyright © 1982 by Thomas Nelson. Used by permission. All rights reserved.

Scripture quoted by permission. Quotations designated (NET) are from the NET Bible® copyright ©1996, 2019 by Biblical Studies Press, L.L.C. http://netbible.com. All rights reserved.

Scripture quotations marked (NIV) are taken from the Holy Bible, New International Version®, NIV®. Copyright © 1973, 1978, 1984, 2011 by Biblica, Inc.™ Used by permission of Zondervan. All rights reserved worldwide. www.zondervan.comThe "NIV" and "New International Version" are trademarks registered in the United States Patent and Trademark Office by Biblica, Inc.™

Dedications

John Passmore said, any writing "is made possible only by a series of 'graces,' gifts from others, gifts the author has done nothing to deserve ... For an author to feel proud of himself for what he has done would be absurd. In relation to any single one of these graces he is, no doubt, a co-operator: no one of them, by itself, explains why he has written as he has written ... A deeper exploration of the situation, however, soon reveals how dependent even [his] 'originality' is on other sources of grace, on genetic inheritance, on upbringing."[1]

I, Van, dedicate this book to the memory of my father and mother,
George Edward and Constance Van Pelt Campbell
Whose love, support, faith, integrity, and love of the life of the mind introduced me to all of the core "graces" which have made me what I am;
And to my wife Karen Campbell,
dearest friend and loyal companion who has continued the grace in ways without number and filled my life with indescribable richness;
And to my daughter Joanna Campbell-Totin with love,
and gratitude for her proofreading and editorial help on numerous writing projects.
And to my son Derek Van Pelt Campbell with love,
and gratitude for the privilege of coauthoring this book with him.
And finally, to the God of my salvation,
Soli Deo Gloria.

---

1. Passmore, *Perfectibility of Man*, Ch. 14.

I, Derek, dedicate this book to my father, the Rev. Dr. George Van Pelt Campbell, who by his example truly demonstrated what it means to love God and love neighbor. As a young boy, I was privileged to accompany him on pastoral visitations and to hear him preach the scriptures. I had no idea at the time that God would call me into pastoral ministry as well. I thank my father for first inspiring my love for God's Word and God's people and count it a great joy to be able to write this book together with him as a living out of that calling.

I also dedicate this book to the people of Union Presbyterian Church who accompanied me on a year-long journey of preaching through the book of Deuteronomy and who offered their invaluable feedback, encouragement, and support.

Contents

Dedications | v

Foreword by Will Ross | ix

Chapter 1	Deuteronomy is Beautiful	1
Chapter 2	Positive Statements of the Ten Commandments	11
Chapter 3	Deuteronomy: Loving God and Neighbor	14
Chapter 4	Commandment 1: "I am the Lord your God"	28
Chapter 5	Commandment 2: "No Other Gods and No Images"	51
Chapter 6	Commandment 3: "Do Not Bear God's Name in Vain"	64
Chapter 7	Commandment 4: "Remember the Sabbath Day"	77
Chapter 8	Commandment 5: "Honor Your Father and Your Mother"	97
Chapter 9	Commandment 6: "Don't Murder"	118
Chapter 10	Commandment 7: "Don't Commit Adultery"	130
Chapter 11	Commandment 8: "Don't Steal"	140
Chapter 12	Commandment 9: "Do Not Bear False Witness"	152
Chapter 13	Commandment 10: "Don't Covet"	162
Chapter 14	The Beginning and the End of Deuteronomy	174
Chapter 15	Beyond Deuteronomy	188

Bibliography | 195

Foreword

THE OLD TESTAMENT HAS a mediocre reputation among much of the evangelical Christian church in North America. There are some who know it thoroughly and profess to love its every jot and tiddle. But in my experience, most don't make much of a serious attempt to get to know it, even if we'll soldier through it in a Bible reading plan. Sure, we like the memorable stories: Noah and the flood, David and Goliath, Daniel and the lion's den. We don't mind most of the Psalms or the Proverbs when we're in need of some comfort or counsel. But the rest, well.

The rest of the Old Testament feels like a long and tedious list of rules, doesn't it? In fact, a lot of the Old Testament actually is a list of rules. When we come to certain books, we might feel like we're dealing with a biblical version of that Terms and Conditions window that inevitably pops up before you create a new account or profile online: Ugh, again? Scroll, scroll, scroll. I have read and agree to these terms. Click. Now on to the real reason I came! Jesus and the New Testament.

Yes. That's an easy mindset to fall into with parts of the Bible. Especially with books like Deuteronomy, which is quite literally all about God's rules. And yet, you hold in your hands a book that makes the provocative assertion that God's law—his rules—are good, actually. Lovely. Even beautiful.

Can rules be beautiful? Popular American culture is almost comically inconsistent on this question. At first blush, the clear answer would surely be a resounding No! Rules are burdensome! They limit creativity and freedom and self-expression. They foster guilt and shame. Rules are at odds with self. In fact, rules may even be inherently unfair because rules imply judgment, authority, control, and power. Such things only lend themselves to oppression, certainly not beauty. Therefore, the culture says, rules are Bad Things.

And yet, our popular American culture also obsessively loves rules. At least, we love rules if they are carefully presented and designed as self-care. You are the lord your god. Therefore, you shall:

Practice positive self-talk.

Drink thirty-two ounces of water daily.

Light a candle.

Start a gratitude journal.

Declutter.

Avoid mindless snacking.

Get at least eight hours of sleep.

Try making sourdough.

Get a houseplant.

Leave yourself affirming notes.

On and on it goes. If the fourteen-billion-dollar value of the American self-help industry is any indication, we cannot get enough rules like these. They enhance wellbeing. They deliver us from anxiety and toxic relationships. They improve our lives.

Yes. It's easy to love rules. As long as the rules love us back.

But this is not the kind of life to which we are called in Christ. The purpose of the rules in Deuteronomy is decidedly not commercialistic self-care. It is closer to God-care. As the book you hold in your hands so capably shows, the law of God is lovely, is beautiful, precisely because it expresses the heart of God for his people. God's law is not a prerequisite for becoming part of his people. It is a guide for those who already are. God's acts of redemption mark us out as his own. His salvation gives us an identity. God's law then helps us know what it should look like for us to express our gratitude for that identity before him and others. In that way, God cares for us by giving us a law that shows us what it means to love God and love neighbor.

This delightful volume by Van and Derek Campbell is a warm and pastoral invitation to reconsider how we think about God's rules. His law is no mere checklist of buzz killing prohibitions and tiresome requirements. It's not a lengthy Terms and Conditions statement. God's law is practical, it is vivifying. As it turns out, rules can indeed be beautiful. At least if you have the right relationship with the rule-giver.

Foreword

I'm grateful to Van and Derek for so effectively showing the purposes and character of God in his law. May this book help you perceive the father's deep love for his people all the more clearly through his law for us in Deuteronomy. And may he empower you by his Spirit to walk according to it and to bear the name of Christ well, for your good and for his glory.

William A. Ross
Associate Professor of Old Testament
Reformed Theological Seminary, Charlotte, NC

Chapter 1

Deuteronomy is Beautiful

It all started with that one brief comment. I, Derek, was a pastor at a small church outside of Pittsburgh, Pennsylvania at the time. Our Sunday morning service had just finished and I was speaking with people after church. I honestly don't remember the passage of Scripture that I had preached on that morning or much of what I said. The main point of my message, though, was that God loves each one of us deeply and shows us boundless grace. One member of the congregation, let's call her Jane, came up to me with a scowl on her face. As if to argue with what I had said, she looked at me and proclaimed, "The God of the Old Testament only seems to be interested in doling out rules. I don't see any grace!" Then, she waited to see how I would respond.

Now, I have learned over many years of working as a pastor that it seldom does any good to argue with people. So, instead, I asked Jane if she would be willing to share more with me about why she felt this way. She agreed to come by my office the following week and talk. Well, that one brief comment turned into a two-hour conversation. Jane shared with me about her past experience in church. She had grown up in a different congregation that was extremely strict. They had many rules about behavior and how someone who believed in God was supposed to act and not act. This congregation did not talk about God's love for Jane, but only how disappointed God would be in her whenever she failed to live how they said that she should. She had not experienced any love or grace at that church, only shame and judgment. In addition, Jane shared with me about how that church had used various verses of Scripture not to testify to God's love, but as a weapon to make sure that Jane lived what they considered to be an appropriate life. In listening to Jane share, I realized both how badly God's word in Scripture had been twisted and abused by what she had been taught and also what a harmful effect that had upon her. No wonder Jane had said, "The God of the Old Testament only seems to be interested in doling out rules. I don't see any grace!" Her view of God did not have any place for love, but only shame, guilt, and judgment.

Fascinating, isn't it, and sad, how Jane's perceptions of the Old Testament and God's rules are so dramatically different from those of the psalmist. The psalmist writes the longest chapter in the Bible celebrating God's rules: "Oh how I love your law! It is my meditation all the day" (Ps 119:97 New King James Version, hereafter NKVJ; all citations in this chapter are NKJV unless otherwise specified). Guilt was not his experience with God's rules: "Great peace have those who love your law" (Ps 119:165). Shame wasn't his reaction: "Happy are those . . . who walk in the law of the LORD!" (Ps 119:1).[1] What has Jane missed to lead her to such a distorted impression of what the psalmist found to be the fountain of life (Ps 119:93, 156)? What Jane was blind to was that the God of the Old Testament gave us his law so that we would love and delight in it (Ps 119:47) because it was the source of life and peace—of happiness. Where might we find such instruction in God's law (besides Ps 119)?[2]

A few days later, as I was thinking and praying about this conversation with Jane, I came across a book written by Daniel Block called *The Gospel According to Moses: Theological and Ethical Reflections on the book of Deuteronomy*. I was deeply intrigued and immediately began pouring through it. As I read, it became increasingly clear to me that I needed to preach on Deuteronomy. I wanted to show the people of my congregation the grace and love of God shining through the pages of the Old Testament. It became clear that Deuteronomy was written "to explain this law" (Deut 1:5) by showing God's grace, his love for us, and how we should love him and others, rather than burdening us with a checklist of duties. Why would the psalmist love God's law? Because he understood its depth and beauty. To grasp this is what this book is about.

---

1. The Hebrew word used here means "happy."
2. The suggestion that our book explains why the psalmist loved God's law so much, as Psalm 119 revels in so beautifully, we owe to Ms. Patricia Anders, editor at Hendrickson Publishing.

THE TEN COMMANDMENTS SHOW US WHO WE ARE

Well, what was originally meant to be an eight-week overview ended up turning into an eleven-month deep dive. Instead of preaching *on* Deuteronomy, I ended up preaching *through* Deuteronomy, covering every single chapter. At the heart of that journey through the book was the Ten Commandments, which we find recorded in Deuteronomy 5. I spent twelve weeks of that eleven-month sermon series on the Ten Commandments — one week on each commandment, plus an introduction and a conclusion. I spent so much time on the Ten Commandments because I realized they were the answer to that original comment Jane had made. The Ten Commandments teach us the heart of who we are and who God is. As Professor John Burgess says, "The Scriptures narrate the story that bestows and shapes our core identity. They help us remember God and therefore that we are God's beloved children. The commandments, too, help us remember. Like Isaiah and Romans, they give us identity markers. They tell us who we really are, because they tell us who God really is — the one who delivers people from the house of bondage."[3]

It is my firm belief that the Ten Commandments are one of the most concise and beautiful presentations of the grace and love of God that we find recorded anywhere in the Bible. They sum up the heart of God for his people. They show us who God is. They teach us about who we are and about what our proper response is to the grace and love that we have experienced from God. In short, the Ten Commandments show us who our God is and who we are as his people.

THE DEPTH OF GOD'S COMMANDMENTS

Often when people speak about the Ten Commandments, they do not think about them as revealing God's and our identity, but rather as a simple checklist. Have I murdered anyone today? No. Okay, check on that command. Have I stolen anything today? No. Ok, check on that command. We find an example of this in the story of the rich young ruler in Matthew's gospel. He asks Jesus what he must do in order to inherit eternal life. When Jesus tells him to keep God's commandments and specifically quotes the Ten Commandments, the man replies, "All these I have kept from my youth. What do I still lack?" (Matt 19:20 NKJV). This young man thought

---

3. Burgess, *After Baptism*, 23.

that God's commandments were just a checklist, and so he brashly declares that he has kept all of them. When we view the Ten Commandments as a checklist in this way, it not only cheapens their meaning but also reduces their importance for and relevance to our lives. It limits their capacity to help us understand who our God is and who we are.

In order to properly understand the Ten Commandments, we need to understand the depth of God's commands. We must understand that the commands are not just a checklist, but that these short phrases have infinite things to teach us about God's identity and ours. Ezekiel Hopkins says it well in his classic essay "Understanding the Ten Commandments":

> The words are but few, called therefore the Words of the Covenant, or the Ten Words (Exod. 34:28); but the sense and matter contained in them is vast and infinite: the rest of Scripture is but a commentary upon them, either exhorting us to obedience by arguments, or alluring us to it by promises; warning us against transgression by threatenings, or exciting us to the one, and restraining us from the other, by examples recorded in the historical part of it.[4]

The Ten Commandments are not just a checklist, but they sum up the entirety of the rest of Scripture. Or, perhaps better put, all of the rest of Scripture is an exposition of the truth of who God is and who we are as his people that we find recorded in the Ten Commandments. There is no end to what we can learn from them and no end to the life-changing impact they can have for us as God's people.

Jesus himself teaches us this when he is asked a trick question by a lawyer in Matthew's gospel. The lawyer asks Jesus which commandment in the law is the greatest. Jesus very directly answers his question. He says, "'You shall love the Lord your God with all your heart, with all your soul, and with all your mind.' This is the first and great commandment. And a second is like it 'You shall love your neighbor as yourself.' " (Matt 22:37–40 NKJV). Notice that these two commands correspond to what are often called "the two tables of the Ten Commandments," that is, the God commandments (commandments 1–4) and the neighbor commandments (commandments 5–10). Love the Lord your God (a quote from Deuteronomy) sums up the first four commandments which describe our relationship to God. The second command, love your neighbor as yourself, sums up commandments 5 through 10, which describe our relationship to one another. However, no

---

4. Hopkins, "Understanding the Ten Commandments," 41.

one would ever view Jesus's great commandment as a simple checklist. Far from a checklist, these two commands show us the core of who our God is for us and the core of who we are called to be in response to his love. Our entire lives and identities are embodied in these two commands. We will never finish loving God with all our heart and loving our neighbor as ourselves.

THE THREE-FOLD NATURE OF THE COMMANDMENTS

Fred Rogers once said that "Peace is far more than the absence of war." Mr. Rogers understood that just because a war is not actively being waged does not mean that peace exists. The same could be said of the Ten Commandments. For example, "you shall not murder" has far more to teach us than simply "don't take another person's life." In order to explore this further, we will look at the three-fold nature of the commands. I am indebted in this to Professor John Burgess who proposes this argument in his book *After Baptism*.[5] Each of the Ten Commandments can be understood at three levels. First, the commandments contain a simple negative prohibition, what we will call the negative minimum. Second, the commandments contain a broader negative implication, what we will call the negative maximum. Third, each commandment contains an opposite positive implication, what we will call the positive maximum.

As an example, let us consider the sixth commandment, "you shall not murder." This commandment can be understood at its most basic on the first level, the negative minimum. The negative minimum is that we should not willfully take the life of another human being. We should not murder other people. This is the first proper meaning of this commandment. It is the negative minimum. You shall not murder.

But is this the limit of this commandment? Is the only thing that this commandment has to teach us, "don't physically murder someone else?" No! It contains far more. In addition to the negative minimum, the commandment also shows us a broader negative implication, the negative maximum. If God calls me not to murder my neighbor, then it follows that God also desires that I should not assault my neighbor. If I assault my neighbor, but do not succeed in actually killing them, I still have violated the commandment of you shall not murder. Similarly, if I do not murder

---

5. Burgess, *After Baptism*, 2005.

my neighbor and I do not physically assault my neighbor, but I berate my neighbor with hateful speech, I am still violating the commandment. The list could go on and on. This is the negative maximum.

So, if I do not actually murder my neighbor and I also refrain from assaulting them, hurling hurtful speech at them or any of the other negative things that the commandment implies, have I then fully kept the commandment of "you shall not murder"? No, because there is still the positive maximum. If God desires me not to murder my neighbor, then it follows that God also desires me instead to do good to my neighbor. Caring for my neighbor and seeking their good is the positive maximum of the command "you shall not murder." Each of the Ten Commandments can be viewed using this three-fold structure.

DEUTERONOMY EXPOUNDS THE TEN COMMANDMENTS IN THIS WAY

We can see this three-fold nature of the commandments in the rest of the book of Deuteronomy. After we find the Ten Commandments recorded in the fifth chapter, the next 21 chapters of the book, chapters 6–27, go on to expound on the meaning of the Ten Commandments, one by one and in order. Deuteronomy carefully elaborates on what the Ten Commandments mean and some of the practical applications of them for the lives of God's people. In that long section of exposition, we find that each of the Ten Commandments is expounded according to the three-fold nature of the commandments.

Let us again consider the sixth commandment, you shall not murder. The book of Deuteronomy expands and expounds on this command in Deuteronomy 19:1–22:8. As we look through these chapters, we find that the book expounds on the sixth command according to the three-fold nature of the commands. First, we see an example of the negative minimum in Deut 19:1–13. This section of Deuteronomy clearly lays out regulations regarding cities of refuge. These are places that someone who has killed someone accidentally may flee to so that they are not murdered in revenge. The cities of refuge show the negative minimum because the stated reason is, "And this is the case of the manslayer who flees there, that he may live." (Deut 19:4, NKJV) In other words, these places of refuge are established to prevent someone from breaking the command "You shall not murder" by seeking revenge while they are angry.

We find an example of the negative maximum in Deut 20:5–8 which says, "The officers shall say to the army: 'Has anyone built a new house and not yet begun to live in it? Let him go home, or he may die in battle and someone else may begin to live in it. Has anyone planted a vineyard and not begun to enjoy it? Let him go home, or he may die in battle and someone else enjoy it. Has anyone become pledged to a woman and not married her? Let him go home, or he may die in battle and someone else marry her.'" This broadens the scope of the commandment from "do not murder someone." Instead, leaders of the military are told to allow anyone who is newly married or has recently built a house to avoid fighting in battle where they might be killed. This is a broader application of you shall not murder. More than just being commanded not to murder, God's people are instructed to actively avoid unfair loss of life.

Finally, we see an example of the positive maximum of the sixth commandment, "you shall not murder" in Deut 21:1–9. This section outlines practices for making restitution for an unsolved murder. The town that is nearest to the place where the person was murdered is to sacrifice an offering in order to set things right. This is more than the negative minimum of not murdering. This is more than the negative maximum of going out of your way to avoid unjust loss of life. This is the positive maximum of the command as the people, through their offering, are seeking to right the wrong. Deuteronomy 21:7–8 demonstrates the positive maximum in the words that the people are commanded to say when they make the sacrifice. They are told to say, "Our hands did not shed this blood, nor did our eyes see it done. Accept this atonement for your people Israel, whom you have redeemed, Lord, and do not hold your people guilty of the blood of an innocent person." We see here the positive maximum of the command in that they are making atonement for the life that has been lost.

JESUS INTERPRETS THE TEN COMMANDMENTS IN THIS WAY

Not only does Deuteronomy expound on the Ten Commandments according to the three-fold nature of negative minimums, negative maximums, and positive maximums, but we also see that Jesus interprets the Ten Commandments in this way as well. We find the most obvious example of this in the Sermon on the Mount. Here we find Jesus apply the three-fold nature to the sixth commandment, "You shall not murder."

First, Jesus says in Matt 5:21, "You have heard that it was said to the people long ago, 'You shall not murder, and anyone who murders will be subject to judgment.' " This is the negative minimum. Jesus repeats and affirms the commandment. It is still valid, and still has merit even as a negative minimum. Yes, God still does not want us to murder each other. Jesus's reaffirmation of the negative minimum is made even more clear when we consider that just a few verses earlier in Matt 5:18, Jesus says, "Do not think that I have come to abolish the Law or the Prophets; I have not come to abolish them but to fulfill them." Jesus begins by repeating and reaffirming the negative minimum.

Second, Jesus broadens the commandment. He teaches us that the commandment is not limited simply to not taking the life of another person but has much broader negative implications. Jesus says, "But I say to you that whoever is angry with his brother without a cause shall be in danger of the judgment. And whoever says to his brother, '*Raca!*' shall be in danger of the council. But whoever says, 'You fool!' shall be in danger of hell fire" (Matt 5:22, NKJV). Here Jesus is teaching the negative maximum. The sixth commandment does not just forbid taking the life of another person, but also forbids hate, name calling, treating another person with anger and more. It should be noted that when Jesus says in Matt 5:22, "But I say to you," he is not negating or speaking against the commandment. Far from it. Jesus is broadening the commandment so that we can see the true heart of what is included in the negative minimum.

Third, Jesus goes on to state the positive maximum of the command. Jesus says, "Therefore if you bring your gift to the altar, and there remember that your brother has something against you, leave your gift there before the altar, and go your way. First be reconciled to your brother, and then come and offer your gift" (Matt 5:23–24 NKJV). The sixth commandment does not just forbid us from willfully taking another's life. It does not stop at forbidding anger, hatred, insults, and other roots of murder. Instead, the sixth commandment calls us to do the opposite of murder. The positive maximum of the sixth commandment is that we are to seek the good of our neighbor. Instead of committing murder, we are called to pursue reconciliation.

THE CHURCH HAS TRADITIONALLY UNDERSTOOD THE TEN COMMANDMENTS IN THIS WAY

Not only does Deuteronomy expound the commandments in this way and not only does Jesus teach the commandments in this way, but the church has also traditionally understood the commandments in this way. While we can find many examples of Christians throughout the history of the church teaching the commandments according to their three-fold structure, we will look at an example from the Heidelberg Catechism. The Heidelberg Catechism was written in 1563 and spends a considerable amount of time teaching on the Ten Commandments as a valuable tool of faith formation for contemporary Christians. It was written in a question-and-answer format, which we abbreviated as "Q." and "A." in each section where we discuss it at the end of chapters. Let us look at what it teaches in regard to the sixth commandment, "You shall not murder." As you go through the following questions, keep an eye out for the three-fold structure of negative minimums, negative maximums, and positive maximums.

Q. What is God's will for you in the sixth commandment?

A. I am not to belittle, hate, insult, or kill my neighbor— not by my thoughts, my words, my look or gesture, and certainly not by actual deeds— and I am not to be party to this in others; rather, I am to put away all desire for revenge. I am not to harm or recklessly endanger myself either. Prevention of murder is also why government is armed with the sword.

Q. Does this commandment refer only to murder?

A. By forbidding murder God teaches us that he hates the root of murder: envy, hatred, anger, vindictiveness. In God's sight all such are disguised forms of murder.

Q. Is it enough then that we do not murder our neighbor in any such way?

A. No. By condemning envy, hatred, and anger God wants us to love our neighbors as ourselves, to be patient, peace-loving, gentle, merciful, and friendly toward them, to protect them from harm as much as we can, and to do good even to our enemies."[6]

---

6. Heidelberg Catechism (1563).

THAT'S BEAUTIFUL!

When we look at the commandments not as simple negative prohibitions, but according to this three-fold structure, then they cease to be a checklist and begin to take on substance. When we see the broader meaning of the commandments, then they have power to truly shape our lives and mold our character. They can truly be life changing.

That is what happened with Jane. I began this chapter by telling the story of Jane, a woman in the congregation that I served at the time who told me after church one Sunday, "The God of the Old Testament only seems to be interested in doling out rules. I don't see any grace!" In that two-hour conversation that I had with Jane, she talked a lot about the Ten Commandments and how she thought they showed how God was just a harsh taskmaster. I talked with Jane about the three-fold nature of the commandments and how the Ten Commandments actually demonstrate the depth of God's love for us. Jane began to get tears in her eyes as she realized that she had been believing lies—lies about who God is and lies about who she is as his beloved child. She looked at me and simply said, "That's beautiful!" I can't think of a better way to sum up the depth of God's commandments to us. That's beautiful!

Chapter 2

Positive Statements of the Ten Commandments

Commandment 1: "I am the Lord your God who brought you out of the land of Egypt." [1]

Positive principle summary: We love because he first loved us.

Full positive principle: The most important thing God requires of his people is that we grow in love for him by remembering his goodness to us, revealed in his word; this will bring lifelong blessing as we remember to love the Lord and our neighbors (10:12–22), not the world (7:1–26), and to live by every command that comes from the mouth of God (8:1–20), not our stubborn ways (9:1–10:11).

Commandment 2: "No other gods and no images"

Positive principle summary: Love for God requires exclusive loyalty to him.

Full positive principle: The supreme command about God, the other side of the coin of "Love the Lord" (Deut 6:4–5), forbids cheating on the Lord with other gods and enjoins devotion to him by behaviors which please him, and results in promising blessing.

Commandment 3: "Do not bear his name in vain"

Positive principle summary: Love for God means representing him well.

---

1. We are calling this commandment 1 because we are using the Jewish numbering of the Ten Commandments, which will be explained later.

Full positive principle: Representing God well includes being pure in worship and practice free from external corruption.

Commandment 4: "Remember the Sabbath"

Positive principle summary: Loving God benefits us and others.

Full positive principle: Giving to the Lord what he deserves for his grace brings blessing and joy to individuals and to their needy neighbors, including the blessing of rest. God's commandments are given to bring about our good and our joy.

Commandment 5: "Honor your father and your mother"

Positive principle summary: We love God and neighbor by honoring the authorities he has authorized.

Full positive principle: We show our love for God and our neighbors by honoring those who extend God's authority over us by (1) obeying their directives, (2) encouraging them to do their jobs well, and by (3) supplying what is due to them to sustain their service to us.

Commandment 6: "Don't murder"

Positive principle summary: We love our neighbors by protecting their lives.

Full positive principle: Loving our neighbor honors them by encouraging respect for and protection of life, by discouraging attitudes and actions which might harm life, and by holding people accountable for their actions which harm life.

Commandment 7: "No adultery"

Positive principle summary: We love our neighbors by respecting the boundaries God has established.

Full positive principle: Loving our neighbor honors them when we practice purity in sexual behavior, avoid cultural practices God forbids, and respect the boundaries God has established.

Commandment 8: "Don't steal"

Positive principle summary: We love our neighbors by treating them with generosity.

Positive Statements of the Ten Commandments

Full positive principle: Instead of taking from others, loving our neighbors honors them by seeking ways to be generous to them, as you would like others to treat you.

Commandment 9: "Don't bear false witness"

Positive principle summary: We love our neighbors by treating them with fairness and respect.

Full positive principle: Loving our neighbors honors them by being fair, which means treating them with dignity, respect, and honesty and not taking advantage of them, especially the weak and vulnerable.

Commandment 10: "Don't covet"

Positive principle summary: We love our neighbors by displaying attitudes which place their wellbeing above our own.

Full positive principle: Loving our neighbor honors them by entertaining and endorsing only attitudes which safeguard our neighbor's well-being above our own, especially for the weak and vulnerable.

Chapter 3

Deuteronomy

Loving God and Neighbor

A COMMUNITY CAN TELL us a lot about who we are. I, Derek, am currently serving as the pastor of the Latrobe Presbyterian Church. This church is located in Latrobe, Pennsylvania, a small town about an hour outside the city of Pittsburgh. If you were to ask someone from Latrobe about the city, they would tell you that there are a lot of things they are proud of about their home. Latrobe was home to professional golfer Arnold Palmer, and there are still many things in the city which bear his name. Latrobe is also home to the first ever banana split, Isaly's chipped ham and the Klondike bar. The first professional football team in America started in Latrobe, and every year Latrobe hosts training camp for the Pittsburgh Steelers. Yet, more than any of these things, if you asked someone from Latrobe about their hometown, they would probably tell you about our most famous neighbor. Fred Rogers was born and grew up in the city of Latrobe.

In fact, Fred Rogers grew up attending the church that I now serve as pastor, the Latrobe Presbyterian Church. There are still many people who attend the church that knew Fred and his family well. They remember little ways that he showed them kindness and was a personal blessing to them. Many of the characters on Mr. Rogers long-running TV show are actually named after people from this church. I will never forget the first time that I met someone at the church named Daniel. Over the course of our conversation, I learned that he was the son of the man after whom Daniel Tiger had been named. I felt like I was in the presence of royalty, although perhaps that accolade would be better applied to King Friday. On more than one occasion, I have introduced myself to a new church visitor after worship who informed me that they found out that Mr. Rogers grew up at this church. They wanted to come and see what made this place so special. I have met people from all around the country and indeed all over the world who have come to see the home of America's most famous neighbor.

I personally am part of an entire generation who grew up watching and, in a very real sense, being discipled by Mr. Rogers. I remember many of the ways that his program blessed me personally and the lessons which it taught me. I remember feeling the great sense of peace which seemed to flow from his calm demeanor. There are many things that could be said about the ways that Mr. Rogers's work was truly groundbreaking, in the subjects that it addressed, the technology that it used and the ways that it impacted our entire society. But, among all these things, the thing that most of us probably think of first when we contemplate the life and ministry of Fred Rogers is the question that he asked at the beginning of each episode of his television program, "won't you be my neighbor?" Mr. Rogers taught all of us about what it truly means to be a good neighbor.

And this question which Mr. Rogers always asked —won't you be my neighbor?—is not random or accidental. You see, Mr. Rogers, in addition to all of the other incredible things that he did, was a Presbyterian minister. He viewed his work in children's television as his ministry. As a minister, Fred Rogers was shaped by the biblical story. It informed everything that he did. And the story of the Bible is really the story of two different and equally important relationships, our relationship with God and our relationship with one another, and what it means to live as a part of those relationships. Fred viewed being a good neighbor as so vitally important because the pages of Scripture taught him that God calls us to be a good neighbor as we live together as a part of the neighborhood. When you drive into the city of Latrobe, you will be greeted be a waving Daniel Tiger standing next to a large sign that says, "Welcome to the neighborhood." We[1] believe that from beginning to end, the biblical book of Deuteronomy is saying the same thing, "Welcome to the neighborhood!" We believe that the core theme of Deuteronomy is how to love God and love your neighbor. Welcome to the neighborhood.

---

1. Throughout the book "we" indicates both co-authors.

DEUTERONOMY IS ABOUT LOVING GOD AND NEIGHBOR

It is a startling fact that the first command to love God in the entire Bible is in Deuteronomy. The text reads, "Hear, O Israel: The LORD our God, the LORD is one. You shall love the LORD your God with all your heart and with all your soul and with all your might" (Deut 6:4–5, English Standard Version, hereafter ESV; citations hereafter are from the ESV unless otherwise indicated)." Since long before Jesus's time, the Jewish community regarded this text as the heart and soul of Judaism and as *the* most important text in the Old Testament (hereafter "OT"). Many Jews still recite it daily. It is so important to Judaism that it has its own name, the "Shema." It is called the Shema because the first word of it in Hebrew (the language in which the OT was written) is *shema*, which means "hear!" as in "now hear this!" What they need to hear is that the "Lord is one" and that loving "the Lord your God" is what life is all about. We agree with the Jewish community's perspective on the Shema. Since it is so important, we would expect that Deuteronomy would explain this paramount obligation that it introduces. Indeed, without an explanation, "love of God" could mean anything anyone wanted to make it. In fact, in Israel's world, child sacrifice was how some showed their love to their god, including sometimes in Israel (2 Chr 28:3; 2 Kgs 21:6; Lev 18:21). So, an explanation seems necessary. We contend, with many others,[2] that the book of Deuteronomy is that explanation.[3]

A second startling fact is that "Deuteronomy has more to say about the love of God and love for God than any other book of the OT."[4] Is this not precisely what we would expect if a major purpose of Deuteronomy

---

2. That Deuteronomy explains the Ten Commandments, particularly in chapters 6–26, is a widespread view, as will become clear as our discussion proceeds. And that the Ten Commandments are about loving God and neighbor is also a common view, which will be documented in due course.

3. The command to "love the Lord" occurs nine times in the Bible: three in Deuteronomy (6:5; 11:1, 13), three in the rest of the Old Testament (Josh 22:5; 23:11; Ps 21:33), and three in the New Testament (Matthew 22:37; Mark 12:30; Luke 10:27). The context makes it clear that Deut 11:1, 33, are repeating Deut 6:5, Josh 22:5 says it is repeating the command from Deuteronomy (there's nowhere else!), and all three NT commands are clearly quoting Deut 6:5. It is reasonable to conclude that Deut 6:5 is the fountainhead of which every Bible command to love the Lord is a repetition. (Note that the phrase "love the Lord" as a non-command also occurs elsewhere.)

4. Lundbom, *Deuteronomy*, 310. Lundbom says this having written a 1,000-page commentary on Deuteronomy, our favorite commentary on the book.

was to explain its most striking demand? Does this not suggest—powerfully—that love is uniquely prominent in Deuteronomy because the book was written to explain its most unique commandment?[5] These two startling facts would seem to justify the conclusion that Deuteronomy is *the* OT book about love of God.

We now turn to Jesus's use of Deuteronomy. When asked what the most important commandment was, Jesus answered, "The most important is, 'Hear, Israel, the Lord our God, the Lord is one. You shall love the Lord your God with all your heart, with all your soul, with all your mind, and with all your strength.' " He then added, "The second is this: 'You shall love your neighbor as yourself.' There is no other commandment greater than these" (Mark 12:28–31). The first portion of Jesus's quotation is from Deut 6:4–5, the original Bible command to love God. Jesus declares that loving God is the preeminent human obligation, thus validating the Jewish community's view of the importance of the Shema. In doing this, Jesus asserts that Deuteronomy houses the most important theme in the entire OT. In maintaining the capital importance of Deut 6:4–5, we are again led to expect that Deuteronomy will provide an explanation of life's foremost duty.

Jesus's other quotation (in Mark 12:31) is from Leviticus 19:18, "you shall love your neighbor as yourself." He asserts that love of God must be followed by love of neighbor. But why does Jesus insist that these two things must go together? It has been widely held that Jesus does so because the Ten Commandments, the acknowledged summary of the Mosaic law, does so. It begins with how we are called to relate to God and moves to how we are called to relate to our neighbors. That is, Jesus is summarizing the Ten Commandments more concisely as love for God and for neighbor. But since positive statements lend themselves to more expansive application, Jesus restates the two parts of the commandments with positive scriptural quotations drawn from the Torah. Jesus is explaining the negative minimums as positive maximums to highlight the depth of their meaning.

We believe this is the correct understanding. For example, New Testament specialist Mark L. Strauss comments on Mark 12, cited above, "The pairing of the two commands, to love God and to love others, finds its precedent in the two tables of the Decalogue (Exod 20:1–17; Deut 5:6–21), with the first four of the Ten Commandments relating to love for God and

---

5. The expectation that his people are to love God occurs eight times in Deuteronomy: 5:10; 6:5; 7:9; 10:12; 11:1, 13; 13:3; 30:6. It appears to occur only eight more times after Deuteronomy: Josh 22:5, 23:11; Neh 1:5; Pss 31:23, 97:10, 116:1, 145:20; Isa 56:8. So, Deuteronomy is *the OT* book about loving God (note also Exod 20:6).

the final six to love for fellow human beings (cf. Mark 10:19)."[6] This is no modern discovery. For example, the Heidelberg Catechism, a German document written for church instruction in 1563, discusses the Ten Commandments extensively. In its question-answer format, question 93 asks, "How are these commandments divided?" Its answer is, "Into two tables. The first has four commandments, teaching us how we ought to live in relation to God. The second has six commandments, teaching us what we owe our neighbor." Jesus summarizes these "two tables" about God and neighbor, originally written largely in negative terms, as positives: love God and love neighbor. Jesus saw the Ten Commandments as the particulars of loving God and neighbor.

If Deuteronomy is intended to explain that the Ten Commandments' most important calling is to love God, then it makes sense that immediately after restating the commandments in Deuteronomy 5, a positive summary of that most important aspect would be articulated. The fact that the command to love God is provided in Deuteronomy when it does not appear in Exodus is another indication that *explaining* the Ten Commandments was a purpose of Deuteronomy in a way that goes beyond Exodus.

This understanding is confirmed when we remember that Deuteronomy states its purpose: "Beyond the Jordan, in the land of Moab, Moses undertook to explain this law" (Deut 1:5). Exodus records the Ten Commandments, but a main purpose of Deuteronomy is to *explain* them. The psalmist understood that there is more to God's law than we immediately see: "Open my eyes, that I may behold wondrous things out of your law" (Ps 119:18).

The need for explanation is also made clear by the fact that three of them (5:17, 18, 19) are only two words long in Hebrew (e.g., "Don't murder") and other longer ones are equally unclear at first sight ("Do not take the name of the Lord in vain"). So, explanations are required. Further, after the Ten Commandments are stated, Deuteronomy 5 ends saying that elaboration of the Ten Commandments is forthcoming. In Deut 5:32, when the people leave Moses after hearing the Ten Commandments, God tells Moses

---

6. Strauss, *Mark*, 542–3. Hooker agrees: "these two Old Testament citations sum up the demands of the Decalogue:" Hooker, *The Gospel According to Mark,* 288. So, also, Williamson: Mark 12:29–32 is "Jesus' summary of the law:" Williamson, *Mark,* 225. France concurs: Jesus's two statements "represent respectively the first and second parts of the decalogue:" France, *The Gospel of Mark,* Mark 12:31, Olive Tree e-book edition. Edwards says Jesus sees "love of God and neighbor as the center and sum of the law:" Edwards, *Mark,* Mark 12:31, Olive Tree e-book edition.

to "stand here by me and I will tell you the *whole* commandment and the statutes and the rules that you shall teach them" (emphasis added). Almost immediately we read, "Now this is the commandment—the statutes and the rules—that the Lord your God commanded me to teach you." (Deut 6:1). So, chapter 6 begins the explanation of the law (as 1:5 says) which Moses authored the book to accomplish, in which he teaches them (as 5:31 and 6:1 state) the *whole* meaning of the Ten Commandments stated in chapter 5.

Miller helpfully explains the centrality of Deut 6:4-5, "love the Lord your God," where

> we come to the pivot around which everything else in Deuteronomy revolves . . . It is the first Command of Moses' instruction . . . [It is] as a bridge between the Commandments and the other instructions given in the statutes and ordinances (chs. 12-26). In turn, the statutes and ordinances explicate in specific and concrete ways the meaning of Deuteronomy 6:4-5 for the life of Israel. That is why Jesus can later say that all the law and the prophets hang on this commandment (Matt. 22:40). One may speak of these verses as a summary of the law or of the Ten Commandments.[7]

All of these considerations show us that Deuteronomy is about love of God and neighbor. Deuteronomy's purpose is to "explain this law" (1:5), which, after a historical introduction, is summarized as the Ten Commandments (chapter 5). Next, the explanation (6:1) of this law begins with the most compact summary of it in 6:5: "love the Lord your God." Finally, chapters 6-26 explain what love of God means, and how it expands to include love of neighbor. Deuteronomy explains that love of God and neighbor is what the law means. The apostle Paul agreed: "love is the fulfilling of the law" (Rom 13:10).

Soren Kierkegaard perceptively said that "Life can only be understood backwards; but it must be lived forwards." The Shema reveals in advance what God says life would reveal to a wise person at the end: that loving God is the heart of who we are called to be and how we are called to live. If our thesis is correct, that would make Deuteronomy a treasure because it expounds what love of God and neighbor mean.

But in a sense, the most convincing evidence will be if Deuteronomy itself seems to be doing this. So, let's look further for this evidence.

---

7. Miller, *Deuteronomy*, 142-3.

HOW DEUTERONOMY EXPLAINS LOVING GOD AND NEIGHBOR

Before we discuss how Deuteronomy explains love of God and neighbor, we must address the issue of how the Ten Commandments are numbered, which is more complex than it appears at first glance.

The Numbering of the Ten Commandments

The Jewish community has always called the Ten Commandments the "Ten Words," which is what Scripture always actually calls them in the Hebrew. Exodus first introduces them by saying, "and God spoke all these *words*, saying . . . " (Exod 20:1; cf. also the summary statement in Deut 5:22). They are also called the "Decalogue," which comes from the Greek words for "ten" and "words." The Jewish community has always considered commandment 1 to be Deut 5:6, "I am the Lord your God who brought you out of the land of Egypt, out of the house of slavery." Referring to them as the "Ten Commandments" seems to derive from early English mistranslations which became tradition and stuck.[8] Then, when Christians read the Ten Commandments as "commandments," they noticed that what the Jews always called commandment 1 was not a "commandment," but a statement. This is vitally important because when we think of them as commandments instead of as God's words to us, then it is easy for them to become obligations and demands, instead of statements of who God calls us to be in and through his love. Calling them commandments instead of words changes them: they become seemingly arbitrary dos and don'ts rather than God telling us who he is and who we are.

---

8. The phrase we call the "Ten Commandments" occurs three times in the Hebrew Bible: Exod 34:28, Deut 4:13, 10:4. The Septuagint (the Greek translation of the Hebrew Bible. begun c. 250 BCE), translated the Hebrew as *rhema* or *logos*, meaning "words." The Latin Vulgate (405 CE) translated the Hebrew with *verba*, "words." The earliest high-quality English Bible translation from Hebrew and Greek was that of Tyndale (1525), which translated Exod 34:28 as "ten verses." Coverdale (1535), Taverners (1539), and the Great Bible (1540) replicated Tyndale. The first translation that mistranslated as "ten commandments" appears to be the Geneva Bible (1557), followed by the Bishops' Bible (1568). When the King James Version (1611) also translated "ten commandments" then displaced all other English translations, "Ten Commandments" became an established error. Interestingly, the Catholic Rheims-Douay Bible (OT, 1610), correctly rendered the Latin Vulgate into English by "Ten Commandments."

Deuteronomy

Because of this misunderstanding of the Ten Commandments, Christians felt compelled to renumber the "commandments" so that Deut 5:7 became the first ("You shall have no other gods before me"). But renumbering them led to confusion about how to divide them to get the required "ten" (e.g., Exod 34:28). Christians eventually developed two different schemes which persist to this day. Below is a chart of these three schemes, both the traditional Jewish understanding and the two different Christian understandings.[9]

Biblical Text	Commandment Numbers	Commandment Numbers	Commandment Numbers
	Jewish	Catholic, Anglican, Lutheran	Eastern Orthodox, Reformed
I am Yahweh your God … (v. 6)	1	Prologue	Prologue
Other gods (v. 7)	2	1	1
Idols (vv. 8–10)	2	1	2
God's name (v. 11)	3	2	3
Sabbath (vv. 12–15)	4	3	4
Honoring Father/Mother (v. 16)	5	4	5
Murder (v. 17)	6	5	6
Adultery (v. 18)	7	6	7
Stealing (v. 19)	8	7	8
Empty Witness (v. 20)	9	8	9
Coveting (v. 21)	10		10
Coveting a wife (v. 21a)		9	
Coveting the rest (v. 21b)		10	

We adopt the Jewish numbering as authentic, which is a distinction with a difference. As a building stands upon its base, the Jewish approach clearly makes grace the foundation to the law. Deuteronomy 5:6 begins the Decalogue saying God has taken the initiative and redeemed his people. It is on that basis that God issues his other commandments. It is because

9. Adapted from Lundbom, *Deuteronomy*, 272. See also Kaiser, *Ethics*, 131, n. 14.

God has established a relationship with his people that he issues them further instructions—especially since they agreed to become his people on that basis (Exod 19:1–8). The Christian renumbering often obscures the foundational nature of grace in God's covenant with his people. Like the barked orders of a drill sergeant, the Christian enumeration makes the "Ten Commandments" sound harsh, since all one hears is demands from God. Deuteronomy, however, regularly sings God's grace, as will become clearer as the book proceeds. The Jewish numbering is important because Deuteronomy expounds each of the Ten Commandments (as we will show below), devoting the most space to the foundational statement of God's grace. Contrary to what many people believe, the Ten Commandments are not arbitrary rules given by an angry God who wants nothing from us but obedience. They are loving instructions given to his beloved people so that they might find life in a relationship with him. That's the *difference* that the Jewish numbering highlights. That's the beautiful truth that Jane learned. The love of God, shown in his grace to his people, is the foundation of their loving response to him.

While we adopt the Jewish numbering, for the sake of simplicity we will continue to use the conventional Christian terms "commandments" including for Word 1.

LOVE AND THE STRUCTURE OF DEUTERONOMY

Like an unfolding flower, Deuteronomy unpacks its own elaboration of the meaning of love for God. A key to understanding this is revealed when we grasp the structure of Deuteronomy, which we elaborate in two ways.

First, Deuteronomy was written to explain the Shema. Commentator Peter Craigie is spot-on when he declares that the Shema "is central to the whole book of Deuteronomy," and continues with, "it is in a very real sense true to say that the entire book is a commentary on the command which stands at the beginning: 'You shall love the Lord your God . . . '" He concludes with, the "obedience [that God wanted] would be possible only when it was a response of love to the God who had brought the people out of Egypt and was leading them into the promised land."[10] Old Testament scholar Eugene Merrill draws exactly the same conclusion. He explains that the Ten Commandments explain the essence of a relationship with God

---

10. Craigie, *Deuteronomy*, 169–70. Miller, *Deuteronomy*, 142–3, agrees.

and that "the essence of the relationship is intimated in the so-called Shema of 6:4–5."[11] He sees Deuteronomy's broad structure like this:[12]

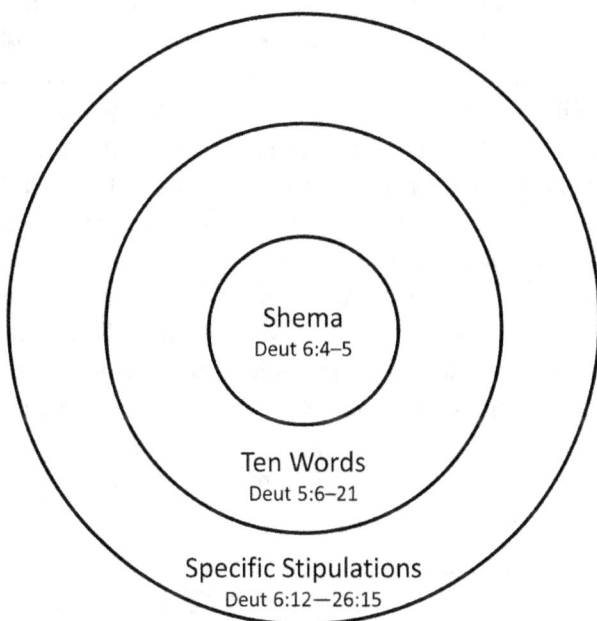

So, Deuteronomy pictures loving God and loving neighbor as the heart of who God created us to be. Living this way is intended to benefit us and others: "that it may go well with you . . . in a land flowing with milk and honey" (Deut 6:3).[13]

But there is a second, more elaborate structure, one which has become clear only in the last century. It is of immense value in understanding the inner working of Deuteronomy. It justifies Merrill's structure pictured above.

Scholars and average Christians were long perplexed by Deuteronomy. The book seemed like "a riddle wrapped in a mystery inside an enigma."[14] It seemed to be a rambling succession of laws, stories, poems and songs (Deut 31:19) with no rhyme nor reason organizing it. Finding order in the

11. Merrill, *Deuteronomy*, 30–31.

12. Merrill, *Deuteronomy*, 31.

13. See the book-length defense of this proposition in the Pauline literature by Charry, *By the Renewing of Your Minds*, 1997).

14. Churchill, *The Gathering Storm*, 403.

laws of Deuteronomy seemed as elusive as dreams. But this situation began to change in 1906 when archeologists discovered evidence of an ancient people mentioned in the Bible called the Hittites. It soon became clear that Deuteronomy was profoundly influenced by the form of a Hittite treaty used in Moses's day (c. 1400 BCE), called a suzerain-vassal treaty.[15] This approach to the book provided an explanation of the *elements* contained in Deuteronomy and the *order* in which they occurred. It became clear that our long-standing perplexity about Deuteronomy was due to our ignorance of the ancient Near East. We hold that Deuteronomy reflects the Hittite treaty form, but that that form is used with a flexibility which (1) suits the author's purposes for Deuteronomy, (2) allows him to incorporate elements which are appropriate to conclude the Torah, of which Deuteronomy comprises the closing section, and (3) permits him to frame the book also as three concluding speeches of Moses, a structure long-recognized in the book.

This chart shows how Deuteronomy fits the structure of a Hittite suzerain-vassal treaty.[16]

Suzerain-Vassal Treaty	Corresponding Sections in Deuteronomy
1. Preamble	Deut 1:1–5
2. Historical Prologue	Deut 1:6–4:40

15. Many scholars have explained the seemingly confused structure of Deuteronomy as a result of successive editions of the book produced over centuries, or layers of tradition, often incompatible, added to whatever was original, and then deduced various criteria for isolating these layers, such as writing style. This approach is not taken here, partly because it is largely speculative. Whatever the prehistory of the text, we have no access to it and no documentary evidence of it. We avoid this approach also because there are other explanations of the data which account for it more simply. The text as it now stands is the only text we have, and we assume that it was crafted by an inspired prophet who intended it to communicate a coherent message. For a brief history and critique of such prehistory scholarship, see McConville, *Grace in the End*, esp. 15–64. For a defense of the unity and coherence of Deuteronomy, see McConville, *Law and Theology in Deuteronomy*, esp. 33–36, 58–67. Many now say that twentieth century ancient Near Eastern treaty discoveries have changed that debate. Wenham (*Song of Power*, 96) concludes that "modern investigation has shown that all parts of the book are a carefully integrated whole." On Deuteronomy as a suzerain-vassal treaty see G. von Rad, *Deuteronomy*, 21–23; Kitchen, Reliability, 492–3. The suzerain is the conqueror-king, and the vassal is the conquered people (or their king). Thus, Deuteronomy presents God as Israel's king and Israel as his subjects.

16. For discussion and elaboration of suzerain-vassal treaties see Kitchen, *Ancient Orient*.

3. General Stipulations	Deut 5
4. Specific Stipulations	Deut 6–26
5. Deposit and Public Reading of the Treaty	Deut 31
6. Witnesses	Deut 32
7. Curses and Blessings	Deut 27–28

Note that all the elements of the Hittite treaty are present, though the "curses and blessings" section comes earlier in Deuteronomy, apparently because Moses did not want to end it there. The material in Deuteronomy 29–30 and 32–34 is added to round out the argument of the Torah as a whole, since Deuteronomy is not a stand-alone document but also the end of the Torah (i.e., Genesis, Exodus, Leviticus, Numbers and Deuteronomy).

The greatest advantage of seeing this structure is understanding the "stipulation" sections. In Hittite treaties, the "general stipulations" section is a brief listing of the obligations ("stipulations") the servant ("vassal") owes to their overlord ("suzerain"). This corresponds in Deuteronomy to the Ten Commandments, showing that they are a summary of the covenant (treaty) obligations of God's people, Israel. The specific stipulations section then elaborates each of the general stipulations with numerous examples to explain in detail what each of the general stipulations meant. This corresponds to chapters 6–26 in Deuteronomy, showing that the bulk of Deuteronomy is an elaboration of the meaning of each of the Ten Commandments.

The chart below shows which section of Deuteronomy explains each of the Ten Commandments.[17]

Text in Deut 5	Command #	Deut Exposition	Topic
Deut 5:6	1	Deut 6–11	"I am the Lord, your God"
5:7–10	2	12:1–13:18	No other gods and no images
5:11	3	14:1–21	Do not bear God's name in vain
5:12–15	4	14:22–16:17	Remember the Sabbath day
5:16	5	16:18–18:22	Honor your father and mother
5:17	6	19:1–22:8	Don't murder
5:18	7	22:9–23:18	Don't commit adultery
5:19	8	23:19–24:7	Don't steal

17. Scholars who adopt this approach have disagreements about the exact limits of the sections. These are ours.

Text in Deut 5	Command #	Deut Exposition	Topic
5:20	9	24:8–25:4	Don't bear false witness
5:21	10	25:5–19	Don't covet

The rest of this book assumes this structure and elaborates each of the Ten Commandments, one by one, in order, by examining how Deuteronomy expounds it. We will devote one chapter to each commandment, ending with a summary of the positive meaning which arises out of how Deuteronomy explains it. We will conclude by showing how the New Testament confirms our conclusions.

Deuteronomy is the first and the foundational biblical exposition of what love for God means. So, it is not a "law book." It is a book about love—love for God and love for neighbor. It is a biblical love letter showing us the depth of what it means to love God and to love our neighbor. It explains the motivations, the mindset, the method, and the matter of love with a marvelous menagerie of models.

WHAT "LOVE" MEANS IN DEUTERONOMY AND THE BIBLE

As a preview of coming attractions, we here survey some of what "love for God" means in Deuteronomy and the Bible. Love means different things to different people. We regularly think of it as an intense *feeling* of deep affection. It is commonly explained as an *action* such as giving to someone else or risking your life to save another person. It has been described as the *choice* to put the welfare of another person above your own, or even to value the life and well-being of an enemy. Indeed, love carries all these meanings in the Bible (see, for example, Gen 29:18; John 15:13; John 3:16; Matt 5:44).

Deuteronomy often connects love and obedience. Old Testament commentator Christopher Wright gets it right: "For Deuteronomy, the command to love is so often linked with the command to obey, in a sort of prose parallelism, that the two terms are virtually synonymous (though they should not be simply identified; 'love' clearly has a distinctive range of affective meaning not entirely equivalent to the practical sense of 'obey'). The simple fact that Deuteronomy's love is one that can be commanded shows that it is not merely an emotion."[18]

---

18. Wright, *Deuteronomy*, 98.

Further, love accompanies fear in Deuteronomy (10:12). "Fear" of the Lord has a wide range of meaning in the book, ranging from terror (5:5) to deep trust. It can mean to stand in awe of God (4:34), and to treat him with reverence, essentially to honor and ascribe worth to him (25:17-19).[19] But its deepest meanings for the believer are loving God, walking in his ways (10:12-13) and exclusive allegiance (6:13; 10:20; 13:4-5). Further, love of God is stimulated by his mercy and grace (Deut 5:6; Ps 116:1), and because of his blessing, help and protection (Deut 4:6; 33:29). Because those who fear the Lord experience his protection, we can say that those who fear God need fear nothing else.

We also grow to love God when we recognize that his laws are given for our good (Deut 5:32-33; 6:1-3). In fact, Jonathan Edwards, one of America's greatest Christian thinkers, and the third president of Princeton University, defined "love," including God's love, as the disposition to do good to others, to be concerned to promote their welfare. It was God's love for his people which caused him to lead them out of Egypt. It is also why Deuteronomy repeatedly states that obedience will make things "go well" for us (e.g., Deut 5:29, 33; 6:3).[20] The psalmist saw this: "happy are those who keep his testimonies" (Ps 119:2). "I have more understanding than all my teachers, for your testimonies are my meditation" (Ps 119:99).

We contend in this book that Deuteronomy is mostly an explanation of what each of the Ten Commandments means, i.e., an exposition of how we are to love God and our neighbor. To begin at the beginning, Deuteronomy begins by stating the book's purpose: "to explain this Torah" (1:5). The Ten Commandments are first presented in Exodus 20, but Deuteronomy was written to explain what those "instructions" (the proper translation of "Torah") really mean. To that task we now turn. We will begin with how Deuteronomy explains commandment 1.[21]

---

19. Block, "Fear of YHWH," 151-54.

20. Edwards, *The End for Which God Created the World*, 439. For a more accessible version, see Piper, *God's Passion for His Glory*, which contains the text of Jonathan Edwards's book.

21. The thorny issue of how to apply the Mosaic law to Christians is addressed briefly in Campbell and Campbell, *Invitation to the Torah*, 138-39.

Chapter 4

Commandment 1: "I am the Lord your God"

Text of commandment 1 in Deuteronomy 5: "I am the LORD your God, who brought you out of the land of Egypt, out of the house of slavery" (5:6).

Commandment 1 expounded in Deuteronomy: 6:1–11:32

Positive principle summary: We love because he first loved us.

Full positive principle: The most important thing God requires of his people is that we grow in love for him by remembering his goodness to us, revealed in his word; this will bring lifelong blessing as we remember to love the Lord and our neighbors (10:12–22), not the world (7:1–26), and to live by every command that comes from the mouth of God (8:1–20), not our stubborn ways (9:1–10:11).

FLOWERS

When I got home from work at the end of the day, I came in the door and saw my wife. She looked tired and worn out. She greeted me with a faint smile and said, "I'm so glad you're home. It has been a really hard day. Two of the kids are sick. I think Billy might have a fever and Susan just threw up all over the bathroom. On top of everything else, my friend Mary called, and I talked with her for almost an hour while trying to take care of sick kids. She is having a really hard time at work right now. Her boss is asking her to do way too much. Anyway, I could really use your help!"

Commandment 1: "I am the Lord your God"

I pulled out a large bouquet of beautiful flowers that I had stopped and purchased for my wife on the way home. I walked over to her and said, "I'm sorry that you had a rough day. I brought these home for you because I thought you could use some encouragement today." My wife smiled and said, "Thank you. It's nice that you noticed I have been dealing with a lot today. These are beautiful, but I could really…" "Oh, you're welcome," I interrupt. "After all, it is my duty as a husband to bring you flowers and do nice things for you. So, I am giving these flowers to you so that I might fulfill my duty and obligations as your husband." The smile quickly vanishes from my wife's face, but I continue, "Not only that, but I also got these flowers on sale! So, I was able to fulfill my duties as a husband and be fiscally responsible at the same time!" My wife begins, "If you really want to be helpful, you could clean the bath…" I plow ahead, "That's not all, though. I know how upset you have been that our gutters look so bad, so this weekend, I am going to rent a pressure washer and really make those gutters shine!" At this point, my wife says, "Honey, can we just talk for a minute? I have had a really hard day and there are some things that I could actually use your help with can you please just listen…" I reply, "Oh, I don't have time to talk right now! There is so much more to do. The lawn needs to be mowed and the basement needs to be organized. Maybe later, if there's time, we could talk for a little bit."

Thankfully, the story above did not actually happen between my wife and me, but it helps us to understand the ways in which we can mistreat God. God created us. God loves us. God sent his son to save us. God desires to have a relationship with us both in this life and in the next. Sadly, though, sometimes we miss God's heart of love and desire for relationship. Sometimes, we can treat God as a taskmaster with a list. We can think that the only thing God cares about is checking his arbitrary boxes. This is perhaps nowhere more evident than when we think about the Ten Commandments. Many people view the Ten Commandments as nothing more than a divine list of duties and obligations, things that we need to check off if we want to keep God happy. However, when we do this, we completely miss the heart of God. The Ten Commandments, Deuteronomy, and indeed of all of Scripture is not listing our obligations to keep God happy and fulfill our duties to him. No. They point us to a loving God who desires a relationship with us. The Ten Commandments proclaim the love of a God who redeems us, who sets us free and who calls us into loving relationship with him. The

Ten Commandments start in love, grace, and freedom, not in lists, duties, and obligations.

We now turn to an examination of the Ten Commandments. Our goal is not a complete exposition of Deuteronomy, which is available in many good commentaries.[1] Instead, we will investigate enough of the structure and meaning of chapters 6–26 to derive a statement of the positive maximum principle of each commandment (summarized in Chapter 2 of this book), explaining its full meaning as it is unpacked in Deuteronomy. Throughout we will devote attention to how love of God and neighbor are elaborated in Deuteronomy.

STRUCTURE OF DEUTERONOMY 6–11

We have already noted that the Jewish community regards Deut 5:6 as "Word" 1, even though Christians use the term "commandments." As already argued, we adopt the Jewish enumeration while using the traditional term "commandment" even for "Word" 1. Commandment 1 is expounded in Deuteronomy 6–11. Commandment 2 also receives some treatment, since it is closely tied to commandment 1,[2] even though it is expounded separately in 12:1–31. Since this may surprise us, here are two reasons to hold that commandment 1 is explained in this section. First, Deuteronomy 5–26 is structured as three units by the phrase, "statutes and rules," which frames the sections and shows that they are expounding the Ten Commandments and their implications:

---

1. Detailed analysis of Deuteronomy is available in the standard commentaries. For such detail we recommend Thompson (1974), Craigie (1976), Weinfeld (1991), Merrill (1994), Wright (1996), Tigay (1996), Christensen (1999), McConville (2002), Block (2012), Lundbom (2013). Our overall favorite is Lundbom: it is the most detailed, quite rich, and excellent on structure, among other strengths. For readers who want to understand the meaning of Deuteronomy for contemporary believers without what they might consider undue detail, the best single volume is Wright. Weinfeld is a very fine contemporary Jewish analysis, though he covers only chapters 1–11, as is Tigay. Our favorites for substantive exegesis under 1,000 pages are Merrill (477 pp.), Block (880 pp.), Craigie (424 pp.), and McConville (538 pp.).

2. It is common to see Deut 6–11 as expounding "You shall have no other gods...", and "You shall make no image..." We are arguing that (1) Deut 6–11 expounds command 1 on the Jewish numbering ("I am the Lord, your God") *and* that (2) command 2 ("no other gods" and "no images") is also expounded here since the two are very closely related (Kaufman, "Structure," 120), command 1 necessarily entailing command 2. This view is taken by Kaufman, "Structure," 110, 118; Kaiser, *Ethics*, 129; and Tigay, *Deuteronomy*, 63.

Commandment 1: "I am the Lord your God"

Chapter 5 is framed by 5:1, 31; it states the Ten Commandments and their reception.

> 5:1: "Hear, O Israel, the statutes and the rules that I speak ..."

> 5:31: "and I will tell you the whole commandment and the statutes and the rules ..."

Chapters 6–11 are framed by 6:1, 11:32; this section expounds commandments 1 and 2.

> 6:1: "Now this is the commandment—the statutes and the rules ..."

> 11:32: "you shall be careful to do all the statutes and the rules ..."

Chapters 12–26 are framed by 12:1, 26:16, 17; it expounds commandments 2–10 in order.

> 12:1: "These are the statutes and rules that you shall be careful to do in the land ..."

> 26:16: "This day the LORD your God commands you to do these statutes and rules."

> 26:17: "You have declared [you will] keep his statutes and his commandments and his rules"

The doubling of "statutes and rules" in 26:16, 17 signals the end of the exposition of the commandments. Deuteronomy explains "statutes and rules" in 5:30–31. There God says to Moses, after Israel hears the Ten Commandments, "say to them, 'Return to your tents.' But you, stand here by me, and I will tell you the whole commandment and the statutes and the rules that you shall teach them." This shows elaboration of the commandments is forthcoming. It is explained as "the whole (meaning of the) commandment (the ten viewed as a unit)" (5:31). The elaboration is called "statutes and rules" (5:31). When Deut 6:1 declares, "Now this is the commandment—the statutes and the rules—that the LORD your God commanded me to teach you," it is a clear declaration that the exposition of the Ten Commandments is beginning.

The second thing that shows that Deuteronomy 6–11 explains commandment 1 is that the phrase, God "brought you out" of Egypt (5:6, 15) occurs eleven times in those chapters and only four times after that section.

Deuteronomy 6–11 contains seven units with the following themes and relationships.

```
┌ 6:1-25: The Shema: Love of God Grows from Constantly Remembering His Goodness
│   ┌ 7:1-26:    Dispossess Canaanites/perish (3x)    Love the Lord        ┐
│   └ 8:1-20:    Possess a good land/not perish (3x)  Remember/Don't forget ┤
│   ┌ 9:1-10:11: You are stubborn (2x)                Remember/Don't forget ┘
│   └ 10:12-22:  Be no longer stubborn                Love the Lord
└ 11:1-25: The Shema: Loving the Lord and his words, and obeying will bring life-long blessing
  11:26-32: Conclusion of Deut. 6-11: Choosing blessing or curses
```

Deuteronomy 6–11 "are the richest instructional, homiletical, and theological materials in the book of Deuteronomy, for they articulate the historical memories and motivations that frame and give context to the commandments to follow."[3] This largest unit in Deuteronomy is framed by two elaborations of the Shema. Beginning and ending this large section with the Shema shows it is the key instruction in the section and shows love of God as the proper response to commandment 1.[4] It is\ followed by a short separate conclusion to Deuteronomy 6–11 which will be analyzed below. The sections between the Shema passages are tightly bound together, elaborating the key subthemes of Deuteronomy 6–11. Note first that chapters 7 and 8 are bound together by a possess/dispossess theme and both mention "perishing" three times. Likewise, Deut 9:1–10:11 and 10:12–22 share a "stubbornness" theme, and while chapter 9 mentions it twice, chapter 10 echoes that by stating it twice in different words: "circumcise the foreskin of your heart, and be no longer stubborn" (10:16). Further, chapters 8 and 9 are differently bound together by a remember/don't forget theme. These two words occur five times in Deuteronomy 8 (8:2, 11, 14, 18, 19), beginning with "remember" (8:2) and ending with "forget" (8:19). The terms are repeated in that order in Deut 9:7. Finally, Deut 7:1–26 and 10:12–22 correspond in urging love for God, though the application of that in chapter 7 is to spurn the Canaanites and their practices while in 10:12–22 it is spurn their own stubbornness, treated in chapter 9. Having

---

3. Brueggemann, *Deuteronomy*, 82.

4. Waltke points out: "Like the analogous Hittite suzerainty treaties, the stipulations consist of the basic stipulation to love the king (Deut. 6:1–11:25), and specific statutes and ordinances that flow from that command (Deut. 12–1–26:15)." See Waltke, *Old Testament Theology*, 483.

Commandment 1: "I am the Lord your God"

examined how Deuteronomy 6–11 is structured to elaborate commandment 1 in detail, we now proceed to briefly show how each unit does this, investigating its structure, content, and positive theological message.[5]

WHAT THE COMMANDMENT MEANS IN DEUTERONOMY 5

Commandment 1 says "I am the LORD your God, who brought you out of the land of Egypt, out of the house of slavery" (Deut 5:6). Again, this is not a "commandment," but it is the first in (the Jewish enumeration of) the Ten Commandments, all of which explain the broad principles of God's covenant (or treaty) with Israel. Renewal of the treaty with each generation was part of the Hittite practice, and here God renews his covenant with the new generation of Israel that has come out of the wilderness wanderings after the exodus from Egypt (Deut 5:1–5).

This is the first commandment because it is the foundation for all the rest. God certainly deserves obedience from all people because he is God. But the stress here is on God's grace that rescued Israel from slavery. God's grace and the gratitude it inspires are the foundation of our relationship with him. God could have pointed out that he formed Israel as a nation when he called Abraham, but he chose instead to focus on his wonderful act of "redeeming" (Exod 6:6) Israel from slavery in Egypt. Instead of being slaves to harsh human masters in Egypt, they now had the privilege of being servants of a far better master, the true God.

Putting God's grace front and center as motivation for obedience in Deuteronomy repeats the same emphasis from Exod 19:3–8. Due to God's goodness, Israel voluntarily responded, "All that the LORD has spoken we will do" (Exod 19:8; see the reiteration in Exod 24:3, 7). This voluntary entering into a covenant relationship is very much like saying, "I do!" in a marriage ceremony. It is an informed choice based upon a previous knowledge of the other person sealed with a commitment.[6] At the risk of sounding like a broken record, we repeat, grace is the prelude and the incentive for obedience. That's why commandment 1 is commandment 1. Craigie

---

5. "Exegesis" is the process of "leading out" the meaning of a text. Its opposite is "eisegesis," reading inaccurate meaning into the text. Detailed exegetical analysis of Deuteronomy is available in the standard commentaries.

6. This imagery is developed in Campbell and Campbell, *Invitation to the Torah*, chapter 6, esp. p. 68.

says, "gospel" [is] placed at the head of the law . . . [God] had acted in love for the people and the obligations imposed upon them in the covenant reflected no less the love of God. This, then, is the context in which the Decalog is to be understood; it was law for a people already redeemed, not designed *per se*."[7] The New Testament sees it no differently.

But what is the source of human love for God? Leon Morris is spot-on: "Our love is a response to God's love."[8] He explains, "in the way we commonly use the term *love* the response cannot be commanded. It is drawn from us by the attractiveness of the loved one . . . We 'fall in love' . . . But we should not understand our love for God in this way. It is different because it is always a response . . . In Deuteronomy it is clear that God's love is the great, basic fact, and that this love awakens a response in those who accept it."[9] Or, as C. E. B. Cranfield expresses it, human love for God is "something dependent on God's prior love, the response of man to God's love, his gratitude."[10] The exodus is the OT paradigm for God's grace and mercy and, until the cross, is the grand illustration of God's deliverance.[11] Commandment 1 precedes commandments 2–10, grace precedes law, and God's love, shown in his redemption of his people from Egypt (Deut 5:6; Exod 6:6), precedes their love for him (Deut 5:10; 6:5). John succinctly sums it up, "We love because he first loved us" (1 John 4:19). The "love" commanded in the Shema (6:5) is a response to the grace of God declared in commandment 1 (5:6).

The term "LORD" in Deut 5:6 refers to God's name, spelled in Hebrew, YHWH (OT Hebrew was written without vowels), and fully spelled "Yahweh." It is God's personal name, not a term for a Deity, and in the OT, it emphasizes his faithfulness to his people. In deference to the Jewish community, which before the time of Jesus had avoided pronouncing "the name," Christian translations adopt the ancient Jewish tradition of substituting "Lord" for God's name. But since there is another Hebrew word for "Lord" (Hebrew *Adonai*), the translators must distinguish the two "Lords" in some way. The common convention is to spell the actual Hebrew word

---

7. Craigie, *Deuteronomy*, 151.
8. Morris, *Theology*, 290.
9. Morris, *Testaments of Love*, 40–41.
10. Cranfield, *TWBB*, 133.
11. Tigay (*Deuteronomy*, 63) explains what motivated suzerain-vassal treaties: "the basis on which subjects entered into such relationships was the past benefactions of the king or suzerain to the subject, often his delivering them from enemies."

Commandment 1: "I am the Lord your God"

for Lord (*Adonai*) as "Lord," while spelling the word that substitutes for YHWH as "LORD" (in all caps, but smaller caps for the letters "ord"). So, whenever we see "LORD" in the OT, it is actually God's name, Yahweh.

HOW DEUTERONOMY EXPOUNDS THE COMMAND

Commandment 1 is expounded in Deut 6:1 – 11:32.[12] Some see this as "the centerpiece of the book," since it expounds the Shema, Deut 6:4–5, as well as commandment 1 (Deut 5:6[13]) It is the lengthiest exposition of a commandment because commandment 1 is the most important commandment.

Deuteronomy 6:1–25: The Shema

Structure and section themes:

A 6:1–9: To foster love of God, remember God's goodness and teach your children

    B 6:10–19: Don't forget or test the Lord

A' 6:20–25: To foster love of God, remember God's goodness and teach your children

Positive message of this section: Love of God grows from constantly remembering his goodness and it results in blessings.

Manner of expounding command 1: Chapter 6 is a chiasm (a form of repetition common in ancient literature with variations on the pattern A, B, C, B', A'), as the similar content in the two outer sections demonstrates. The framing sections establish the main thrust: love of God grows from remembering his goodness, recorded in Scripture. This is especially clear in 6:20–25, which elaborates 6:5–9. The repeated exhortation to "teach your children" is best obeyed by one who resolves, "your servant will meditate on your statutes" (Ps 119:23).

Deuteronomy 6:1–25 begins the exposition of commandment 1 by saying that Deut 5:6 ("I am the Lord, your God, who brought you out of Egypt") should result in love of God because of his goodness to Israel. This is especially clear in 6:20–25. But all three sections focus on remembering

---

12. Kaufman, "Structure," 121.

13. Miller, *Deuteronomy*, 65. Miller is including Deut 5–11 in this statement.

God's commandments and his goodness to Israel. This beginning is the beginning because it is the central idea of Deuteronomy 6–11, and the central implication to be drawn from God's goodness which constitutes commandment 1. In beautiful prose, Moses urges constant preoccupation with God's goodness and his words. The chiastic structure frames (begins and ends with) this message to reinforce it by repetition. The central section (6:10–19) is one unit framed by "the land God swore to your fathers" (6:10, 18)[14] though it has two parts: "Do not forget the Lord" (6:10–15) and "Do not test the Lord" (6:16–19). It examines the other side of the coin: the proper response to meditating on God's goodness (loving the Lord) is the primary defense against doubt, and thus disobedience. Remembering God's goodness is not only a delight; it makes it hard not to fall in love with him.

Deuteronomy 7:1–26

Structure and section themes:[15]

7:1–5: *Possess* the land and *destroy* larger nations
    7:6–11: God's *loved*, holy people, his treasured possession
    7:12–16: God's *loved*, richly blessed people
7:17–26: *Dispossess* larger nations, *destroy* their worship so you are not *destroyed*

Verbal repetition studs the passage. In sections 1 and 4, Israel will *possess* the land and *disposs-ess* (7:1, 17) larger nations (7:7, 17), and will *destroy* them and their means of worship (using three Hebrew words meaning "destroy" in the passage: 7:2, 4, 24, 26 [2x]). The inner sections repeat God's love for Israel (7:7, 9, 12, 13, also using three Hebrew words).

Positive message of this section:

For Israel to be a holy (7:7) people—set apart for the Lord as his treasured possession and richly blessed—she must be untainted by the Canaanites.

---

14. Lundbom, *Deuteronomy*, 317.

15. Lundbom, *Deuteronomy*, 328, documents some of the verbal repetition. See also McConville, *Grace*, 62.

Commandment 1: "I am the Lord your God"

MANNER OF EXPOUNDING COMMANDMENT 1:

Chapter 7 elaborates commandment 1 and commandment 2 ("no other gods") since commandment 1[16] should lead to exclusive loyalty to the Lord. It stresses, negatively, that a holy people must avoid Canaanite worship practices, and positively, that they will possess the land and dispossess its inhabitants.

Deuteronomy 8:1–20: Man Does not Live by Bread Alone

Structure and section themes:[17]

A Exhortation: obey, to inherit the land sworn to the fathers (8:1)

  B Remember the wilderness, a place of humbling, testing, manna (8:2–6)

    C A good land (8:7–9)

      D You will eat and be full (8:10)

        E Exhortation: Do not forget (8: 11)

      D' You will eat and be full (8:12a)

    C' A good land (8:12b–13)

  B'Don't forget the wilderness, a place of humbling, testing, manna (8:14–17)

---

16. The command to "destroy" the Canaanites raises ethical questions. Ancient Jewish scholars took the command as hyperbole: it didn't actually demand killing them all but emphasized being untainted by them. Christians have normally taken it straightforwardly and have tried to explain the hard questions about the killing by pointing out such things as God commanded it as his judgment on the Canaanites' sin (Gen 15:16), that it applied only to foreigners *in the land*, and that it is not authorized for contemporary Christians. On the Jewish history of interpretation, see Tigay, *Deuteronomy*, esp. Excursus 18. For Christian considerations which help explain this challenge, see Block, *Deuteronomy*, 218-22, and Copan, *Moral Monster*, 158-197. Wright argues something like the ancient Jewish approach: "A better explanation seems to be that it is an absolute and irrevocable renouncing of things or persons, a refusal to take any gain or profit from them" (Wright, *Deuteronomy*, 109; Copan agrees, *Moral Monster*, 168-85). The strongest argument in favor of Wright's view is that the command is immediately followed by instructions that are unnecessary if the Canaanites were dead, i.e., it seems to assume they are not killed. See further, Gundry, *Show them No Mercy*.

17. Adapted from Wright, *Deuteronomy*, 121.

A′ Exhortation: Remember God, to confirm the covenant sworn to the fathers (8:18–20)

Craigie calls attention to two "double themes:" (a) remember/forget and (b) wilderness/promised land, which are oft repeated and are closely interwoven.[18]

Positive message of this section: Do not forget that man does not live by bread alone (8:3).

Manner of expounding command 1:

Chapter 8 elaborates commandment 1 by providing an extended meditation on God's goodness when he brought Israel "out of the land of Egypt, out of the house of slavery" (8:14, repeating 5:6). It illustrates how to "remember" (8:2, 18) God's goodness. It also belabors God's goodness in many good gifts and provisions for his people during that time. The takeaways are to remember (and not forget) God's many good gifts and to obey him (8:2, 6, 11, 20). Chapter 8 also elaborates commandment 2 (8:19): going after other gods will spoil the rich blessing of God.

Deuteronomy 9:1–10:10

Structure and section themes:

Moshe Weinfeld observes that "This section revolves around the concept of the miraculous 'forty days and forty nights' spent by Moses on the mount of God."[19] This exact phrase occurs in 9:9, 11, 18, 25; 10:10, each introducing a new paragraph, but nowhere else in the book. This establishes the boundaries of the sections.

>9:1–8: Inheriting the land, but "not because of your righteousness" (3x: 9:4, 5, 6)
>>9:9–10: forty days and forty nights to establish the covenant
>>9:11–17: the forty days and forty nights ended with the covenant annulled[20]

---

18. Craigie, *Deuteronomy*, 184.
19. Weinfeld, *Deuteronomy*, 426, adapted.
20. Lundbom, *Deuteronomy*, 370; McConville, *Deuteronomy*, 184.

Commandment 1: "I am the Lord your God"

9:18–24: forty days and forty nights of intersession that God not destroy Israel

9:25–10:9: forty days and forty nights of intersession to renew the covenant[21]

10:10–11: Inheriting the land because the Lord was unwilling to destroy you

Positive message of this section:

God blesses his people in spite of their stubbornness because of his promises and his reputation.

Manner of expounding commandment 1:

This long passage has two emphases. The bulk of the passage fixates on Israel's continual stubbornness (9:6, 13) and rebelliousness (9:7, 23, 24). Exhibit A is the golden calf incident discussed in Deut 9:12–21 (the story is found in Exod 32). In other words, we have met the enemy, and it turns out to be us. The core issue behind this is stated in 9:23: Israel did not believe God.[22] So grievous was this to God that it annulled the covenant with Israel and God considered destroying the nation (9:3, 14, 19, 25, 26; 10:10). The second preoccupation of the passage is *why* God did not destroy Israel but renewed the covenant: (a) Moses's intersession, which reminded God of (b) his promise to their fathers (9:5, 27), and (c) his reputation (9:27–29).

This section expounds commandment 1 by showing that despite God's grace and faithfulness, Israel's default position is unbelief, resulting in stubborn rebellion. It seems that God's people are willing to disbelieve, wanting to disbelieve, waiting to disbelieve. But the value of our bearing this truth in mind is that it can help us to skip straight to obedience.

The text also expounds commandment 1 by showing that despite the nation's unbelief and resultant stubbornness, God's grace and faithfulness is persistent and is greater than Israel's sin. Stated positively, "blessing is a product of grace."[23] The passage also expounds commandment 2 by showing that unbelief tends toward breaking the first and primary commandment

---

21. Thompson, *Deuteronomy*, 144; Lundbom, *Deuteronomy*, 381.

22. Note the same assessment by God of Moses's disobedience in Num 20:1–12: the root cause was disbelief.

23. Merrill, *Deuteronomy*, 188.

regarding God: no graven images. Trust is a must for blessing, but not for God's faithfulness to his promises.

Deuteronomy 10:12–22

Structure and section themes:

The unit is framed by the phrase, "and now" (1:12, 22b) associated with commands to fear the Lord, thus forming an *inclusio* (an ancient literary device which begins and ends a passage the same way to mark its boundaries)[24]

> 10:12-13   And now, Fear the Lord
>
> 10:20-22   Fear the Lord, and now

Lundbom shows the passage is structured around four imperatives, each followed by a reason:[25]

> Command: 10:12-13, Fear the Lord
>   Reason: 10:14, Because the Lord owns the earth and chose you
> Command: 10:16, Circumcise your heart
>   Reason: 10:17-18, Because the Lord is great, unbribable and executes justice
> Command: 10:19a, Love the sojourner
>   Reason: 10:19b, Because the Lord loves the sojourner, and you were a sojourner
> Command: 10:20, Fear the Lord
>   Reason: 10:21-22, Because God is your praise who has done great things for you

Note that the opening and closing imperatives seem to be parallel in that both include five parts:

> 10:12-13: Fear, walk, love, serve, keep.
>
> 10:20-22: Fear, serve, hold fast, swear, praise.

---

24. Lundbom, *Deuteronomy*, 389.
25. Lundbom, *Deuteronomy*, 388-89.

Commandment 1: "I am the Lord your God"

Positive message of this section:

What God requires of Israel is to fear the Lord by loving him, walking in his ways, and loving their needy neighbors because of his awesome character and his goodness.

Manner of expounding commandment 1:

The structure and the alternating of commands with reasons makes the message clear: God's people should fear the Lord because of who he is and what he has done for them.

Craigie recognizes that this section "may be seen as a positive sermon on the negatively stated first commandment: 'You shall not have other gods besides me.' "[26] Strengthening this conclusion, 10:20 is almost an exact quote of Deut 6:13, which adds to it (6:14), "You shall not go after other gods." But, as we noted above, commandment 2 is closely tied to commandment 1. The first duty commanded in Deut 10:12 is to "fear the Lord." The fear of the Lord was last commanded in Deuteronomy 6 where it expounded commandment 1. The mention of Egypt (5:6; 10:19, 22) reinforces this conclusion. In exquisite language, this section echoes many themes from Deuteronomy 6–10 and restates four imperatives which arise from commandments 1 and 2. It buttresses them with reasons that motivate obedience: first, because of God's greatness (10:14, 17–18) then because of his goodness to Israel in liberating them from Egypt and keeping his promises to them (10:19b, 21–22). This passage says when we come to forks in the road, take the fork labelled "fear the Lord," not "stubbornness" (10:16).

Deuteronomy 11:1–25: The Shema Repeated

Structure and section themes: Deuteronomy 11 has two sections: 11:1–17 and 11:18–25.

The first passage (11:1–17) is a chiasm:

    11:1: love and keep
        11:8: keep
    11:13: keep and love

26. Craigie, *Deuteronomy*, 204, adapted.

A more detailed structure is as follows.[27]

> 11:1: Requirement = love God and keep his commandments
>> 11:2–7: Reason: God's wonders shown in Egypt and the wilderness
>>> 11:8: Requirement = keep the commandments
>>> 11:9–12: Reason: to inherit a land better than Egypt
>> 11:13: Requirement = keep the commandments and serve God
> 11:14–17: Reason: to experience blessing in the land

Positive message of this section:

Believers should love God and keep his commandments to experience blessing.

Manner of expounding commandment 1:

The message of this text is that believers should love God and keep his commandments to experience blessing. *The* blessing in view is inheriting the promised land by God's power and experiencing blessing there. The word "land" occurs 11 times in these 17 verses. The text elaborates upon commandment 1 as Deuteronomy 6 does: by connecting the obedience which grows from God's grace and mercy (Deut 5:6) with long life and blessing in the land (e.g., Deut 6:1–3). It is "a land flowing with milk and honey" (Deut 6:3; 11:9), a phrase that occurs only in these passages until it recurs several times at the end of the book.

The second unit is 11:18–25.

Structure and section themes:

Lundbom observes the striking feature of this passage: it repeats the words which elaborate the Shema "from 6:6–9, making an *inclusio* with chs. 6–11," though the major elements are reversed in order.[28] So 11:18–25 is the formal conclusion of Deuteronomy 6–11, though it will be followed by a conclusion which parallels this section with the next one, Deuteronomy

---

27. Craigie, *Deuteronomy*, 207–08.
28. Lundbom, *Deuteronomy*, 407. So also, Weinfeld, *Deuteronomy*, 448.

Commandment I: "I am the Lord your God"

12–16. Because the text elaborates the Shema in Deuteronomy 6, "these words" that are to be upon the heart of God's people (11:18) are the Shema (Deut 6:4–5).[29] In fact, Deut 11:18 restates Deut 6:6:

> Deut 6:6: these words that I command you today shall be on your heart
>
> Deut 11:18: You shall therefore lay up these words of mine in your heart

Thus, the Shema and its elaboration frames Deuteronomy 6–11 and serves as the statement of the section's essence. Meditating on God's grace and goodness should increase our love for him.

Deuteronomy 11 repeats Deuteronomy 6, but in reverse order, as the chart below shows.

Structure of Deut 6:1–25	Structure of Deut 11:1–25
A: 6:1–9: your days long, words on your heart, teach your children, frontlets	C': 11:1–7 Obey, remembering God's goodness in Egypt and the wilderness
B: 6:10–19: In the good land, don't forget the Lord, no other gods, so you don't lose the land	B': 11:8–17: Life in a land of milk & honey; obedience > rain, etc., but don't turn lest you lose the land
C: 6:20–25: God's goodness in Egypt and the wilderness, so obey!	A': 11:18–25: words on your heart, frontlets, teach your children, your days multiplied

Positive message of this section: Loving the Lord and his words will bring lifelong blessing.

Manner of Expounding commandment I:

Parallel to Deuteronomy 6, chapter 11 ends the exposition of commandment 1 by saying that Deut 5:6 ("I am the Lord, your God, who brought you out of Egypt") should result in love of God because of his goodness to Israel. But while chapter 6 shows that connection by teaching us "to foster love of God, remember God's goodness," chapter 11:18–25 assumes that connection and concentrates on the results that follow from meditating on God's goodness. It promises conquest of the land and long life in it. Thus, it expounds commandment 1 by focusing on the long-term results which eventually flow from it. For contemporary Christians, this equates

---

29. Merrill, *Deuteronomy*, 210.

to lifelong blessing. The lie that blessing comes from disobedience is as old as the Garden of Eden (Gen 3:4), but Deuteronomy is trying to convince us that obedience to the lover of our souls is the road to life and blessing.

Deuteronomy 11:26–32: Conclusion of Deut 6–11: Choosing blessing or cursing

Structure and section themes:

Deuteronomy 11:26–32 is framed by the phrase "I am setting before you today" (11:26, 32), which is literally the opening and the closing phrase of the section.

Positive message of this section:

God's history with his people should motivate us to choose blessing by obeying him.

MANNER OF EXPOUNDING COMMANDMENT 1:

This closing section of Deuteronomy 6–11 serves two functions in the structure of the book. First, it is a fitting conclusion to Deuteronomy 6–11. It ends the unit where it began, declaring the centrality of obeying "the statutes and the rules" (6:1; 11:32). Second, it ends the exposition of commandment 1 with the same conclusion that summarizes Deuteronomy: choose blessing rather than a curse (11:26; 30:11–20) by choosing to obey the Lord. Deuteronomy 6–11 has argued that the proper response to God's mercy and grace (Deut 5:6) is to love the Lord (Deut 6:5; 11:1), which results in obedience (6:1–4; 11:27, 32). This unit concludes the exposition of commandment 1 by emphasizing that the result of obedience is blessing, restating Deut 6:3, "that it may go well with you." It also concludes its exposition of commandment 2 by summarizing the proper response to God's mercy and grace (Deut 5:6): exclusive devotion to the Lord (11:28, do not "go after other gods"; cf. 5:7).

We may summarize Deuteronomy 6–11, restating the message of each passage:

6:1–25: The Shema: love of God grows from constantly remembering his goodness

7:1–26: A holy people must be untainted by the world

8:1–20: Do not forget that man does not live by bread alone

9:1–10:11: Despite our stubbornness, God is faithful to his promises

10:12–22: What God requires of his people is loyalty and loving our needy neighbors

11:1–25: The Shema: Loving the Lord and his words and obeying brings lifelong blessing

11:26–32: Conclusion of Deuteronomy 6–11: Believers must choose blessing or cursing

WHAT COMMANDMENT 1 MEANS AS A POSITIVE PRINCIPLE FOR CONTEMPORARY CHRISTIANS

Commandment 1 begins the Ten Commandments because it is the foundation. The framing of the section by the Shema answers that, communicating that love of God grows from constantly remembering his goodness and that the result of that is long-term blessing. The conditions or blessings that elaborate this are, in order, being untainted by the world (chapter 7), living by the words of God (chapter 8), recognizing our tendency to stubbornness (9:1–10:11), and remembering that God wants absolute loyalty and loving our needy neighbors (10:12–22).

In summary, a detailed positive principle statement of commandment 1 can be articulated as: The most important thing God requires of his people is that we grow in love for him by remembering his goodness to us, revealed in his word; this will bring lifelong blessing as we remember to love the Lord and our neighbors (10:12–22), not the world (7:1–26), and to live by every command that comes from the mouth of God (8:1–20), not our stubborn ways (9:1–10:11).

A briefer summary of the positive message of commandment 1 is: God's love for us spurs love for him, which shows in obedience and brings well-being.

The most succinct statement of the positive principle is, *We love because he first loved us* (see 1 John 4:19).[30] This positive statement is elaborated in Deuteronomy 6–11 by these key emphases: (1) God's love for his people inspires his people's love for him; (2) love for God is demonstrated by obedience to his commands; (3) a further motive for obedience is understanding that God's commands serve our good, as the psalmist trumpets throughout Psalm 119; (4) loving God inspires love for our needy neighbors.

For contemporary Christians, the meaning is clear: choose life! The psalmist knew where to find life: "I will never forget your precepts, for by them you have given me life" (Ps 119:93). This is also the main application of Deuteronomy as a whole: it was written "to explain" God's laws (Deut 1:5), and it states as much at the end of the book:

> I call heaven and earth to witness against you today, that I have set before you life and death, blessing and curse. Therefore choose life, that you and your offspring may live, loving the LORD your God, obeying his voice and holding fast to him, for he is your life and length of days, that you may dwell in the land that the LORD swore to your fathers, to Abraham, to Isaac, and to Jacob, to give them (Deut 30:19–20).

Toward the conclusion of Deuteronomy, we find Moses speaking to the people of Israel. He gives them the instructions above, telling them, "Now choose life." The entire book of Deuteronomy in many ways comes down to this simple command to choose life and not death. Likewise, the intent of the book that you are currently reading is not simply to be an academic exercise or to put forth sound scholarship about Deuteronomy, although that is certainly important. The intent of this book is to help God's people "choose life" through seeing the beauty and grace of God shining forth in the pages of Deuteronomy. The psalmist commended God's law for

---

30. The King James Version (1611) translated, "We love *him* because he first loved us." While that is true, the best manuscripts do not contain the word "him," as reflected in the newer translations (such as NIV and ESV). Bruce explains, "But in context 'we love' is the more suitable reading as it is the better attested one. We love God, it is true, but in loving God we inevitably love his children. In taking the initiative in loving us, he not only showed us how to love one another (cf. 3:11), but he imparted the desire and the power to follow this example of his. Our Lord made it plain that the two great Old Testament commandments of love to God and love to one's neighbor are two sides of one coin (Mark 12:29–31)" (Bruce, *Epistles of John*, 114.) Bruce's last observation suggests what we believe: Deuteronomy is the basis of John's statement in 1 John 4:19.

just this purpose: "Your word is a lamp to my feet and a light to my path" (Ps 119:105).

Remember also that Moses wrote these words out of his own bitter experience of choosing death rather than life. The low point of his life is recorded in Num 20:1–11. There he chose poorly. Overcome by fury at his continually difficult people, he struck the rock to which God had instructed him to speak, instantly earning a one-way ticket back from the brink of the promised land to a grave outside it. What he had dreamed of all his adult life was suddenly and unalterably taken away. He had traded life in a land "flowing with milk and honey" for death in a wilderness. His unbelief led to disobedience and death, rather than life (Num 20:12). It is his own galling experience that he pleads with his people to avoid. Winston Churchill once said that history would be kind to him because he intended to write it—which he did. Moses also wrote his own history; however, his goal was not to make the record reflect well on him, but to repent in print! Baring his soul, he sought to stun his audience with the cruel impact of his own unbelief, imploring them to instead "choose life."

Commandment 1 uses God's love and grace, displayed in the exodus, to motivate gratitude, love, and obedience to the Lord. But a display of God's love and grace greater than the exodus captures the heart of God's New Testament people. Merrill explains:

> For the Christian the moment of greatest significance is no longer creation or the exodus—as important as these are in salvation history. Central to his faith and experience is the resurrection of the Lord Jesus Christ, a re-creating and redemptive event that eclipses all of God's mighty acts of the past.[31]

Thus, the New Testament ("NT") does not reiterate commandment 1 in its OT form. Instead, it cites the life, death, and resurrection of Jesus as the greatest proofs of God's love and grace (e.g., John 3:16). The NT continues the OT idea that God's love and grace motivate love of God and obedience to him, but the proof is God's greatest act in history, the redemption brought by Jesus. John wrote, "In this is love, not that we have loved God but that he loved us and sent his Son to be the propitiation [satisfaction] for our sins." The love and grace of God are magnified in the NT, as they were in commandment 1 of the OT. But the exodus has been eclipsed by Jesus's redemption.

---

31. Merrill, *Deuteronomy*, 152.

To assist believers in choosing life, as Deuteronomy urges, each of the chapters that expound one of the Ten Commandments will end with the Heidelberg Catechism statement about the commandment followed by two sets of questions for the reader to consider. These questions are aimed at two specific groups: individuals for private devotional use, and Bible study leaders and pastors for expounding Deuteronomy. It is our hope that these questions at the end of each chapter will help you to "choose life."

The Heidelberg Catechism was organized according to the Reformed numbering of the commandments, so it has nothing for our commandment 1. But because commandment 1 is about the grace of God that calls forth our gratitude, and because the OT example of that grace is eclipsed by Christ's cross, we cite here the Introduction of the Heidelberg Catechism. Intended for youth to memorize, the catechism consists of questions followed by their answers.

HEIDELBERG CATECHISM

Q. What is your only comfort in life and in death?

A. That I am not my own, but belong body and soul, in life and in death to my faithful Savior, Jesus Christ. Christ has fully paid for all my sins with his precious blood, and has set me free from all the power of the devil. He also watches over me in such a way that not a hair can fall from my head without the will of my Father in heaven; in fact, all things must work together for my salvation. Because I belong to him, Christ, by his Holy Spirit assures me of eternal life and makes me wholeheartedly willing and ready from now on to live for him.

Q. What must you know to live and die in the joy of this comfort?

A. Three things: first, how great my sin and misery are; second, how I am set free from all my sins and misery; third, how I am to thank God for such deliverance.

Commandment 1: "I am the Lord your God"

QUESTIONS FOR PERSONAL DEVOTIONS:

1. This chapter argues that grace precedes law in the Ten Commandments, recorded in Deuteronomy 5. How does this affect your understanding of who God is and your relationship with him?
2. Does understanding that grace precedes law change your personal understanding of the rest of the Ten Commandments?
3. What are some personal steps that you could take to remember God's grace to you? (similar to the practical steps we find outlined in Deuteronomy 6)
4. What are the "Canaanites" in your life? What are the things that, as Deuteronomy 7 warns us, can pull you away from your identity as God's beloved?
5. What can you learn from Deut 7:7–9 about God's love for you?
6. In what ways do the words of Deut 8:1–5 challenge what you trust in most?
7. How do you find the attributes of God listed in Deut 10:12–22 shape your view of him and of who you are through faith?
8. What else might God be saying to you through this section of Deuteronomy?

QUESTIONS FOR TEACHING AND PREACHING:

1. What other passages in the Old and New Testaments show or demonstrate the idea that grace precedes law? How does this understanding that grace precedes law affect how you will preach or teach the Ten Commandments?
2. How does the Shema in Deuteronomy 6 expound the same idea that God's grace precedes law? How can you preach and/or teach the importance of remembering God's grace?
3. In his temptation in the wilderness, Jesus quotes three times from Deuteronomy 6–8. How does the experience of God's people in these three chapters of Deuteronomy relate to Jesus's experience in the wilderness? How can both of these help in preaching and teaching to the circumstances that people find themselves in today?

4. How might the words of Deut 7:7–9 encourage people in their relationship with God? Where else do you see similar ideas expressed in Scripture?

5. How do the words of Deut 8:3 that "man does not live by bread alone" challenge where we sometimes put our trust?

6. Deuteronomy often repeats that the Lord's instruction is "for our good." (See Deut 10:12–13) How does this encourage you in your preaching and teaching?

7. How will you encourage people in your preaching and teaching to choose life and not death? (Deuteronomy 11)

Chapter 5

Commandment 2: "No Other Gods and No Images"

Text of commandment 2 in Deuteronomy 5: "You shall have no other gods before me. You shall not make for yourself a carved image, or any likeness of anything that is in heaven above, or that is on the earth beneath, or that is in the water under the earth. You shall not bow down to them or serve them; for I the LORD your God am a jealous God, visiting the iniquity of the fathers on the children to the third and fourth generation of those who hate me, but showing steadfast love to thousands of those who love me and keep my commandments" (5:7–10).

Commandment 2 expounded in Deuteronomy: 12:1–13:18.

Positive principle summary: Love for God means exclusive loyalty to him.

Full positive principle: The supreme command about God, the other side of the coin of "love the Lord" (Deut 6:4–5), forbids cheating on the Lord with other gods and enjoins devotion to him by behaviors which please him, and results in promising blessing.

WINDOWS TELL THE STORY

The stained-glass windows were some of the most beautiful that I had ever seen. They were not the biggest. They were not the most elaborate. They were not from Tiffany or some other renowned glass studio. No, these windows were beautiful for a different reason. They were beautiful, because they told the story of redemption through Jesus Christ that we find in the Scriptures. There were seventeen of them in all. The first window depicted Adam and Eve and the fall of humanity into sin in the Garden of Eden. From there the windows went in order around the sanctuary. They depicted the story of the sacrifice of Isaac and Moses receiving the tablets of the Ten Commandments on Mount Sinai. The windows showed the leadership of David as king, the prophecy of Isaiah calling the people back to faith, and other stories from the OT. Then, the windows continued around the sanctuary telling the story of Jesus and how he came to save us. The windows showed his birth as a baby in Bethlehem, his journey to the temple as a young man, his baptism at the start of his ministry, and his teaching and healing of the sick. Finally, the stained-glass windows finished their story with the crucifixion of Jesus on Good Friday and his resurrection on Easter Sunday.

These windows were some of the most beautiful that I have ever seen, simply put, because they told the story of the Scriptures. This was the original purpose of stained-glass windows in churches. For centuries of human history, there was a large percentage of the population that was illiterate and could not read their own names. Yet, when they came to church, they could look upon these holy images and learn the story of salvation. The seventeen beautiful windows that I mentioned are found at a small country church where I used to serve as pastor. They continue the ancient tradition of declaring, without words, the story of salvation. I ended up preaching a seventeen-week sermon series at that church on those windows. We would put a picture of the next window on the front of the bulletin and for seventeen weeks, together we learned the story of salvation in Jesus Christ.

When we come to the second commandment in Deuteronomy, some people think that the prohibition against "graven images" is simply God telling his people to never to depict him in art of any kind. When we view the second commandment through this lens, it has several negative consequences. First, it makes this powerful commandment into nothing but a box on a checklist. Have I drawn a picture of God today? If not, then I have kept the commandment. This commandment, according to some, has nothing more to say to our daily lives than that. If this is true, all of the growth in faith in Jesus that resulted at that church from looking at the stained-glass windows together was a direct violation of God's commandments! Second, God is the one who gave us beauty and artistic expression. God created the entire universe, with its diverse flowers and trees, lakes and oceans, sunsets, and starry skies. Why would God prohibit us from using art and beauty in worship? Is prohibiting stained-glass windows and artistic beauty really the point of commandment 2 about "graven images," or is the meaning something that teaches us about how to live a life of faith? Let's take a look.

WHAT THE COMMAND MEANS IN DEUTERONOMY 5

In a world full of "gods" and constant temptation for Israel to conform to the beliefs and practices of her neighbors, commandment 2 begins with the most important commandment about God himself. Its purpose is that Israel know, and know that she knows, that the Lord alone is her God and that her allegiance is to him alone. Some argue that Deut 5:7 ("no other gods") and 5:8-10 ("no carved image") are two separate commandments. But Imes makes a persuasive case that Deut 5:7-10 is part of the same unit. She points out this structure:[1]

A (motive), v. 6			I am YHWH your God
	B (prohibition), v. 7		You are not to have any other *gods*
		C (central prohibition), v. 8	You are not to make a carved image
	B' (prohibition), v. 9a		You are not to bow down to or serve *them*
A' (motive), v. 9b-10			I am YHWH your God

She then points out that the plural "them" in 5:9 has only one plural it can be referring to: the plural "gods" in 5:7. So the correspondences in the structure and the plurals show these are part of one unit, not two, just as the Jewish community has traditionally held. So, Deut 5:7-10 constitutes commandment 2.[2] But Imes makes another perceptive observation. That the

---

1. Imes, *Bearing YHWH's Name*, 133.

2. Imes also uses this structure to argue that 5:6-10 is commandment 1, i.e., "I am the Lord your God...." is the beginning of commandment 1. Since the Jewish community thought of 5:6 as commandment 1, we take the inclusion of 5:6 in this structure to indicate that these two commands are closely bound together, one leading to the other, which also explains why Deut 6-11 expounds both commandment 1 (5:6) and commandment 2 (5:7-10).

plurals "gods" (5:7) and "them" (5:9) refer to the same thing shows that the statement sandwiched between them, "you shall not make a carved image" (5:8), refers to images of the false gods being discussed, not of YHWH.[3] This understanding is confirmed by the statement, "For I the Lord your God am a jealous God" (Deut 5:9). Since jealously is directed at interlopers, it is other gods that are in view. That is, God expects exclusive loyalty to himself. We can find an example of this in Psalm 115, a psalm that is concerned about the glory due to God's name. The psalm warns about making idols, but the idols spoken of are "silver and gold, made by human hands. They have mouths, but cannot speak, eyes, but cannot see. They have ears, but cannot hear, noses, but cannot smell. They have hands, but cannot feel, feet, but cannot walk, nor can they utter a sound with their throats. Those who make them will be like them, and so will all who trust in them." (Ps 115:4-8) Clearly the application of the commandment in this passage is warning against placing your trust in images of false and impotent gods. This should be taken as a warning against trusting in useless idols, not a prohibition of making Christian art.

Commandment 2 begins with, "You shall have no other gods before me." This command is likely not emphasizing monotheism ("there is only one God"): that is taught elsewhere (Deut 4:35, etc.). It is forbidding worship of anyone or anything other than God. The Hebrew text actually says, "You shall have no other gods *before my face*." The phrase could mean "in my presence," or, more likely, "besides me." Either way, it means that "Yahweh alone must be worshipped."[4] This is confirmed by Deut 6:12-14 which repeats commandments 1 and 2: "brought you out of the land of Egypt"[5] Calvin also points out that God properly deserves our worship, our trust in every situation and every problem, and our thanksgiving for all the good we receive. To give any of these to another so-called god, to another person, or even to ourselves, is to put in God's place a false object of worship. It is idolatry! The commandment is not emphasizing God's sole Deity—though other texts declare that—but his sole sovereignty over Israel.[6]

---

3. Imes, *Bearing YHWH's Name*, 134; see also the more accessible *Bearing God's Name*, 47-8.

4. Lundbom, *Deuteronomy*, 278-9.

5. Calvin, *Institutes* 1:382.

6. Wright, *Deuteronomy*, 68.

Commandment 2: "No Other Gods and No Images"

Forbidding making, bowing down to and worshipping images (5:8–10) serves "as a commentary on"[7] "no other gods" (5:7). The images of gods are not to copy "any likeness of anything that is in heaven above, or that is on the earth beneath, or that is in the water under the earth" (5:8). This is forbidden because "this would lead to the unthinkable position of a creature being regarded as the creator, and of humans, the very image of God and sovereign of all the universe, bowing down before that over which they were commissioned to be master" in Gen 1:26–8.[8] The story of the golden calf in Exodus 32 is perhaps the key example of this exact sin occurring in the Torah.

Deuteronomy 5:9 forbids "serving" images of gods. The command used here is the same command used in Gen 2:15 where Adam is put in the Garden of Eden to (literally) "serve and to keep" it. There it means that Adam "serves" God and "keeps" his command by doing his labor in the garden. All of life is to be service to God, including our daily labor at home or in agriculture or in business. Commandment 2 means that we are not to give to any other the "service" that belongs to God. Merrill elaborates: "To bow down is to recognize the sovereignty of a god, but to serve is to express commitment to that sovereignty in a practical, tangible way. Israel had been redeemed from bondage or service in Egypt in order to serve Yahweh. To serve other gods, then, was to reverse the exodus and go back under bondage, thus betraying the grace and favor of Yahweh."[9]

Deuteronomy 5:9 speaks of God "visiting the iniquity of the fathers on the children to the third and fourth generation of those who hate me." This does not mean that God punishes innocent children for what their parents have done, since Deut 24:16 forbids this. Instead, four generations was considered the normal lifespan. "Someone living to be seventy or eighty will likely see the birth, and maybe even the maturity, of the fourth generation."[10] So, as Block observes, "in the ancient world a domestic unit could consist of up to four generations, all under the leadership of the father." The father who worships other gods will teach his household to "hate" God (i.e., to reject his covenant-lordship), which will bring the results of "the iniquity of

---

7. Block, *Deuteronomy*, 162.

8. Merrill, *Deuteronomy*, 147. On the "*as* image of God" meaning the function to rule God's creation in his stead, see Merrill, *Everlasting Dominion*, 169–72.

9. Merrill, *Deuteronomy*, 147–8.

10. Lundbom, *Deuteronomy*, 280.

the father" upon his household in his lifetime.¹¹ The alternative is boundless blessing on future generations who are taught to follow the Lord (5:10), since "thousands" outnumbers the family of any father in one generation. Verses 9–10 emphasize again that disobedience to God brings bad results while obeying him brings good. Winston Churchill once defined politics as the ability to foretell what would happen in the future, and the ability afterwards to explain why it didn't happen.¹² Not so with Scripture: God's promises won't fail to transpire.

Block nails the gravity of commandment 2:

> This first principle of covenant relationship (vv. 7–10) represents 'the Supreme Command' which Moses has in mind whenever he uses the singular expression 'the command' in connection with the plural forms 'the decrees and laws" (5:31; 6:1; 7:11). This principle will find its obverse in the Shema (6:4–5). The following ... commands represent specific ways of demonstrating one's exclusive devotion to Yahweh.¹³

WHAT THE COMMANDMENT MEANS IN DEUTERONOMY

Commandment 2 is expounded in Deut 12:1–13:18. We have seen that commandment 2 is about Israel's exclusive loyalty to her God. Its exposition in Deuteronomy 12 is like déjà vu all over again, as Wright rightly writes:¹⁴ "Chapter 12 is concerned with Israel's exclusive loyalty to Yahweh in its worship and thus reflects" Deut 5:7–10. Chapter 13 is sometimes seen as expounding commandment 3¹⁵ but it seems better to consider it a second part of the exposition of commandment 2.¹⁶

The two imperatives of commandment 2 ("no gods," "no images") are closely bound together, so both are treated throughout Deuteronomy 12–13. For example, "you shall not *serve* them" (5:9) is taken up in 13:2, 4, 6, 13, though it also frames chapter 12 (12:2, 30). Nevertheless, Deuteronomy 12–13 largely expounds the two prohibitions of 5:7–10 in reverse order. The

---

11. Block, *Deuteronomy*, 162; so also, Craigie, *Deuteronomy*, 154.
12. Peter, *Peter's Quotations*, 220.
13. Block, *Deuteronomy*, 163.
14. Wright, *Deuteronomy*, 159.
15. Kaufman, "Deuteronomic Law," 122.
16. Merrill, *Deuteronomy*, 229, 232; Driver, *Deuteronomy*, 151.

Commandment 2: "No Other Gods and No Images"

dangers of images of false gods (5:8-10) is the emphasis of Deuteronomy 12, while worship of other gods (5:7) is accented in Deuteronomy 13. This is the structure of commandment 2 and its exposition in Deuteronomy:

A 5:7: no other gods	
	B 5:8-10: no images
	B' 12:1-31: no images
A' 13:1-18: no other gods	

Deut 12 is structured as a chiasm.

A 12:1: Introduction: "be careful to do"

    B 12:2-4: Prohibitions about worshipping God as the heathen do

        C 12:5-28: The true place and methods of worship

    B' 12:29-31: Prohibitions about worshipping God as the heathen do

A' 12:32: Conclusion: "be careful to do"

Like a stool with three legs, chapter 12 is structured in three parts, all of which expound "no images." The outer frame (the parallel beginning and ending: A and A') functions to underscore the gravity of the instruction (since underlining was not an ancient convention for emphasis).[17] The inner frame (the parallel B and B') stress what commandment 2 *prohibits*, i.e., it states what *should not be done*. The central section (C: 12:5-28), as is often the case with chiastic structures, is the core of the instruction. In this instance, it is both the longest section, and it accentuates *positive* obligations that develop what "you shall not worship the Lord in that way" (12:4, 31) means in practice.

After the outer frame's (12:1, 32) exhortation to "be careful to do" these things, the inner frame (12:2-4 and 12:29-31) restates "no carved images" (5:8-10) as "You shall not worship the Lord your God in that way" (12:4, 31). Deuteronomy 12:2-4 instructs Israel to destroy the pagan sites of worship and the objects of veneration which they will encounter when they enter Canaan. Deuteronomy 12:29-31 restates the same thing more directly: "you shall not be ensnared" by saying, "How did these nations

---

17. Since few could read in the ancient world, books were written to be read out loud to the audience. Thus, the clues we use to help readers understand, such as underlining, bold print, etc., were not used. The clues were aimed at the ear, such as repetition, playing with sounds of words (wordplay), rhyming, and chiastic structures. See, e.g., Alter, *Art of Narrative*; Bar-Efrat, *Narrative Art in the Bible*.

serve their gods—that I also may do the same" (12:30). Part of this was using idols and another part was burning children on altars as an offering to the gods (12:31).

The normal pattern in Deuteronomy is that the Ten Commandments are elaborated in terms of negative *and* positive implications, i.e., the negative minimums entail positive maximums, as we saw in Chapter 3. After the inner frame has developed the negative implications, the central section develops positive ones. The central section is made up of two parts, 12:5–14 and 12:15–28[18] which state positive obligations and permissions related to "no images." The first unit is framed by its core concept: sacrifices are to be offered "at the place that the LORD will choose" (12:5, 14). The intent, in part, is to discourage Israel worshipping where, and thus how, their pagan predecessors had done, which always involved images. The positive principle is that proper worship is to be conducted only as God authorizes.

The second unit of the central section (12:15–28) deals with the eating of non-sacrificial animals. This may seem an odd insertion at this point, but Tigay clarifies its importance: "Previously, only game animals could be slaughtered nonsacrificially"[19] according to the Sinai revelation in Lev 17:1–16, and that was only with the participation of a priest. Block elaborates,

> This arrangement was workable as long as the people were in transit and lived around the Tabernacle positioned in the middle of the camp. However, once they settled in the land, such restrictions would be problematic. Without modifications to the Sinai legislation, everyday diet would be restricted to wild game and vegetarian foods and the people would have to be satisfied with eating the meat of domesticated animals only at celebrations at the central sanctuary.[20]

So, God here relaxes the former restriction. Israelites may now (in anticipation of a settled life in Canaan) kill and eat domestic animals as a part of their regular diet in any place and without participation by a priest. The one restriction is that the blood must not be eaten.

Tigay clarifies the significance of this concession: "This verse establishes a major change in religious and dietary practice."[21] The positive

---

18. Wright, *Deuteronomy*, 161–2.
19. Tigay, *Deuteronomy*, 124.
20. Block, *Deuteronomy*, 316.
21. Tigay, *Deuteronomy*, 124.

Commandment 2: "No Other Gods and No Images"

contribution of this seemingly intrusive paragraph is seen by noting an observation Jesus later made about commandment 4: "The Sabbath was made for man, not man for the Sabbath" (Mark 2:27). Likewise, here, the burdensome implications that the Leviticus legislation would impose in the new conditions in Canaan are mitigated out of God's love for his people. It would almost be accurate to say, "Exclusive worship of God was made for man, not man for exclusive worship of God." Almost. This section of Deuteronomy 12 shows that the principle Jesus observed operates in the Decalogue more broadly: God's rules take into account human needs and the conditions of real human life. This is mirrored later in Ps 103:14, "For he knows our frame; he remembers that we are dust." Or perhaps closer to home, the concession here is an important acknowledgement of commandment 1: God's grace and love for his people grounds and permeates all the Ten Commandments.

Deuteronomy 12 affirms twice that obedience means that it will "go well with you" (12:25, 28). Churchill said, "It is always wise to look ahead, but difficult to look further than you can see."[22] This promise of Scripture enables believers to look ahead farther than they can see because God, who can look ahead, has told us what the future holds: obedience brings benefits.

Chapter 13 extends the discussion of commandment 2.[23] Each section is about someone who attempts to "draw [people] away" (the word is used also in 13: 5, 10, 13) from the Lord saying, "let us go after other gods" (13:2, 6, 13). The three sections are:

13:1–5: a prophet/dreamer who does a miracle

13:6–11: a friend/relative in personal conversation

13:12–18: a worthless fellow enticing a town

The overall benefit is summarized at the end: resisting temptation will bring blessing (13:17–18).

---

22. Langworth, *Churchill by Himself*, 576.

23. Kaufman ("Deuteronomic Law," 124–5) sees chapter 13 as one of the most difficult to correlate with the Ten Command exposition scheme he advocates. We believe that is because he sees it as expounding commandment 3, "Do not use the name of the Lord in vain," rather than commandment 2, "no other gods." Driver recognizes that the chapter deals with "special cases of seduction into idolatry." See Driver, *Deuteronomy*, 151; also, Merrill, *Deuteronomy*, 229, 232.

WHAT THE COMMANDMENT MEANS AS A POSITIVE PRINCIPLE

Commandment 2 forbids worshipping other gods. This is the Supreme Command[24] about God. As Block noted, this is the other side of the coin expressed in the Shema (6:4–5), the command to love the Lord, as we saw in the exposition of commandment 1 in chapters 6–11. In a nutshell, love for God, the greatest command and privilege of a human (Deut 6:4–5) expresses itself in exclusive loyalty to him (Deut 5:7–10; Deut 12–13). This is analogous to marriage, where love is expressed by exclusive loyalty to the beloved, to keep oneself only unto him/her as long as you both shall live. Chapters 12–13 elaborate love for God as forbidding cheating on the Lord with other gods and enjoining devotion to him by behaviors which please him, promising blessing as the result.[25]

We can state the positive message of commandment 2 as, *love for God requires exclusive loyalty to him*. We could also say, "This is love for God, that we keep his commandments" (1 John 5:3).

WHAT THE COMMANDMENT MEANS FOR CHRISTIANS

Exclusive loyalty to God is affirmed in the NT as fervently as in the OT. This is reinforced, for example, in the numerous NT passages that forbid idolatry (e.g., 1 John 5:21). The negative view of images is repeated in Acts 17:29 and Gal 4:8. But perhaps the greatest NT advance on this commandment is that Jesus is seen as the perfect image of God (Col 1:15–23; 2 Cor 4:4). Why would one worship a statue of a false god when the very image of the one true God is available for us to worship and follow in the person of Jesus Christ (see 1 Cor 8:15–16)?

The Heidelberg Catechism says the following for this commandment (seeing it as commandments 1 and 2). Though it differs a bit in its understanding of the Bible text, it is still valuable.[26] Notice that it treats both positive and negative aspects of the Ten Commandments, consistent with

---

24. Block, *Deuteronomy*, 163.

25. See Campbell and Campbell, *Invitation to the Torah*, 53–76, for elaboration of the marriage imagery in the Pentateuch.

26. Heidelberg Catechism (1563).

Commandment 2: "No Other Gods and No Images"

what we argued in chapter 3, as it does regularly when it expounds the commandments.

HEIDELBERG CATECHISM:

93. Q. How are these commandments divided?

A. Into two tables. The first has four commandments, teaching us how we ought to live in relation to God. The second has six commandments, teaching us what we owe our neighbor.

94. Q. What does the Lord require in the first commandment?

A. That I, not wanting to endanger my own salvation, avoid and shun all idolatry, sorcery, superstitious rites, and prayer to saints or to other creatures. That I sincerely acknowledge the only true God, trust God alone, look to God for every good thing humbly and patiently, and love, fear, and honor God with all my heart. In short, that I give up anything rather than go against God's will in any way.

95. Q. What is idolatry?

A. Idolatry is having or inventing something in which one trusts in place of, or alongside of, the only true God who is self-revealed in the divine word.

96. Q. What is God's will for us in the second commandment?

A. That we should not represent or worship God in any other manner than God has commanded in the Word.

97. Q. May we not then make any image at all?

A. God cannot and may not be visibly portrayed in any way. Although creatures may be portrayed, yet God forbids making or having such images if one's intention is to worship them or to serve God through them.

98. Q. May not images be permitted in the churches as teaching aids for the unlearned?

A. No. We should not try to be wiser than God. God wants us to be instructed by the living preaching of the Word not by idols that cannot even talk.

We note here that Christians genuinely disagree about what this commandment means and acknowledge that what we have argued in this chapter is inconsistent with how many Christians have understood this commandment, which is also reflected in the Heidelberg Catechism statement above.

QUESTIONS FOR PERSONAL DEVOTIONS:

1. Are there some things that you can be tempted to put in the place that only God should occupy in your life?
2. Why are these things tempting to you?
3. What have you been taught about the meaning of "idolatry" in the past? How did this affect your view of God?
4. What are your "high places"? (Deut 12:2)
5. How could the exposition of Deut 5:7–10 in 12:1–13:18 help to shape your faith?
6. How does obedience to the second commandment illustrate God's love at work in our lives?
7. What else might God be saying to you through this section of Deuteronomy?

QUESTIONS FOR TEACHING AND PREACHING:

1. Discuss the words "serving" and "keeping" as they are used in Genesis and Deuteronomy and how that affects your understanding of idolatry.
2. Is the chapter's presentation of the meaning of "graven images" similar to or different from your understanding? How could this affect the way that you teach and preach on this command?
3. Is the chapter's presentation of Deut 5:9 ("third and fourth generation") similar to or different from how you have heard this verse presented before? How will this understanding influence your teaching and preaching?
4. How are the second commandment and the Shema (Deut 6:4) two sides of the same coin?

5. How do you see commandment 2 expounded in Deuteronomy 12? How could you teach or preach God's grace from the laws given in Deuteronomy 12?

6. How could the story of the golden calf in Exodus 32 illustrate the meaning of the second commandment?

7. How does the second command help us to love God and to love our neighbor?

8. Can you think of a personal story that would help to illustrate the meaning of idolatry presented in this chapter?

9. What else might God be saying to you and your community through this commandment?

Chapter 6

Commandment 3: "Do Not Bear God's Name in Vain"

Text of commandment 3 in Deuteronomy 5: "You shall not take the name of the LORD your God in vain, for the LORD will not hold him guiltless who takes his name in vain" (5:11).

Commandment 3 expounded in Deuteronomy: 14:1–21.

Positive principle summary: Love for God means representing him well.

Full positive principle: Representing God well includes being pure in worship and practice from external pollution.

A TRIP TO BEST BUY

My friend Matt and I, Derek, walked into our local Best Buy. Matt works in an office and does a lot of work on his computer. He called me toward the end of the workday and said that his computer had developed a problem and that he needed to get it repaired. He asked me if I would be interested in going to Best Buy with him. Matt knows that I can never resist a trip to go and look at tech stuff. So, Matt picked me up and we went to Best Buy. We walked into the store and started browsing things in the aisles, because we still had about ten minutes before Matt's appointment with a computer tech. While we were standing in the aisle devoted to printers and ink cartridges, someone came over and asked me what I thought about a particular printer. I just so happened to own that same printer at home. So,

Commandment 3: "Do Not Bear God's Name in Vain"

I began to tell them what I thought about the printer. I talked about the pros and the cons, what I liked, and what I didn't like. The person listened attentively and thanked me for my help. Another person standing in the next aisle happened to overhear this conversation. When the first person left, they came over and asked me about a different product. This was strange, I thought. Why were all these people asking me technology questions? I knew a little bit about this kind of stuff, but certainly not as much as some people. I tried to answer the person's question as best as I could.

When I had finished talking with this person, it was time for my friend's appointment with the computer tech. He left and went to get his computer fixed while I continued to browse in the aisle. During the time that Matt was getting his laptop serviced, four more people came over and asked me questions. This was crazy! What was going on here? Why were so many people coming and asking me questions? Then, I realized what was going on. I had just gotten home from work when my friend picked me up, and I was still wearing the clothes that I had worn to work that day, a pair of khaki pants and a blue polo shirt. It just so happened to be the right shade of blue that with the khaki pants, I looked just like an employee at the store. No wonder all of these people had come and asked to talk to me.

I had, even without realizing it, represented this Best Buy store to six different people. They had formed opinions about this store and how helpful or not helpful its employees were, and I didn't even work there. Suddenly, I hoped that I had been a good representative of this store where I did not even work. What if they thought that I had been rude or unhelpful? That wasn't the store's fault. It is a serious thing to represent something. It is an especially serious thing to represent something larger and more far-reaching than yourself. The way that we serve as a representative can shape and form the experience of others and their perceptions of what we represent.

While the God of Israel is often called simply "God" (Hebrew '*Elohim*), his Hebrew name is "YHWH." Hebrew was written with no vowels, but supplied with the proper vowels for pronunciation, the name is properly spelled "Yahweh." This name of God is called the "Tetragrammaton," a Greek word meaning "four letters." Commandment 3 intones, "You shall not take the name of the LORD your God in vain, for the LORD will not hold him guiltless who takes his name in vain" (Deut 5:11).

God's name should be very special to his people. The ancient Jewish community was so concerned to obey this commandment that long before Jesus's time, they made it a tradition to never pronounce it. While Christians have not followed this practice, it demonstrated a sound intent to avoid ever misusing God's name. Since they could not utter it, over time they came up with various circumlocutions to refer to God's name, including "the Place," "the Command," and "the Holy One, Blessed be He." When reading Scripture aloud in public, they regularly substituted "the Lord" (i.e., pronouncing Hebrew *Adonai* instead of "Yahweh"). A common circumlocution was "the name," which in Hebrew is *ha shem*. *Shem*, the Hebrew word for "name," happens to rhyme exactly with "name." Knowing this makes it easy to remember the idea communicated by commandment 3: do not shame the name! The heart of the third commandment is that we would live our lives in such a way that we would bring honor and praise to our Heavenly Father instead of bringing shame and disrepute on the name of God. Do not shame the name!

WHAT THE COMMANDMENT MEANS IN DEUTERONOMY 5

God desires that we love him, and he delights in his people referring to him with honor and respect. Commandment 3 commands that we not shame the name. But exactly what does that prohibition prohibit? The most natural reading of the Hebrew text here is, "Do not carry (or bear) the name of the Lord in vain." But since we do not think of names as something we "carry," this has caused confusion. Imes explains[1] that the commandment[2] has usually been understood to prohibit misusing God's name in the way we use it in speech.[3] Scholars have drawn that conclusion by assuming that the cryptic language here means, "Do not lift up [your hand in a verbal oath in which you swear by] God's name in vain."[4]

To understand this commandment, there are two things that need examination: (1) "do not take" and (2) "in vain." Imes makes a persuasive (book-length) case that the proper meaning of the verb normally translated

---

1. Imes, *Bearing God's Name*, 49, 51. This book is more accessible than her academic work, *Bearing YHWH's Name*, usually cited here.
2. Craigie notes this (*Deuteronomy*, 155–6) while arguing it is broader, including using God's name in magic or to otherwise try to manipulate God.
3. See Imes, *Bearing YHWH's Name*, 3, 10.
4. Imes, *Bearing YHWH's Name*, 7.

Commandment 3: "Do Not Bear God's Name in Vain"

in commandment 3 as "to take" is "to carry or bear," so that the proper translation is, "Do not carry/bear the name of the Lord in vain."[5]

What's problematic about, "*take* the name in vain"? Imes points out that the object of "take" (Hebrew *nāasā'*) is "name," not "hand," which would be the case if it meant to "lift up the hand in a spoken oath,"[6] as it is usually understood. She also says, "In the Hebrew Bible, *nāasā'* never refers to oath taking, and never refers to speech without explicit contextual clues."[7]

But the more important issue is the positive considerations which suggest that "*carry/bear* the name" is the proper rendering. First, the standard Hebrew lexicon, lists "to carry" as the primary meaning of the term.[8] Second, the Septuagint (the Greek translation of the Hebrew Bible, c. 250 BCE) translates the Hebrew *nāasā'* in Exod 20:7 and Deut 5:11 with the Greek word *lambano*, "to carry," which "never refers to taking an oath."[9]

But the strongest evidence is the closest linguistic parallel to commandment 3, which is in Exodus 28. There we read, "Aaron shall bear the names of the sons of Israel in the breast piece of judgment on his heart, when he goes into the Holy Place, to bring them to regular remembrance before the LORD" (Ex. 28:29; see also v. 12). Both are in the Torah and the vocabulary is the same: Aaron "bears" (*nāasā'*) the names (*shem*) of the tribes on his breastplate. The clear meaning here is "carry the names." So, in the passage closest in language and context to commandment 3, *nāasā'*[10] means to "carry."[11]

Another important text is the priesthood's blessing upon Israel recorded in Num 6:24-27:

> The LORD bless you and keep you;
> the LORD make his face to shine upon you and be gracious to you;
> the LORD lift up his countenance upon you and give you peace.

---

5. Imes, *Bearing YHWH's Name*, 108.
6. Imes, *Bearing YHWH's Name*, 92.
7. Imes, *Bearing YHWH's Name*, 100.
8. HALOT (Hebrew and Aramaic Lexicon of the Old Testament) 1:724.
9. Imes, *Bearing YHWH's Name*, 95. In fact, the prevailing tendency of the Septuagint is to translate *nāasā'* with *lambano* when *nāasā'* means to "carry" or "bear" something, and *lambano* often means "to carry," especially in the Torah. See Imes, *Bearing YHWH's Name*, 95.
10. Imes, *Bearing YHWH's Name*, 91-2.
11. Imes, *Bearing YHWH's Name*, 92.

What is most interesting is the follow-up statement: "So shall they *put my name* upon the sons of Israel" (6:27). Imes explains this: "the blessing functioned as an oral branding, affixing the divine name . . . upon the people who consequently belonged to Yahweh."[12] This shows the sense in which Israel bore the name of God. The daily repetition of this blessing through Israel's history reminded them that they bore God's name and so were his representatives to the world. Thus, Deut 28:10, "all the peoples of the earth shall see that you are called by the name of the LORD" (see also Jer 14:9).

These reasons lead to the conclusion that the proper translation of commandment 3 is "You shall not bear/carry the name of the Lord in vain." One way to picture this is to think of an army going to battle. Often, a standard bearer would be visible in the very front line of troops.[13] They would be carrying a tall pole with their lord's insignia prominently displayed. This means that the army was quite literally carrying the name of their lord with them into battle. This allowed everyone to see who this group of soldiers represented. Therefore, whatever the group of soldiers did in battle was done in the name of their lord. While this word is not meant to convey any militaristic or battle sense in Deuteronomy, this picture can help us to grasp the basic meaning of the Hebrew word.

The second issue to be resolved is the meaning of "in vain." The term "in vain" has a range of meaning from "empty" to "false" to "for nothing."[14] Imes concludes from a detailed survey of its use in the Hebrew Bible that it warns God's people "not to bear his name 'ineffectually' or 'falsely' (hypocritically),"[15] i.e., in a way that dishonors his name. This is how it is normally understood. Believers shame the name by living in a way that is false to his name, or hypocritical for those who claim to honor God. Just as an employee at an event wearing a company name tag represents their company and can make a good or a bad impression for the company, so believers wear a tag than names them as followers of Christ—the name "Christian"—and can honor or embarrass him by how they speak and act.

When viewed together, commandments 2 and 3 communicate the first two imperatives concerning God (Deut 5:7–11).[16]

---

12. Imes, *Bearing YHWH's Name*, 169.
13. I owe this observation to my daughter, Joanna Campbell-Totin.
14. Imes, *Bearing YHWH's Name*, 100–104.
15. Imes, *Bearing YHWH's Name*, 104.
16. Imes, *Bearing God's Name*, 52.

Commandment 3: "Do Not Bear God's Name in Vain"

1. Commandment 2: Worship only Yahweh.
2. Commandment 3: Represent him well.

That is, Israel is to give their exclusive loyalty to their God, Yahweh, and because they bear his name, they must represent him appropriately (Deut 5:11).

So, commandment 3 means, "Do not shame the name! Instead, represent God well in all you do."

Charles Spurgeon captured it well:

> If we live carelessly, the world will soon see it, and with its hundred tongues, it will spread the story, exaggerated and emblazoned by the zeal of slander. They will shout triumphantly, "See how these Christians act! They are hypocrites." Thus will much damage be done to the cause of Christ and much insult offered to his name. The cross of Christ is in itself an offence to the world; let us take heed that we add no offense of our own.[17]

WHAT THE COMMANDMENT MEANS IN DEUTERONOMY

We have seen that commandment 3 prohibits bearing God's name in vain, i.e., carrying his name as his child and yet living in a way that dishonors his name. Christians do not want to shame the name. Commandment 3 is expounded in Deut 14:1–21.[18] We must first show that 14:1–21 is a unit, then that it elaborates commandment 3, and finally how it does so.

Several considerations demonstrate that Deut 14:1–21 is a unit. It is framed by the declaration, "you are a people holy to the Lord" (14:2, 21c).[19] This framing communicates that as God is holy, so Israel must be holy, bearing his name in a way that is consistent with his holy character. This is followed by an inner frame which contrasts a two-fold designation of Israel

---

17. Spurgeon, *Strengthen My Spirit*, November 18.
18. Kaufman ("Deuteronomic Law," 124–5) sees commandment 3 expounded in Deut 13–14. In the last chapter we defended chapter 13 as part of Deuteronomy's exposition of commandment 2. Merrill, *Deuteronomy* (note 34, 234–5), limits commandment 3 to Deut 14.
19. The next unit, Deut 14:22–16:17 is structured differently, around the term "year" (14:22, 28; 15:1, 9, 12, 18, 20; 16:16; it does not occur again until 24:5).

and a two-fold designation of someone who is not Israel (14:2, 21b). The structure is:

A 14:2a: you are a people holy to the Lord your God

    B 14:2b: (Israel) chosen, a treasured possession

        C 14:3–21a: You shall not eat any abominable thing

    B' 14:21b: (not Israel) sojourner, foreigner

A' 14:21c: you are a people holy to the Lord your God

The basic argument is revealed by the structure: *because* they are holy, i.e., "set apart" from the nations as God's possession (the two frames), Israel is not to eat the forbidden things (the center). As Merrill observes, "To be God's people requires a lifestyle commensurate with that high and holy calling."[20] So, we conclude that 14:1–21 is a unit.[21]

We must now demonstrate that this section expounds commandment 3. Chapter 14 begins by declaring "You are *the sons of* the Lord your God" (14:1). This echoes the priest's blessing from Num 6:27: "So shall [the priests] put my name upon *[literally] the sons of* Israel, and I will bless them." The priests placed God's name upon the Israelites, so they carried his name.

Further, the name "Israel" is best understood as meaning, "God fights for you." The "el" at the end of "Israel" is the short form of "God" (Hebrew *'Elohim*). It often appears in Jewish names, such as "Daniel," meaning "God is my judge."[22] So by bearing the name "Israel," they carried God's name before the world. The name they carry in "Israel" is not his name "Yahweh" but the more generic term "God." But since everyone knew that Israel's God's name was "Yahweh," the name "Israel" was a way of carrying God's name.

Next Israel is called a "holy people" and God's "treasured possession" (14:2). These terms consciously echo Exod 19:4–6, when Israel was invited to become God's people and thus God's "treasured possession" and a "holy nation" (Exod 19:5–6). What was the purpose of this relationship in Exodus 19? It is so that they "shall be to me a kingdom of priests" (Exod 19:6).

---

20. Merrill, *Deuteronomy*, 235.

21. This is confirmed by the further discussion of the passage's structure below.

22. "Daniel" is a little Hebrew sentence: "Dan" means "judge," "i" makes it possessive, and "el" is the short form of "'*Elohim*" ("God"). The resultant meaning of the name is "My judge [is] 'El(ohim)."

Commandment 3: "Do Not Bear God's Name in Vain"

Israel is to represent God to the nations as priests represent people to God, and to draw the nations to their Lord. That is, they are to "bear his name," to represent him to the nations. The point of Deuteronomy 14 is that Israel is to be distinct from the nations around her in her practices lest they "bear his name in vain."

Further, Deuteronomy 14 begins and ends with the affirmation that Israel is "holy," that is, set apart, distinct from, the other nations. To bear God's name is to represent his holiness. The central focus of Deut 14:3–21 is that Israel distinguishes between "clean" and "unclean" in food because the unclean is "an abomination" to the Lord (14:3). Craigie states, "The practices prohibited are those which characterized certain facets of foreign religion."[23] Driver is correct: Israel "should conform their character to His, and do nothing that is unworthy of the close and intimate relation in which they stand towards Him."[24] We conclude that Deut 14:1–21 expounds commandment 3.

We will now investigate how it expounds the intent of not "bearing God's name in vain." The structure is more complex than discussed above. The passage begins and ends with imperatives which are parallel in form and correspond to the imperative which introduces the central section of the chapter:

1. 14:1   You shall not cut . . .

2. 14:3   You shall not eat . . .

3. 14:21d You shall not boil . . .[25]

These three commands expound three examples which explain how not to bear God's name. Again, Merrill masters the logic of the passage:

---

23. Craigie, *Deuteronomy*, 229.

24. Driver, *Deuteronomy*, 156.

25. The meaning of Deut 4:21c, "Do not boil a kid in its mother's milk," is much debated. Merrill states (*Deuteron-omy*, 239), "It is reasonable to conclude that the boiling of a young goat in its mother's milk was part of a Canaanite festival ritual that so epitomized that depraved cultus that it came to symbolize all that was evil and detestable in it. Both uses of the prohibition against it in Exodus are in festival contexts and, indeed, this is the case here in Deuteronomy as well, though here the festival instructions follow rather than precede it (Deut 14:22–29). Its position in Deuteronomy is to allow it to serve as a framing device matching the prohibition of 14:1." Lundbom (*Deuteronomy*, 477) however, notes that "it has been argued more recently that [the Hebrew here] means 'suckling kid,' which would give the reading: 'You shall not boil a kid (still) at its mother's milk' (Schorch 2010)."

The uniqueness of Israel is first spelled out in the opening frame of the inclusio and then elaborated once more in the closing frame. Thus, the prohibition "Do not cut yourselves or shave the front of your heads for the dead" (v. 1) matches formally "Do not cook a young goat in its mother's milk" (v. 21). The recognition of this function of the respective prohibitions sheds a great deal of light on the rather enigmatic character of these two taboos and also contributes to the connection between them and the material they enclose, namely, the instructions concerning the clean and the unclean.[26]

So, while the opening and closing prohibitions are obscure, the first has to do with avoiding practices of pagan religion while the bulk of the passage (14:3–21) is clear and exhorts Israel to eat only what is not offensive to their God.

Interestingly, the imperatives "do not eat" (A) and "eat" (B) follow a pattern:

A, B, B, A 14:3–7

A, B, B, A 14:8–10

B, A, A, B 14:11–20

A, B   14:21

Note that each imperative occurs seven times. One effect is to balance the prohibitions and the authorizations so that the passage does not convey a negative impression. God's provisions are as numerous as his restrictions. Further, seven-fold repetition is a common feature of the Hebrew Bible. After Genesis 1, the number seven becomes symbolic of completion or fullness, since the creation story records seven affirmations that God's work is "good" in the seven-day sequence.[27]

In summary, the three imperatives which structure the passage elaborate "not bearing God's name in vain" as involving (1) not imitating the practices of other religions, and (2) not engaging in practices which offend the Lord. Both external and internal purity are expected of those who bear God's name. Both are aimed at distinguishing a "holy" people from those not devoted to the Lord.

---

26. Merrill, *Deuteronomy*, 235.
27. E.g., Wenham, 96, on *Genesis* 1:9.

WHAT THE COMMANDMENT MEANS AS A POSITIVE PRINCIPLE

Commandment 3 can be articulated in the negative as "do not shame the name!" In the positive it means "represent God well." But we saw that that representation includes (1) not imitating the practices of other religions, and (2) not engaging in practices which offend the Lord, i.e., being pure of external corruption and pure in internal functioning.

The succinct positive statement of commandment 3 is *love for God means representing him well*.

Perhaps it is from Jesus's favorite book's exposition of commandment 3 that Jesus fashioned his query, "Why do you call me 'Lord, Lord,' and not do what I tell you?" (Luke 6:46), or "If you love me, you will keep my commandments" (John 14:15).

WHAT THE COMMAND MEANS FOR CHRISTIANS

New Testament believers bear God's name by being called "Christians." What we do can reflect upon Jesus poorly because we are called by his name, as Spurgeon said, and as Rom 2:24 states: "The name of God is blasphemed among the Gentiles because of you."[28] The principle is stated over and over again: we must not shame the name of our savior, Jesus.[29] One example is, "To this end we always pray for you, that our God may make you worthy of his calling and may fulfill every resolve for good and every work of faith by his power, so that the name of our Lord Jesus may be glorified in you" (2 Thess 1:11–12).

Commandment 3 is reaffirmed in the NT when believers are expected to be holy, reflecting their God in their character. Romans 12:1–2 makes the same point as commandment 3, "I appeal to you therefore, brothers, by the mercies of God, to present your bodies as a living sacrifice, holy and acceptable to God, which is your spiritual worship. Do not be conformed to this world, but be transformed by the renewal of your mind, that by testing you may discern what is the will of God, what is good and acceptable and perfect."

Love for God means representing him well: do not shame the name!

---

28. Paul is citing Isa 52:5, and perhaps also the result of David's misbehavior in 2 Sam 12:14

29. See, for example, 1 Cor 5:11; Col 3:17; 1 Tim 6:1; Jas 2:7.

The Heidelberg Catechism says what follows regarding commandment 3. While differing in its precise interpretation of the commandment, it is nevertheless instructive.

HEIDELBERG CATECHISM:

99. Q. What is God's will for us in the third commandment?

A. That we neither blaspheme nor misuse the name of God by cursing, perjury, or unnecessary oaths, nor share in such horrible sins by being silent bystanders. In a word, it requires that we use the holy name of God only with reverence and awe, so that we may properly confess God, pray to God, and glorify God in all our words and works.

100. Q. Is blasphemy of God's holy name by swearing and cursing really such serious sin that God is angry also with those who do not do all they can to help prevent and forbid it?

A. Yes, indeed; for no sin is greater or provokes God's wrath more than the profaning of the divine name. That is why God commanded it to be punished with death.

101. Q. May we swear an oath in God's name if we do it reverently?

A. Yes, when the government demands it, or when necessity requires it, in order to maintain and promote truth and trustworthiness for God's glory and our neighbor's good. Such oaths are approved in God's Word and were rightly used by Old and New Testament believers.

102. Q. May we also swear by saints or other creatures?

A. No. A legitimate oath is calling upon God, as the only one who knows my heart, to witness my truthfulness and to punish me if I swear falsely. No creature deserves such honor.

QUESTIONS FOR PERSONAL DEVOTIONS:

1. Have you ever encountered someone who claimed to be a Christian that lived in such a way that they "shamed the name"?

Commandment 3: "Do Not Bear God's Name in Vain"

2. How did this encounter affect you and your faith? Does it still affect you?
3. How can you represent God's name well to those around you?
4. How does being "a people holy to the Lord" (Deut 14:2) encourage you to observe commandment 3?
5. What are some practices or activities that you could refrain from or choose to participate in in order to carry the name of God well and not in vain?
6. How is the understanding of commandment 3 presented in this chapter similar to or different from what you have heard before? How does this understanding impact your faith and daily life?
7. What else might God be saying to you through this section of Deuteronomy?

QUESTIONS FOR TEACHING AND PREACHING:

1. The third commandment is often taken as a prohibition against using the name of God in a curse. How does this chapter expand your understanding of this commandment? How will this influence your teaching and preaching of the third commandment?
2. How does the chapter's presentation of the words "to take" and "to carry" affect your understanding of the third commandment?
3. How is the example of Aaron in Exodus 28 helpful for understanding the meaning of the third commandment in Deuteronomy 5?
4. How could you relate being "a people holy to the Lord" (Deut 14:2) and the third commandment in your teaching and preaching?
5. How do you see the third commandment expounded in Deuteronomy 14 and how could this be helpful to our faith today?
6. How do you speak to people who have been hurt by others living in such a way that they "shame the name"?
7. What are some practical ways that you can teach and preach to others about how to represent the name of God well in their families, work, and communities?

8. If you are a part of a tradition or denomination that practices a benediction, how could the priestly blessing in Num 6:24–27 inform this practice and help to live out the third commandment?

Chapter 7

Commandment 4: "Remember the Sabbath Day"

Text of commandment 4 in Deuteronomy 5:

> Observe the Sabbath day, to keep it holy, as the LORD your God commanded you. Six days you shall labor and do all your work, but the seventh day is a Sabbath to the LORD your God. On it you shall not do any work, you or your son or your daughter or your male servant or your female servant, or your ox or your donkey or any of your livestock, or the sojourner who is within your gates, that your male servant and your female servant may rest as well as you. You shall remember that you were a slave in the land of Egypt, and the LORD your God brought you out from there with a mighty hand and an outstretched arm. Therefore the LORD your God commanded you to keep the Sabbath day" (5:12–15).

Commandment 4 expounded in Deuteronomy: 14:22–16:17.

Positive principle summary: Loving God benefits us and others.

Full positive principle: Giving to the Lord what he deserves for his grace brings blessing and joy to individuals and to their needy neighbors, including the blessing of rest. God's commandments are given to bring about our good and our joy.

WHAT DOES IT MEAN TO KEEP THE SABBATH?

While some of the Ten Commandments that we find in Deuteronomy seem pretty straightforward and self-explanatory, the fourth commandment certainly does not fit this category. When we read the command to keep the Sabbath, many people are probably very confused about what a Sabbath is and how we are supposed to keep it. The Sabbath is not a concept that is very familiar to many people in our world today. I admit that when I, Derek, think of the Sabbath, the first thing that comes into my mind is my grandmother.

My grandmother lived in the southern part of the United States. She attended a very strict church. This church had a lot of rules that she and my grandfather were supposed to follow. She took these rules seriously and tried to live by them. They were important to her. Because they lived far away from us, whenever we went to visit them, we would always end up being there over the weekend. This meant going with them to their strict church two times whenever we were there on a Sunday, sometimes three if there was a special prayer meeting or missionary speaker. During the hours when we were not in church on a Sunday, it seemed that there were only three other activities that were permissible on the Sabbath — eating, sleeping and reading your Bible. The Sabbath seemed to be mainly about the things that you were not allowed to do, even though this is one of the few commandments that is stated in a positive form, not a negative one.

This kind of understanding is not uncommon and not new. At the church that I, Derek, am currently serving, we recently discovered some records of church meetings that had been lost for a long time. These records are from the early 1800s and shed some interesting light on what happened at the church during that period. One of the most interesting entries was actually about an ancestor of one of the current church elders. It seems that this man was a farmer and was in the process of bringing in his crops. He probably felt that it was going to rain and was worried about losing the rest of his hay. So, he decided to take his chance and bring in the crop on a Sabbath day. The records tell of how he was caught in the act by an elder at the church. The elder reported this man's activities to the board of elders. He was brought before the elders and was placed under church discipline for his "willful violation of the Sabbath as commanded by God." Is this really what God intended in the fourth commandment? Did God mean for us to simply keep very strict lists of what we could and could not do on the Sabbath day or is there more going on in this commandment? Let's see.

Commandment 4: "Remember the Sabbath Day"

WHAT THE COMMANDMENT MEANS IN DEUTERONOMY 5

People look forward to weekends; relatively few look forward to Sunday as anything but a holiday. Some people see Sunday as the "Sabbath."[1] The Sabbath concept has had significant influence in Western, and American, history. The concept of a seven-day week originated in the Hebrew Bible (the "Old Testament"), and the Sabbath commandment in the Bible is the first record in human history of the idea that people deserve a day of rest each week. Both of these are gifts of the Jews to the world.[2] But what is a "Sabbath" and what does it have to do with Christians today? These issues are the focus of this chapter.

Yogi Berra once said, "You can observe a lot just by watching."[3] We believe the Sabbath commandment is like that. What at first seems utterly familiar, upon inspection reveals a lot. So, let's observe. The word "Sabbath" comes from a Hebrew verb which means "to stop"; Merrill points out that it "means both 'to cease' and 'to rest,' for both meanings occur in the respective versions of the fourth commandment."[4] So a Sabbath day means a day to rest (from labor).

The Sabbath commandment is carefully structured.[5]

A Observe the Sabbath			5:12
	B as the Lord your God commanded you		5:13
		C six days you shall labor but the seventh day is a Sabbath	5:14
		C' remember that you were a slave, but the Lord your God brought you out	5:15

1. Actually, the seventh day of the week is Saturday, which is the day Jews and some Christians, including nearly 20 million Seventh Day Adventists worldwide, choose to worship. Many Christians see Sunday as the "Christian Sabbath" and most Christians worship on Sunday.

2. Craigie, *Deuteronomy*, 157.

3. Peter, *Peter's Quotations*, 295.

4. Merrill, *Deuteronomy*, 150. See also Tigay, *Deuteronomy*, 68.

5. Lundbom, *Deuteronomy*, 285 and Lohfink, *Theology*, 253, note some of this structure.

	B' therefore the Lord your God commanded you		5:15
A' keep the Sabbath			5:15

Note first the *inclusio* that constitutes the first and last phrases (in Hebrew): "observe/keep the Sabbath!" That this is called a "command" reinforces its solemnity; the term "command" is used in the Ten Commandments only here (2x in 5:12b, 15) and in commandment 5 (5:16).

Note, too, the parallel built into C and C' above. In C, six days of labor is countered by a day of rest. Likewise, being a slave in C' is countered by being "brought out" of that condition.[6] The implication is that as a day of rest is a refreshing alternative to labor, being brought into God's service is a refreshing alternative to slavery in Egypt.

This is the second of the three commandments which is stated in the positive, along with commandments 1 (5:6) and 5 (5:16). That fact is striking! Why this variation? Kaiser lifts the veil:

> The Decalogue could have been stated positively throughout as well as negatively, for moral law is always doublesided. Every moral act is at the same time also a refraining from a contrary mode of action that could have been taken . . . Since it is easier to state in fewer words a command in a negative form . . . most of the decalogue takes this form. But our freedom in grace is so large that it would be difficult to give a set of moral prescriptions in the positive form with the scope and succinctness with which the Decalogue is presently cast.[7]

Such good reasons for the negative formulation of most of the Ten Commandments highlight those that are stated in the positive. Clearly, they were worded so intentionally. So, it must be our intention to discern the author's intention in intending this. And discern we can.

First, the positive framing of the commandment corresponds to the inner mood of commandment 4. The thrust of the two central sections (C and C' above), the bulk of the commandment, is positive, reminding God's people that we are granted rest on a regular basis (5:13–15) and that we have been rescued from slavery by God to a better sort of labor for him

---

6. I have translated the *waw* (Hebrew for "and," or "but") both times as "but" since they are parallel and are identical in the Hebrew (5:14, 15).

7. Kaiser, *Toward OT Ethics*, 83–84.

(5:15). Jesus emphasized the positive meaning of the Sabbath when he said, "The Sabbath was made for man, not man for the Sabbath" (Mark 2:27).

Second, that the first and fourth commandments are stated positively frames the commandments about God[8] in the positive as a reminder that the obligations God sets forth here have more positive implications than negative ones. As we have seen, the Ten Commandments are largely formulated in the negative for brevity, but they imply positive maximum obligations, as we learned in chapter 3. Even more importantly, the Decalogue—and all of God's commands—are given to bring about our good, as Deut 6:1–3, declares,[9] among other texts. Framing commandments 1–4 positively reinforces this message.

Third, commandments 1 and 4 emphasize the positive by reiterating God's deliverance of Israel from Egypt. Thus, God's grace, elaborated in commandment 1, is repeated here, framing commandments 1–4 (5:6, 15). God's grace to his people serves not only as the foundation of the Ten Commandments but also frames the commandments about God (5:6, 15), redoubling that happy emphasis.

Fourth, the Sabbath serves as a regular reminder to remember (Deut 5:15) God's redemption from Egypt, and in this parallels the New Testament's Lord's Supper as a regular reminder of Jesus's redemption: "Do this in remembrance of me" (1 Cor 11:24). What's in a positive turn of phrase? Much, indeed.

But this striking juxtaposing of positive and negative formulations of the commandments suggests another important implication. Kaiser writes that the positive ones "might serve as the basis for dividing up the decalogue into three sections [which] govern the other seven commands."[10] This suggestion is attractive because it accounts for this obviously intentional variation. More importantly, Tigay points out that positive commandments require "more than simple avoidance of prohibited acts."[11] That is, stating a

---

8. See the discussion below about whether commandment 4 is to be grouped with commandments 2–3.

9. See the book-length defense of this proposition in the Pauline literature by Charry, *Renewing of Your Minds*.

10. Kaiser, *Toward OT Ethics*, 84. Kaiser cites John J. Owens as the source of this idea. Since multiple, overlapping structures are common on the Bible, this is not incompatible with dividing the Decalogue in other ways.

11. Tigay, *Deuteronomy*, 68.

commandment in the positive implies its more open-ended obligations and thus seems to signal its greater importance.[12]

We therefore agree with Kaiser and propose that each positive commandment begins a section which the following negative commandments unpack. The three positive commandments signal the key emphases in the Decalogue and are the foundational ones.[13]

Lohfink points out an additional feature which buttresses this conclusion. While commandments 6–10 are almost identical in Deuteronomy as in Exodus, there is one significant difference. In Deuteronomy, unlike in Exodus, commandments 6–10 are bound together by the word "and," "binding them into a single unit."[14] This also suggests that the negative commandments 6–10 form a unit which elaborates on the positive principle in commandment 5.

Recognizing these features yields the following structure:[15]

---

12. Old Testament specialist Patrick Miller points out that there are three obligations, all of which are open ended. Sabbath observance entails (1) rest and refreshment, (2) setting the day apart to God, and (3) recalling the redemptive work of God in the exodus. Miller, *Deuteronomy*, 81–83.

13. Several additional considerations confirm this proposal. While they are never called "the Ten Commandments" (except in mistranslations, most importantly in the King James Version of 1611), in fact, two are referred to as "commands:" commandments 4 and 5. Commandment 4 is framed by "the Lord your God commanded you" (5:12, 15) and commandment 5 repeats that exact phrase (5:16). The basic meaning is a reminder that these commands were given to Israel earlier, at Sinai (Exodus 20). But that could have been said of *all of* the Ten Commandments! Why do these two alone say, "the Lord your God commanded you"? In answer, note four things. First, the "command" designation occurs only with positive commandments (5:15; 5:16). Second, the words here called as "commands" are the longest commandments in their respective sections. Third, Levinson assumes the reference to the earlier command should mean an exact repetition; however, "The ostensible precise repetition nonetheless here diverges from the original" (Levinson, *Jewish Study Bible*, 377). Finally, in fact, these "commands" are the ones which differ most markedly from their statement in Exodus 20, while the other seven commandments are virtually identical to their statements in Exodus. (Brueggemann, *Deuteronomy*, 68, notes this for commandment 4.) All these considerations signal that commandments 4 and 5 are the key ideas in the Ten Commandments (along with commandment 1). So, while the term "commandment" is regularly *overapplied* to the Ten Commandments, it is *underapplied* to the two commandments which actually use the term!

14. Lohfink, *Theology*, 257. Kaiser, *Toward OT Ethics*, 84.

15. Lohfink, *Theology*, 257, notes the long-short alternation though he divides the material differently.

Commandment 4: "Remember the Sabbath Day"

A Commandment 1: Positive		5:6	"I am the Lord your God"	short
	Commandment 2: negative	5:7–10	"No other gods and no images"	long
	Commandment 3: negative	5:11	"Do not bear the name in vain"	short
B Commandment 4: Positive		5:12–15	"Keep Sabbath and rest"	long
C Commandment 5: Positive		5:16	"Honor your parents"	short
	Comm. 6–10: negative	5:17–21	"No murder, adultery, steal, lie, covet "	long

The positive commandment 1 governs the negative commandments 2 and 3, communicating, "I brought you out of Egypt, *therefore* you should obey commands 2–3."[16] This logical connection between commandment 1 and commandments 2–3 is widely acknowledged. This suggests that the same connection exists between commandment 5 and commandments 6–10, as Kaiser suggests.[17] Commandment 5 governs commandments 6–10, communicating, roughly, "One should honor their parents, and those who learn early in life to honor them are less likely to dishonor others by killing them, etc."[18] In fact, the last phrase of Deut 5:16 may suggest this: "that it may go well with you in the land." If God's people honor their parents and if, therefore, murder, adultery, stealing, etc., are minimized, life will go better for God's people.

Commandment 4 is unique among the positive commandments in the Decalogue in that it does not govern other commandments. Like commandment 1 and commandment 5, however, it does move from a positive statement to a lengthy negative elaboration, though it is internal to commandment 4, in 5:14. It is also unique in that it is the longest command in the Decalogue, signaling its importance.[19] But it is also distinguished from commandments 2 and 3, with which it is regularly grouped, in that it does not deal specifically with an obligation to the Lord. Though it is regularly seen as the last of the commandments about God, this perception is not

---

16. Kaiser, *Toward OT Ethics*, 84.
17. Kaiser, *Toward OT Ethics*, 84.
18. McConville, *Deuteronomy*, 129, says that commandment 5's respect for parents is "symbolic of respect for the whole social organization."
19. Block, *Deuteronomy*, 164; Tigay, *Deuteronomy*, 68.

strictly accurate. The Sabbath commandment is not an obligation to God as such, but an exhortation about human activity to be done "as the Lord your God commanded you" (5:12, 15). It is a command to rest. In this it precisely parallels commandment 5, "honor your father and mother as the Lord your God commanded you" (5:16). Both are motivated by God's "command" (said only of these two commandments) though neither is an obligation about how God is to be treated, as are commandments 2 and 3.[20]

If commandment 4 is not to be coupled with commandments 2–3, the obligations to God specifically, how is it to be regarded? It is a transitional commandment between those about God (commandments 2–3) and those about neighbors (commandments 5–10).[21] Wright calls commandment 4, "the pivot of the Decalogue that, along with the fifth commandment, directs attention both to God and to human society."[22] Its separation from commandments 2 and 3 is signaled by being framed as a positive commandment. Its distinction from commandments 5–10 is established by the fact that commandment 5 is also framed positively, beginning a new section that is distinctly neighbor-oriented. Commandment 4 stands as a bridge between commandments 2–3 and commandments 5–10. It is tied to commandments 2–3 by being a final "bulwark against idolatry,"[23] which was the major thrust of those commandments. As Wright observes, in our materialistic world, people often "endow work and the whole economic enterprise with a significance beyond its God-given role . . . The command to rest from work on the Sabbath day forces a pause in this compulsive process and reminds us that time, like the earth itself, belongs to God."[24] But commandment 4 is also related to commandments 5–10 in several ways. It alone shares with commandment 5 the phrase "as the Lord your God commanded you." Further, the primary object of the commandment is about human well-being. Also, the provision that all in Israel should rest (5:14) focuses on human well-being, acting as a brake on the "tendency of

---

20. It is also called a "Sabbath to the Lord" (5:14) and it is grounded in the fact that the Lord your God "brought you out" of Egypt (5:15), but these are supporting clauses, not commandments.

21. Miller, *Deuteronomy*, 72, says, "The sabbath commandment in the Deuteronomic formulation is both the *bridge* from God to neighbor, in that it deals in some sense with relations to God and responsibilities in the human sphere, and the *center* of the Decalogue" (emphasis in the original).

22. Wright, *Deuteronomy*, 75.

23. Wright, *Deuteronomy*, 74.

24. Wright, *Deuteronomy*, 74.

human economic exploitation and oppression," thus "preserving the social liberation that *reflected the character of Yahweh*."[25] Finally, by addressing human well-being for all, it is the commandment which begins the transition from loving God to "Love your neighbor as yourself."[26] All of this reinforces the conclusion we drew earlier: the Ten Commandments are properly divided into three sections, and are dominated by the positive, not the negative, reversing the popular stereotype.

The result of our analysis shows the logic of the Ten Commandments as this:

A. Commandments 1–3: Because of God's grace we should love the Lord our God;

B. Commandment 4: Doing as God commands brings individual and societal blessing;

C. Commandments 5–10: Doing as God commands yields loving our neighbor as ourselves.

Finally, the first command in the Sabbath injunction, "Observe!" commonly means "celebrate," and is used of keeping holidays.[27] What is celebrated is the opportunity to rest.

WHAT THE COMMANDMENT MEANS IN DEUTERONOMY

Commandment 4 is expounded in Deuteronomy 14:22–16:17.[28] The section is structured around things required at stated intervals. As the Sabbath of commandment 4 is celebrated every seventh day, so other requirements

---

25. Wright, *Deuteronomy*, 76, emphasis in the original. Wright reports (p. 76) that Harold Macmillan, British Prime Minister from 1957 to 1963, described the Sabbath as the first and greatest worker-protection act in history. Christensen, *Deuteronomy*, 403, is likely correct: the fact that wives are not mentioned in what is otherwise a rather comprehensive list is probably "an attempt to avoid the suggestion that the law applies to necessary domestic activities." So also, Craigie, *Deuteronomy*, 157.

26. Miller, *Deuteronomy*, 83.

27. Tigay, *Deuteronomy*, 68.

28. This varies slightly from Kaufman's section, but we will argue the justification for this change. Merrill and Tigay see this as a unit.

at periodic intervals are elaborated in Deut 14:22–16:17. These passages deal with tithes, offerings, feasts, and remissions.[29] Note the time signatures:

> 14:23 ("year by year"),
> 14:28 ("every three years"),
> 15:1 ("At the end of every seven years"),
> 5:12 ("in the seventh year"),
> 15:20 ("year by year;" section begins at 5:19),
> 16:1 ("Observe the month"),
> 16:9 ("you shall count seven weeks"),
> 6:13 ("you shall keep . . . seven days"),
> 6:16 ("Three times a year").

But why emphasize things required at intervals? Merrill explains,

> A major responsibility of any king in vassalage to a Hittite ruler was the periodic presentation of tribute to him, tokens of his submission and loyalty. This was no less true of Israel, which, in line with the sovereign-vassal nature of the Sinaitic covenant, must bear appropriate offerings to the Lord on stated occasions. This was part and parcel of true worship, a vital aspect of what it meant to give recognition to the Lord as the only God and to respond to him accordingly. This tribute is an expression of obedience to the fourth commandment, that which celebrates redemption from the bondage of Egyptian slavery to the happy service of the Great King, the Lord.[30]

Merrill continues, "The entire section under review addresses (1) the matter of the procedure for presenting tribute (14:22–29), (2) its use in regard to other Israelites, especially the poor (15:1–11) and indentured (15:12–18), (3) special instruction concerning animal sacrifices (15:19–23), and (4) the three major festival times when tribute was taken to the Lord at the central sanctuary (16:1–17)."[31] Here is a list of the sections and their subjects:

1. 14:22–27	Yearly: tithe the yield of your seed and eat it, "*the Lord your God blesses you*"
2. 14:28–29	Every three years: tithe your produce for others to eat
3. 15:1–11	Every seven years: release debts
4. 15:12–18	Every seven years: release servants

29. Lundbom, *Deuteronomy*, 417.
30. Merrill, *Deuteronomy*, 239.
31. Merrill, *Deuteronomy*, 239.

5. 15:19-23	Yearly: give first-born of the flocks and eat it
6. 16:1-8	Yearly in month of Abib eat at Feast of Passover/Unleavened Bread (16:1, 16)
7. 16:9-12	Yearly, seven weeks after harvest begins: eat at the Feast of Weeks
8. 16:13-15	Yearly, eat for seven days, at Feast of Booths, when processing the harvest ends[32]
9. 16:16-17	Three feasts per year: give as one is able *"according to the blessing of the Lord"*

Note several things about this section. In the nine sections, the word "bless" (Hebrew *bārak*) occurs nine times, though not in each unit. Further, the entire section is bounded by an *inclusio*, a standard boundary marker in Deuteronomy,[33] in that the Lord's blessing is mentioned in the first and the last section (14:24; 16:17). In addition, the terms "eat," or "feast" occur in *every* one of the nine sections (a total of sixteen times) except for 15:1-11 and 15:12-18. Finally, a form of the command "rejoice" occurs four times (14:26; 16:11, 14, 15). Since repetition is a major device that Bible writers used to help the audience follow their train of thought, what can we deduce from the repetition of the terms "bless," "eat/feast," and "rejoice"?

The passage communicates first that what we give to the Lord comes from his blessing (14:24; 16:10, 17). We are also shown that obedience to the Lord *brings us* blessing (14:29; 15:10; 15:18). Most striking, every gift given to the Lord in the passage brings benefit to the offerer or a needy person, whether the Levites (14:27, 29; 16:11, 14, 15) or "the sojourner, the fatherless and the widow" (14:29, 16:11, 14). Finally, the end result of everything in the passage is "rejoicing" (14:26, 16:11, 14, 15), which forms an *inclusio* in the passage. Tigay's observation points in the right direction when he observes that the gifts given to the Lord "are not given to the clergy or the sanctuary. They are eaten by their owners or given to the poor."[34] The same message is reinforced in the two paragraphs which are not about eating.[35] They also benefit others by a release from debt (15:1-11) or from servitude (15:12-18). We are at last ready to state the principle that animates commandment 4 and its elaboration. *Like the Sabbath*

---

32. Lundbom, *Deuteronomy*, 514.
33. Lundbom, *Deuteronomy*, 504.
34. Tigay, *Deuteronomy*, 141.

35. Two texts in 15:4 and 15:7, 11, seem in conflict. The "if" clause in 15:5 clarifies it. If Israel obeyed well there would be no poor, but 15:7, 11 assume—or predict—that Israel will never obey well enough to inherit that blessing!

commandment in 5:12–15, *every section in 14:22–16:17 is about how obedience to the Lord brings benefit to the person who obeys or to others around them*. What stands out in *every* section where an offering is given *to the Lord* is that the giver or a needy neighbor eats what is given. In the two sections about releases, it is also clear that benefit comes to both the giver (15:4, 6, 10; 15:18) and the receiver (15:1; 15:12) of the release. And note that in both cases of release, like the gifts given in the other sections, the release is done for the Lord (15:2, 5; 15:15). It is noteworthy that the generosity commanded of God's people (15:8, 13–14) mirrors the generosity of God in providing the blessings from which they give back to him (16:17), and his generosity in promising blessing to them (15:4, 6, 10).

These considerations demonstrate that Wright is right about how the Sabbath commandment and its exposition are consistent. "The Sabbath commandment focused on the needs especially of the dependent sections of the population (5:14) and was motivated by God's redemptive action on behalf of Israel when they were oppressed slaves. Chapter 15 is saturated with the same social concern and the same motivation."[36] In fact, this is the animating spirit of 14:22–16:17.

The way Deuteronomy elucidates commandment 4 reinforces—in spades—the theme that obedience to God is good for us. While this is stated many times in the book (e.g., Deut 5:29, 6:1–3), commandment 4 trumpets this by repetition: even what we give to God turns about and enhances us. What a good God we worship!

But commandment 4 also leads to an even more dazzling realization. By repeatedly returning to how obedience to God brings benefits to others, commandment 4's full import teaches us that love of God must lead to love of neighbor. It is in commandment 4 that this vital connection is made. Notice that the Ten Commandments do not simply paste on obligations to neighbor after those to God. Instead, commandment 4 is carefully crafted as the bridge between commandments 1–3 and commandments 5–10, in order to join the two sections and unveil their connection.

We see this bridge function in something we noted earlier, that commandment 4 is unique in pointing both back to God and forward to our neighbors. The second major clue is the seemingly odd repetition that what we give to God keeps benefitting others. But two other considerations reveal why this should be so.

---

36. Wright, *Deuteronomy*, 187.

Commandment 4: "Remember the Sabbath Day"

One is the heart of God. Jonathan Edwards defined "love" as the disposition to do good to others, to act for their benefit.[37] This definition is confirmed and perfectly displayed in John 3:16, "For in this way God loved the world: that he gave his one and only Son" (NET Bible). So, it is natural for God, it is God's essential nature, to take that which is his and give it to others for their wellbeing. The meaning of commandment 4 here is that our offerings to God must, because of who our God is, flow from him to benefit those he loves.

Another reason for this is also elaborated by Jonathan Edwards. He taught that the essence of "true virtue" for humans is love, since it is the root of the disposition to bring all good to others.[38] In other words, human virtue is to imitate God, who is love (1 John 4:16). Jesus commanded such imitation: "This is my commandment, that you love one another as I have loved you" (John 15:12). John declared the other side of the coin: "If anyone says, 'I love God,' and hates his brother, he is a liar" (1 John 4:20). So, the exposition of commandment 4 in Deuteronomy reveals that what we give to God benefits others, both because it is God's nature and because we who represent him imitate his love toward others.

So, while the NT forcefully affirms these things, we are asserting that commandment 4 is ground-zero for the original idea. Commandment 4 shows that what we give to God turns around and benefits our neighbors, and it does so as the introduction to our instructions about how to continue to benefit others in commandments 5–10. Essentially, commandment 4 announces that those who honor God honor a God who gives to others, so they must do the same.

Following commandment 3, commandment 4 discloses that representing God well entails imitating his love for others. So, the internal logic of the ordering of commandments 2–10 is:

> Love of God requires exclusive loyalty to him (commandment 2),
> and loyalty to him means representing him well toward others (commandment 3),
> and representing him well means imitating his love for others (commandment 4),
> the principles of which are explained in commandments 5–10.

---

37. Edwards, *The End for Which God Created the World*, 439.
38. Edwards, *The End for Which God Created the World*, 442.

The end result is to recognize that when Jesus said that love of neighbor must follow love of God (Mark 12:28–32), he is stating the precise meaning of commandment 4, once we grasp its position at the center of the Decalogue.

WHAT THE COMMANDMENT MEANS AS A POSITIVE PRINCIPLE

We may summarize: obeying the Sabbath commandment and its elaborations demonstrates submission to the Lord as Israel's king by giving him the tribute he deserves;[39] shows gratitude to God for one's goods and one's freedom;[40] but is fundamentally humanitarian, benefitting the giver and showing compassion for the poor, since what is done for and given to the Lord invariably benefits his people.[41] The Sabbath commandment states one example of how giving God the tribute he deserves benefits the giver and those around them. The elaborations in Deut 14:22–16:17 only enlarge upon the blessings that come to the individual and their needy neighbors when they honor God as he has commanded. It is almost as if giving to the Lord is giving to oneself—and others!

Even more to the point are Jesus's words, "The Sabbath was made for man, not man for the Sabbath" (Mark 2:27). Now that we have examined commandment 4 and its exposition in detail, it is apparent that Jesus's comment is not an offhanded remark about the Sabbath commandment, but a considered, deliberate proclamation of its exact essence. Commandment 4 *means* that giving God what he rightfully deserves benefits the giver and those around them. Loving God results in loving our neighbors.

Each section related to commandment 4 is about obligations which occur at regular intervals, suggesting that how we handle our time matters to God, that life is punctuated by opportunities to render to God the proper tribute that such a glorious benefactor deserves. But that is not the core issue.

The essence of commandment 4 may be stated as a positive principle this way: *giving to the Lord what he deserves for his grace brings blessing and joy to individuals and to their needy neighbors, including the blessing*

---

39. Merrill, *Deuteronomy*, 239.
40. Walton, "Deuteronomy," 223–24. Note five mentions of freedom from Egypt in the section (15:5; 16:1, 3, 6, 12).
41. Block, *Deuteronomy*, 173.

Commandment 4: "Remember the Sabbath Day"

of rest. God's commandments are given to bring about our good and our joy. At the center of the Ten Commandments, the longest one proclaims that everything God commands us to do is ultimately for our good and the good of others, as well as for God's glory. In its most succinct form, the positive meaning of commandment 4 is, *the Sabbath was made for man, not man for the Sabbath* (Mark 2:27).

WHAT THE COMMANDMENT MEANS FOR CHRISTIANS

How the Sabbath commandment applies to contemporary Christians is a particularly contentious and difficult issue.[42] Based upon our exposition, we offer the following observations and proposals for consideration, acknowledging that not all Christians will agree.

First, the Sabbath commandment is not repeated in the NT as binding upon Christians after Jesus's death.[43] After the Gospels, the NT records no instructions or reports about believers observing the Sabbath. The Sabbath disappears for Christians. The book of Acts uses the term "Sabbath" ten times, all of which are descriptive, not prescriptive. All three instances in which the apostle Paul attended the synagogue on the Sabbath (Acts 13:14–44; 17:2; 18:4) seem to be instances of attending so he could interact with Jews and share the gospel. If anything, the Sabbath is replaced by Sunday meetings, though it is not explained that way. There are two NT texts

---

42. Carson calls the Sabbath issue "one of the most difficult areas in the study of the relationship between the Testaments, and in the history of the development of doctrine." Carson, *From Sabbath to Lord's Day*, 17. For a detailed and thoughtful defense of the view that Christians do not live under the Jewish Sabbath but must observe the Sabbath as a creation ordinance taught in the biblical creation account and incumbent upon all of humanity, see Beale, "Sunday Sabbath Day Observance." He acknowledges that the issues are difficult. Further, his view requires accepting several controversial conclusions. For a book-length defense of the view that NT believers do not live under the Sabbath commandment either as a Christian continuation of the Jewish Sabbath or as a creation ordinance, see Carson, *From Sabbath to Lord's Day*. Carson and his coauthors argue that the NT application, clear especially in Hebrews, is that trusting in Christ for salvation inaugurates the believer's rest, which will be consummated in eternity, and which the creation account and the Jewish Sabbath were always shadows of (see esp. Carson chapters 2, 6, and 7. We are persuaded by Carson.

43. "Sabbath" occurs about sixty-nine times in the NT. Fifty-six are in the Gospels. Ten are in Acts, never as an imperative, all of which are descriptive ("x happened on the Sabbath"). After Acts, the term occurs three times: 1 Cor 16:2 (where it means "week" in "first day of the *week*:" BDAG, 910); Col 2:16, Heb 4:9.

about believers meeting "on the first day of the week." The first, Acts 20:7, reports that the believers gathered. In 1 Corinthians 16:2, perhaps some 20 years later, such gathering had apparently become a regular procedure: "On the first day of every week, each of you is to put something aside and store it up, as he may prosper."[44] This suggests that the believers met then, and so offerings were to be given then. That's all the evidence. But there is no effort to clarify this or provide a theological rationale.

In light of all this, and in line with our earlier treatment of the relation of the believer to the Mosaic law, we propose that NT Christians are entirely free from the Sabbath regulations of the Mosaic covenant.[45]

However, the Sabbath commandment and its exposition in Deuteronomy are Scripture which teaches all believers (2 Tim 3:16–17). Further, the Sabbath concept predates the Mosaic law, beginning in Gen 2:1–3. It seems at the least that the principle that God gave rest to humans as a blessing and that resting on a regular basis is to be guarded as a gift from God has perpetual application.[46] In fact, many have learned from experience that people who overwork themselves can collapse from emotional exhaustion.[47]

---

44. See Lacey's discussion in Carson, *From Sabbath to Lord's Day*, 183–86.

45. As noted above, a detailed defense of this view is found in Carson, *From Sabbath to Lord's Day*.

46. For a thoughtful reflection on American busyness and the idolatry it masks, and how resting can counteract that idolatry, see Davis, "Sabbath as Counter-Formational Practice" in Carson, *From Sabbath to Lord's Day*. One need not agree with everything here to profit from the essay.

47. Merrill points the way to application of this command in conclusions drawn from the text of Deuteronomy. He observes that the motive for observing the Sabbath in Exodus is changed in Deuteronomy. Exodus cites God's rest after creation (20:11), while Deuteronomy names liberation from slavery in Egypt (5:15). He then helpfully elaborates, "The principal theological truth to be seen here is the changing theological emphasis of the unchanging God. For the people freshly delivered from Egyptian overlordship by the mighty exodus miracle, God as Creator is a central truth. Therefore it is most appropriate that the Sabbath focus on him as creator and the cessation of that creative work, the very point of the Exodus commandment. From the perspective of the Deuteronomy legislation some forty years later, creation pales into insignificance in comparison to the act of redemption itself. With the benefit now of historical retrospection and with the anticipation of the crossing of another watery barrier—the Jordan—and the uncertainties of conquest, Israel was to recall its plight as slaves and its glorious release from that hopeless situation. Sabbath now speaks of redemption and not creation, of rest and not cessation. All this gives theological justification for the observance by the Christian of Sunday rather than Saturday as the day set apart as holy. For the Christian, the moment of greatest significance is no longer creation or the exodus—as important

Commandment 4: "Remember the Sabbath Day"

We conclude that regular rest as God's wise provision is a perennial principle. Apparently, Christians abandoned the Sabbath but celebrated Jesus's resurrection by a Sunday celebration. So, we also conclude that honoring God by celebrating Jesus's resurrection and redemption on Sunday is appropriate.[48] We conclude, finally, that since the NT provides no further instruction, any further specifics are left to the conscience of the individual believer.

There is, however, one imperative about the Sabbath in the NT Epistles: "Therefore let no one pass judgment on you in questions of food and drink, or with regard to a festival or a new moon or a Sabbath. These are a shadow of the things to come, but the substance belongs to Christ" (Col 2:16; cf. Romans 14). Believers are free to do with the Sabbath concept as their conscience dictates. Paul likely writes these words for the Jewish believers in the Roman congregation, who, growing up with the Sabbath, might still desire to observe it after they became believers. But the fact that he forbids any judgment and leaves it to the believer's conscience shows that in Paul's mind there is no Sabbath mandate, even for Jewish believers. That's the sum total of the Sabbath "requirements" laid down for NT Christians.

There is one other text in the Epistles that speaks of the Sabbath. The "substance" that the Sabbath foreshadowed in Christ is explained in Heb 4:9: the Sabbath pictured the rest from labors which believers will experience in the eternal state.[49] While we begin to experience it now, the fullness awaits the future.[50] So, this suggests, in line with the "already and not yet" emphasis of the NT, what the substance of the believer's Sabbath rest is. The deepest application of the Sabbath to NT believers is that we *continually* celebrate what the Sabbath foreshadowed, both the current rest in Christ by faith in him for salvation and the final rest of God's people in "a better country, that is, a heavenly one" (Heb 11:16). The hallowing of the seventh day at creation and the Jewish Sabbath were shadows anticipating the rest

---

as these are in salvation history. Central to his faith and experience is the resurrection of the Lord Jesus Christ, a re-creating and redemptive event that eclipses all of God's mighty acts of the past. Thus by example if not by explicit command Jesus and the apostles mandated the observance of the first day of the week as commemorative of his triumphant victory over death." See Merrill, *Deuteronomy*, 152.

48. See Lacey's analysis in Carson, *From Sabbath to Lord's Day*, 180–84, as well as Merrill's observation in the previous note.

49. Bruce, *Hebrews*, 76–9.

50. See Bruce, *Hebrews*, 75. The "rest" here begins by faith in Christ for salvation, but its fulfillment is in eternity.

intended by God for his people. That rest, experienced in the Garden of Eden, was then taken away by sin. Christians look forward expectantly to the restoration of that Edenic rest in the eternal state of God's people, through the redemption brought by the death and resurrection of Jesus.[51]

The application of the Sabbath to Christians is not an easy issue. Our discussion is meant to provide a case for our conclusions, recognizing that capable and sincere Christians nevertheless come to different conclusions.

Since Christians don't have further directions about the Sabbath, we are all free to follow our conscience. Rest regularly! Honor the Lord on "the Lord's Day" (Rev 1:10)," at least. "Do not neglect to meet together" with other Christians (Heb 10:25). But no further instructions means "no instructions." So, if anyone asks us what they are required to do on the Sabbath, we will not answer. Well, maybe we will quote Jesus: "The Sabbath was made for man, not man for the Sabbath" (Mark 2:27).

HEIDELBERG CATECHISM:

Our conclusions are very much in line with the Heidelberg Catechism.

103. Q. What is God's will for us in the fourth commandment?

A. First, that the gospel ministry and education for it be maintained, and that, especially on the festive day of rest, I regularly attend the assembly of God's people to learn what God's Word teaches, to participate in the sacraments, to pray to God publicly, and to bring Christian offerings for the poor. Second, that every day of my life I rest from my evil ways, let the Lord work in me through the Spirit, and so begin in this life the eternal Sabbath.

QUESTIONS FOR PERSONAL DEVOTIONS:

1. The word Sabbath means "to stop." What things might you need to stop?
2. How could stopping some of these things, even temporarily, allow you to experience God's grace more fully in your life?

---

51. See Lincoln's excellent discussion in Carson, *From Sabbath to Lord's Day*, chapter 7.

Commandment 4: "Remember the Sabbath Day"

3. How does the inclusion of servants, animals and foreigners in the Sabbath commandment inform your view of those around you and how you are called to love your neighbor?
4. Why is it important that the Sabbath is commanded to be a regular/weekly practice?
5. What expectations/pressures could having Sabbath as a regular/weekly practice help to counteract in your life?
6. How does regular stopping our labor remind us that God, not we, are in control?
7. Consider the relation between the Sabbath commandment and Ps 46:10?
8. How can the exposition of the Sabbath commandment that we find in Deuteronomy chapters 14 through 16 inform how we treat those around us today?
9. What else might God be saying to you through this section of Deuteronomy?

QUESTIONS FOR TEACHING AND PREACHING:

1. Why is it important that servants, animals, and foreigners are included in the Sabbath commandment? How does this affect your teaching and preaching of the fourth commandment?
2. What are some ways that you have seen members of your congregation/community of faith struggle to keep the Sabbath commandment?
3. Deuteronomy 5:14 states that, "the seventh day is a Sabbath to the Lord your God." Discuss the importance of the words "to the Lord" (not "for" or "from") and how this relates to the idea of offering something to God.
4. What is the significance of God's deliverance from Egypt, which is mentioned in the first of the Ten Commandments, being repeated in the Sabbath commandment?
5. In giving the Sabbath commandment, Deuteronomy 5 calls us to remember the slavery of God's people in Egypt. Compare this to passages in the NT that call us to remember that we have been freed from

slavery to sin through faith in Christ. How could you teach or preach on this?

6. The Sabbath commandment contrasts service to God with slavery in Egypt. What is keeping the people of your congregation/community of faith in spiritual slavery and preventing them from experiencing God's grace more fully?

7. Where do you find ideas similar to the exposition of the Sabbath commandment in Deuteronomy chapter 14 through 16 present elsewhere in the Old and New Testaments? How might these passages inform our understanding of the Sabbath commandment?

8. How does the regular reminder of the Sabbath commandment correspond to the regular reminder of the Lord's Supper in the life of the church?

9. How does the Sabbath commandment discourage the exploitation and oppression of those around us and how can you communicate this in your teaching and preaching?

Chapter 8

Commandment 5: "Honor Your Father and Your Mother"

Text of commandment 5 in Deuteronomy 5: "Honor your father and your mother, as the LORD your God commanded you, that your days may be long, and that it may go well with you in the land that the LORD your God is giving you" (5:16).

Commandment 5 expounded in Deuteronomy: 16:18–18:22.

Positive principle summary: We love God and neighbor by honoring the authorities God has authorized.

Full positive principle: We show our love for God and our neighbors by honoring those who extend God's authority over us by (1) obeying their directives, (2) encouraging them to do their jobs well, and (3) supplying what is due to them to sustain their service to us.

FLOWERS

Think back several chapters to the, thankfully, imaginary story that I, Derek, told about coming home to my wife after she had a terrible day. In that story, I told her that I had brought her flowers because as her husband, it was duty and obligation to do so. I shared that story as an example in a sermon once, and there were several women in the congregation who I think were ready to murder me on the spot. That story is so terrible because it takes a relationship that is meant to be close and intimate and personal and replaces it with a list of dos and don'ts, of boxes to be checked off. As we have gone through the different commandments, we have seen how this type of thinking is harmful and also how it misses the heart of what God was trying to teach his people in the commandments. In short, it misses grace and love and replaces it with duty and obligation.

As we now turn to the second table of the Ten Commandments, the neighbor commandments, this story of "obligation flowers" is just as helpful as when we started the first table. God calls us to honor our father and mother. In doing so, God is calling us to relationship, to be a part of a covenant community. God is not calling us to duty and guilt and obligation and "because I said so." God is calling us to learn and grow together in respectful relationship and community. If we miss the heart of this commandment, then we will miss the heart of all that follows.

I am also aware that this can be a very emotional and difficult commandment for some people to hear. It can be a struggle for some to know how to apply this commandment. Some people never had the opportunity to know their father or their mother. Some people had largely negative examples of father and mother. Some people were hurt and mistreated by their father and/or mother. Some people come from blended families where their relationship to father and mother is complicated. Some people have lost their father or mother or both. While hearing this commandment can strike people in many different ways, let's see if we can get to the heart of what it really means.

WHAT THE COMMANDMENT MEANS IN DEUTERONOMY 5

Commandment 5 is very close in wording to its expression in Exod 20:12, though it is a bit longer in Deuteronomy. Deuteronomy adds, "as the Lord your God commanded you," referring to its first statement at Mt. Sinai. As discussed in Chapter 7, since that reminder could have been said of all the Ten Commandments, the fact that it is specified in Deuteronomy only of commandments 4 and 5 highlights their special importance. Further, as treated under commandment 4, commandments 1, 4, and 5 are the only ones framed as positives, again showing their special significance. Our earlier conclusion was that commandment 5 begins the section of the Ten Commandments which addresses human obligations to other people

Commandment 5: "Honor Your Father and Your Mother"

and governs commandments 6–10.[1] In fact, it is the most important commandment related to humans.[2] Weinfeld points out that commandment 5 "is in fact considered by the [Jewish] sages to be the foremost among the commandments for which man is rewarded in this world."[3] He cites a Mishnah[4] text which reads, "The following are the things for which a man enjoys the fruits in this world while the principal remains for him in the world to come: Honoring one's father and mother . . . "[5]

We argued earlier that the Ten Commandments are arranged in descending order of importance. The most important comes first, both in the overall arrangement of the commandments (obligations to God come first, before the commandments about our neighbors), and in the arrangement of the commandment lists about God and those about neighbors. That would require that commandment 5 be the most important one in commandments 5–10, which corresponds to what we have just argued. But how could commandment 5 about honoring parents be of greater importance than commandment 6, which forbids murder? The answer is this. The commandments about God are more important than the commandments about humans (they come first), and the first commandment about humans sets the stage for honoring of God to carry over into honoring human beings rightly. If children learn in the home, from their earliest memories, to honor their parents, they are more likely to honor others in general, and to be reluctant to dishonor others by disobeying God's commandments.[6] Learning early in life to respect authority is the best route to a social order in which respect for others is practiced. Hence, commandment 5 is the critical foundation of commandments 6–10.

The first word in this short commandment is "honor" (Hebrew *kābed*), meaning to grant special esteem to them. The root meaning of the Hebrew noun is "heavy, or weighty" while its metaphorical use means to consider someone or something weighty, significant, important.[7] It is com-

---

1. See Kaiser, *Ethics*, 84.
2. See Merrill, *Deuteronomy*, 153.
3. Weinfeld, *Deuteronomy*, 312.
4. The Mishnah is the collected sayings of the Jewish rabbis from c. 200 BCE to 200 CE, written down about CE 200.
5. Blackman, Mishnah, *Pe'a* 1:1.
6. Wright observes, "The fifth commandment focuses on the honor due to parents, who are the first form of social authority encountered in life" (*Deuteronomy*, 203). See also Craigie, *Deuteronomy*, 159.
7. See Wright, *Deuteronomy*, 87, note on 5:16.

monly used in the Hebrew Bible of God, meaning to esteem him as the most important, weighty, significant one, that is, to honor him.

Merrill explains,

> Honor, however, is not something that can be commanded if it remains only an attitude or disposition. Therefore, and very much in line with the underlying root meaning of the verb, to honor demands action that betokens the inner spirit ... The command to honor therefore is a command to demonstrate in tangible, empirical ways the respect people must have for their parents.[8]

It is interesting that Lev 19:3 repeats this commandment, substituting "fear" for "honor," showing that the commandment means to "respect," or "revere" one's parents (the normal meaning of "fear" in the OT). The Hebrew term for "dishonor" means "to treat lightly," and is used of one who "curses or insults" his father or mother (Exod 21:17; Lev 20:9).[9] Lundbom is helpful: "In Proverbs, honoring parents means adhering to their teaching and showing them respect when they are old (Prov 1:8; 4:1–5; 23:22–25)."[10]

A story in Deut 21:18–21 illustrates the opposite of respecting one's parents.[11] It describes an incorrigible son characterized by flagrant and sustained disobedience, who will not accept correction. The description approaches that of a sociopath, one who disregards accepted attitudes and behaviors and does whatever he desires with no sense of obligation to others or conscience. Instead, the exhortation to honor parents aims to foster children who care about others, accept correction, and live harmoniously with their family and society. It is not endorsing all that particular parents may do, or affirming that parents always fulfill their roles admirably, but it is commanding a respect for authority figures which accepts limits on personal behavior for the sake of others and which teaches people to coexist with others based upon the same regard for them that one has for oneself. It is aimed at respect for the position that parents (and other authorities: see below) occupy and for cooperation toward the beneficial results they attempt to bring about, not affirming (nor excusing) the shortcomings that humans inevitably display.

It is also interesting that Lev 19:3 reverses the order in which the parents are named. This suggests that while it is traditional to designate the

---

8. Merrill, *Deuteronomy*, 153.
9. Weinfeld, *Deuteronomy 1–11*, 309.
10. Lundbom, *Deuteronomy*, 287.
11. Lundbom, *Deuteronomy*, 287, points out this parallel.

Commandment 5: "Honor Your Father and Your Mother"

father first, honoring him as the head of the family, the mother being named first communicates that she is to enjoy equal respect as a parent, which is also clear from the fact that in all three texts, both parents are named.[12] This also shows that women were not considered mere chattel property in the Hebrew Bible, whatever other ancient Near Eastern cultures thought.

Tigay is perceptive when he says, "this commandment, like the Decalogue as a whole, is not addressed merely to youngsters; see v. 14."[13] This is demonstrated in Deut 21:18–21.[14] He continues,[15] "Care for one's aged parents is one of the fundamental duties spelled out in adoption contracts and other documents of the ancient Near East. The Akkadian cognate[16] of *kābed*, "honor," is one of the verbs used to describe such care." Wright reminds us that the family in ancient Israel included several generations living together, so commandment 5 applied to the entire family, not just small children.[17]

Noting the similarities we pointed out above between commandments 4 (the Sabbath) and 5 (parents) and that these two are paired in Exodus 20, Deuteronomy 5, and Lev 19:3, Tigay suggests that "observing the Sabbath is a means of honoring God and is thus a counterpart to honoring parents."[18]

Wright develops the importance of this commandment: "the family, or 'father's house,' was the basic unit of Israel's society in three ways:" socially, economically, and spiritually. He adds, "whatever threatened the family ultimately threatened the wider social basis of the whole covenant relationship."[19] Commandment 2 emphasized that failure by parents could affect their children and grandchildren (5:9; see also 6:6–7). Craigie elaborates, "Here, the reciprocal side of that responsibility is stated . . . [for parents] to teach effectively, there must be a receptive audience. If children

---

12. So Tigay, *Deuteronomy*, 70, who also points out that the Talmud sees the Torah as affirming the equality of father and mother.

13. Tigay, *Deuteronomy*, 70. So Wright, *Deuteronomy*, 76, who also notes that it does apply to children also, and that Paul uses it primarily that way in Eph 6:1–3 does not suggest that we limit it to that valid use.

14. McConville, *Deuteronomy*, 128.

15. Tigay, *Deuteronomy*, 70.

16. A "cognate" is the equivalent word in a similar, or related, language.

17. Wright, *Deuteronomy*, 77.

18. Tigay, *Deuteronomy*, 70.

19. Wright, *Deuteronomy*, 77.

did not honor their parents . . . they would not be able to learn about the covenant relationship with God."[20]

Tigay also observes that "This is the only command in the Decalogue for which a reward is promised."[21] Further, to "that your days may be long," Deuteronomy adds to the Exodus wording a second expression of blessing, "that it may go well with you."[22] To be distinguished in these two ways is further confirmation of this commandment's special gravity. This also supports our earlier assertion that it governs commandments 6–10 which follow it.

Of special importance is the fact that commandment 5 is primarily about *our obligation to others*. The aim of commandment 5 is primarily to benefit one's parents, while the obedience of the children to commandment 5 is the means to that ultimate end. We could also say that the commandment's desired end is the parent's well-being while the child's obedience to it is the instrument which produces the result. Let us illustrate by borrowing an analogy from Jonathan Edwards,[23] who distinguishes an "ultimate end" or goal from a "subordinate end" or goal. An ultimate end is the final result one has in view while a subordinate end is a goal one pursues in order to achieve the ultimate end. For example, if one goes to the pharmacy to get medicine when one is ill, the end, or goal of *that trip* is to secure the medicine. But the end result one desires is not to have the medicine, but the health that the medicine can bring. So, the trip to the pharmacy pursues a subordinate end—to secure the medicine—which aims at the ultimate end—health. The trip to the pharmacy is a vital goal, but it is subordinate to the final goal, health.

Now it is vital to grasp that the ultimate end, or goal, of commandment 5 is the well-being of parents while the subordinate end is the obedience of the children (young and older) to it. Just as no trip to the pharmacy means no medicine and thus no health, so no obedience of children to commandment 5 means no actions which result in the honoring of parents. The ultimate end commandment 5 aims at is the well-being of parents while the subordinate end is children obeying the commandment so as to facilitate their parents' well-being.

---

20. Craigie, *Deuteronomy*, 158.
21. Tigay, *Deuteronomy*, 70. The apostle Paul also noted this: Eph 6:2.
22. Tigay, *Deuteronomy*, 70.
23. Edwards, *The End for Which God Created the World*, 405.

Commandment 5: "Honor Your Father and Your Mother"

The reason we have belabored this is that commandments 5–10 are all of this character. That is, commandments 5–10 articulate the subordinate ends, or goals, while neighbor well-being is the ultimate end of each of them. Commandment 6 fundamentally means, "Do not murder your *neighbor*." Commandment 7 means, "Do not damage your *neighbor* by committing adultery with their spouse and thus destroying their family." Commandment 8 means not primarily, "It is lamentable *for you* if *you* were to sink to the disreputable level of becoming a thief" (though, of course, that is true). It means, "Thou shalt not harm thy *neighbor* by stealing from them." Commandment 9 is particularly clear in this regard. It does not fundamentally mean, "Do not *be* a liar" (though that is the subordinate end). It is concerned with lying that harms your *neighbor*, hence its wording: "Do not bear false witness *against your neighbor*." It clearly means, "Do not harm your neighbor's reputation or have them punished for something they did not do *because you bore false witness against them*." Commandments 5–10 are all principles aimed at promoting the good of our neighbor. And our part in each commandment is to avoid the actions prohibited that will harm their well-being, and so ultimately to promote their good—i.e., to love them—as will become clearer as we proceed. Commandments 5–10 express the subordinate goals while the ultimate end of them all is protecting our neighbor from harm and promoting his or her well-being. That is, commandments 5–10 aim at love of neighbor, defined as seeking their well-being. Thompson notes this important consideration: "The last five commandments cover fundamental requirements for life in society."[24] We will return to this emphasis below.

Commandment 10 may seem a bit different, but it really is not. "Do not covet," aims at the inner motives of the audience, but the difference is simply that it aims at the roots which give rise to the actions which damage our neighbors. Its immediate goal, that we avoid coveting, is the subordinate end, while its ultimate end is the same as the others: to avoid harm to our neighbor. Notice that the first prohibition concerning coveting is about our neighbor's spouse. The point is that if one's inner cravings for another's spouse become actions, commandment 7 (adultery) is violated, and our neighbor is harmed. The other things we are not to covet are our neighbor's possessions. Why? Because if our inner cravings spill over into actions, we violate commandment 8, and our neighbor is damaged by our stealing. So, while commandment 10, too, expresses the subordinate goal, its ultimate

---

24. Thompson, *Deuteronomy*, 117.

end is to prevent the damage to our neighbor that will arise if we do not control our cravings.

In sum, commandments 5–10 state the subordinate goals which are the divinely revealed means toward the ultimate goal: love of neighbor, i.e., seeking their well-being.

Commandment 5 heads the neighbor-oriented obligations, which it governs. It kicks off the love emphasis toward neighbor by addressing our obligation to our parents—the first and most important neighbors we all encounter in life. The commandment states the first neighbor-love obligation as a positive instruction to stress that positive actions of love are the ultimate goal of commandments 5–10, even though most are stated as negative minimums. By instructing us to "honor" our parents, we perceive that the obligation is expansive, open-ended, and ongoing. Paul saw this expansive nature of the commandments when he wrote, "Leave no debt outstanding to anyone, except the debt of love to one another" (Rom 13:8).[25]

The fact that commandment 5 governs commandments 6–10 has a final, determinative implication. Its positive commandment is to "honor" others. We propose that this obligation is the integrating theme which animates and clarifies the meaning of commandments 6–10. That is, honoring others is the positive meaning of each of the commandments which are stated as negative minimums. Commandments 6–10 define the key spheres, after parents, in which honoring others is required and thus define "love" of neighbor. "Honor" means to choose to value them, to grant them esteem, to respect them. If one values, esteems and respects others, one would not murder them, or do the other things prohibited in commandments 6–10. So, stated differently, love of neighbor can be defined as honoring them in the spheres specified in commandments 5–10.[26] Our

---

25. Translation of Cranfield, *Romans*, 673.

26. Several considerations support this conclusion. First, "honoring" is the only positive commandment in commandments 5–10, and its positive nature makes it more expansive and open-ended than negative minimums. This by itself suggests that commandments 6–10 provide the particulars. Similarly, the fact that it is termed a "commandment" and yet it is so cryptic—one word in Hebrew!—suggests again that particulars must be supplied so that the "commandment" can be obeyed by the pious. Third, the fact that parents are specified but that Deuteronomy later expands this honoring to other groups shows that the obligation of honoring others is not limited to parents but extends far more broadly. Fourth, it is obvious that the term "honor" would be a fitting way of summarizing each of the commandments following commandment 5: "honor your neighbor by respecting his right to life," "honor your neighbor by respecting his marriage as inviolable," "honor your neighbor by valuing his reputation so as to refuse to

exposition of commandments 6–10 in the following chapters will apply this conclusion in detail.

WHAT THE COMMANDMENT MEANS IN DEUTERONOMY

Commandment 5 is expounded in Deut 16:18–18:22,[27] which discusses leadership and authority in Israel. It elaborates the principle stated in commandment 5 regarding parental authority in regard to other authorities. Merrill helpfully explains,

> With the transition from a patriarchal, familial structure in Egyptian and wilderness times to that of a village-centered culture following the conquest, Israel's understanding of authority patterns also changed. While one must continue to honor his parents, there are other, more comprehensive hierarchies that also must be given due consideration. [Israel experienced the] need for government at increasingly higher and broader levels. The result in due time would be the rise of monarchy itself.[28]

Wright elaborates the connection to commandment 5: "Parental authority ... is a model for other forms of authority and leadership in society (as is seen in the use of "father" for various kinds of honored or important persons in many societies)."[29] Lundbom points out the unit's structure. It "sets forth regulations concerning the four major officeholders in Israelite society."[30] Respect for authority is here extended to the institutions outside of the family which represent God's authority among his people. We can chart the structure this way:

A. Judge (16:18–17:13); "abomination" (2x: 17:1, 4)

B. King (17:14–20)

C. Priest (18:1–8)

---

bear false witness against him." Finally, the fact that commandments 6–10 are joined by "and" shows that they are a unit, as we have seen, and supports the conclusion that these are all manifestations of one principle, that of honoring others.

27. Merrill, *Deuteronomy*, 257; also noted by Wright, *Deuteronomy*, 203.
28. Merrill, *Deuteronomy*, 257.
29. Wright, *Deuteronomy*, 203. So also, Christensen, *Deuteronomy* 1:124.
30. Lundbom, *Deuteronomy*, 519.

D. Prophet (18:9–22); "abomination" (3x: 18:9, 12, 12)

The entire unit is framed by repetition of the word "abomination" which proves to be a key theme regarding judges and prophets. In 16:18–17:13 (unit A), we are told what judges are to do and why they might need to take legal action.[31] Thus, 16:21–17:1 describes "abominations" (17:1) which either (1) characterize pagan worship (16:21–22) or (2) are forbidden by God's covenant (17:1; see Lev 1:3, 10; 22:17–25; Deut 15:21).[32] The following words take up these two offenses in reverse order, which we can chart this way:

A pagan worship: 16:21–22	
	B transgressing God's covenant: 17:2
	B' offending God's covenant: 17:1
A' serving other gods: 17:3	

In the last unit, 18:9–22 (unit D), we are told why Israel needs prophets (18:15–22). The word "abomination" occurs three times in the first part of the passage (18:9, 12, 12), establishing prophets because God has not authorized Israel to derive insight by "abominable" means such as sorcerers and necromancers (18:9–14). So, these two authority figures frame the section as guards against "abominations."

The first authority named is the judge. The section is bound together by the repetition of "town" across the unit (16:18; 17:2, 5, 8 [not visible in v. 5's English translation]). The unit has two sections, the first about what local judges do (16:18–17:7) and the second about what more senior judges do in the hard cases (17:8–13).[33] This provision institutionalizes Moses's legal division of labor first introduced in Exod 18:13–27.

Wright draws out important implications for a biblical view of justice from 17:2–7. The rules applied equally to men and women, so chauvinism was to be excluded. Further, full investigation was required to prove any charges, which assumes that the accused is presumed innocent until proven guilty. Finally, the regulations wisely required two or more witnesses to

---

31. Wright, *Deuteronomy*, 205 notes this.

32. References from Lundbom, *Deuteronomy*, 519.

33. Merrill, *Deuteronomy*, 262, calls this the "supreme court of last resort." He also notes there that apparently both a Levitical priest and a judge are mentioned (17:9) because the nature of the case would determine whether a religious or nonreligious official would preside.

Commandment 5: "Honor Your Father and Your Mother"

establish guilt, since convicting based on one witness obviously lent itself to abuse. He concludes, "the *procedural* concerns of Deuteronomy's judicial instructions are impressive and point to objectives still worth striving for."[34] Human authority should reflect God's character.

That Deut 16:18–17:13 is expounding the "honor" (5:16) due to these non-parental authorities is evident when the passage ends with a solemn and lengthy adjuration that their judicial pronouncements be respected and followed (17:10–13).

The next section of the passage (17:14–20, unit B) deals with kingship. In one sense, this seems unexpected, since monarchy was far in the future in Moses's day. But as Merrill observed, kingship was the logical culmination of the trajectory which extended authority beyond the family for a nation soon to be established in a land.[35] The prime directive here is that the king be devoted to the Torah (17:18), which requires that he be an Israelite (17:15). Indeed, of the several expectations articulated here, devotion to reading and obeying Torah is by far the most extensive (17:18–20). About ancient Near Eastern societies (hereafter "ANE"), Lundbom notes, "In other ANE societies the king is the lawgiver; in Israel the lawgiver is Yahweh."[36] This demonstrates that the monarchy in Israel was to be an extension of God's authority among his people. Here Israel is granted permission to establish a monarchy, but the king is to be chosen by the Lord (17:15), and he is to operate according to God's standards rather than the standards of the other nations (17:16–17).

This passage about kingship explains how one of the future offices is to be set up and how it extends God's authority into Israel, but how does it advance the principle of honoring leadership appropriately? The answer lies in a paradox written into the text. Israel states that they want a king "like all the nations" (17:14). God grants the desire for a king but declares in some detail that the king they must authorize is to be distinctly *unlike* those in the other nations! Wright explains,

> The three restrictions (vv. 16f.) are remarkable because they quite explicitly cut across the accepted pattern of kingship throughout the ancient Near East. Military power, through the building up of a large chariot force (the point of having great numbers of horses), the prestige of a large harem of many wives (frequently related

---

34. Wright, *Deuteronomy*, 206.
35. Merrill, *Deuteronomy*, 257.
36. Lindbom, *Deuteronomy*, 541.

to international marriage alliances), and the enjoyment of great wealth (large amounts of silver and gold)—these were the defining marks of kings worthy of the title. Weapons, women, and wealth: why else be a king? But Deuteronomy starkly declares, "Not so in Israel." . . . the king they are to have is to be as unlike the kings of other nations as one can imagine. Clearly the issue is not merely if Israel should have a king or not, but what kind of king that should be. What matters fundamentally for Deuteronomy is whether or not the whole covenant people of Israel will remain wholly loyal to Yahweh their God. The value of a king is assessed solely by the extent to which he will help or hinder that loyalty.[37]

Understanding this, the answer becomes clear. Note that the establishment of kingship is described as an initiative of the people: it is *how they do it* that is the issue here (17:14–15). The way Israel was to show proper honor (Deut 5:16) to the office of king was to set over themselves only a king who ruled in such a way as to honor the Lord and his authority. Setting up a king of this sort honored kingship by establishing a kingship that honored God's kingship and therefore deserved the respect and honor of the citizenry. All the prescriptions stated in this passage were to help establish kingship as an extension of God's authority, such that honoring the king's authority was an expression of honoring God's authority.

Miller goes further. After showing that many of the things expected of a king are also incumbent upon all Israel (e.g., 7:17c echoes 8:13–17), he summarizes, "Deuteronomy's primary concern was that the king be the model Israelite . . . The fundamental task of the leader of the people, therefore, is to exemplify and demonstrate true obedience to the Lord for the sake of the well-being of both the dynasty and the kingdom. King and subject share a common goal: to learn to fear the Lord).[38]

Deuteronomy 18:1–8 (unit C), deals with priests. But the honor accorded them is of a different sort. It deals with support for the priests and Levites, i.e., the provisions for their food, since they devoted their full time to ministering before the Lord for Israel's people and they have no allotted inheritance of land on which to raise their own food. Since their "inheritance" (cf. 18:1, 2, where "inheritance" is used four times) is the Lord, this paragraph declares one proper way to "honor" (Deut 5:16) these leaders, i.e., by providing their material needs.[39]

---

37. Wright, *Deuteronomy*, 209.
38. Miller, *Deuteronomy*, 149; p. 208 in the Kindle edition.
39. This provision resonates with 1 Tim 5:17–18, though the precedents drawn upon

The final section (unit D) is about God appointing a prophet (18:14–22). The overall point is that Israel is to show honor to future prophets by heeding their words since they are from God (18:18–19), and by executing prophets who falsely claim to speak for the Lord (18:20–22), since such prophets dishonor the Lord.[40]

Now that we have shown that 16:18–18:22 urges honoring human authorities beyond one's parents as extensions of God's authority, we must address another question: why did the Ten Commandments chose parental authority as its example? Surely the answer is obvious: while the offices of judge, king, and the future line of prophets are all yet to be established, parental authority is already active. Further, it is the first experience of authority which humans encounter and can thus serve as an example of authority that is universally understood. Thus, it best serves as a simple imperative representing the larger category of ways that God's authority is extended into human experience. These conclusions were stated earlier as intuitive ones; we now see that they are well-justified by how Deuteronomy elaborates "honor your father and your mother."

We have seen above how commandment 5 speaks to love of neighbor. We may still ask how its exposition in Deut 16:18–18:22 contributes to our practice of love. The answer is stated below when we summarize the positive statement of commandment 5. There we will see that honoring authorities beyond the family in the social order contributes to their well-being and that of society.

WHAT THE COMMANDMENT MEANS AS A POSITIVE PRINCIPLE

Commandment 5 is easy to state as a positive principle because it is already stated in the positive. But our summary statement must also account for the ways it is elaborated in Deut 16:18–18:22. It will help to outline that passage and how it elaborates the concept of honoring authorities.

---

there are from Deut 25:4 and 24:15, both of which are expounding commandment 9, dealing with fairness: see the discussion of commandment 9 below.

40. When the passage speaks of prophets who falsely claim to speak for God, it makes it clear that the passage is referring to a line of prophets rather than a single prophet in the future. But the way that Deut 34:10–12 continues this discussion reveals that a deeper meaning is embedded here.

A. Judge (16:18–17:13): honor them by obeying them and disciplining the presumptuous

B. King (17:14–20): establishing godly kings honors God's authority

C. Priest (18:1–8): honor them by providing their material needs impartially

D. Prophet (18:9–22): honor them by obeying them and disciplining the presumptuous

It is interesting that units A and D have the same structure. First, one honors the judge or the prophet by respecting and obeying their words. But second, both passages end by laying down the principle that discipline is to be brought down upon those who dishonor the office of judge or prophet by disobeying their words (17:13–12; 18:19), or who dishonors the office of prophet by fraudulently claiming to speak for God (18:22), or who speaks for another god (18:20). Interesting also is the repetition of the Hebrew root term "presumptuously" in both sections (17:12, 13; 18:22). Those who do these things are judged "presumptuous" or "arrogant" and given such a severe penalty (17:12; 18:20) because "any decision made on the basis of ritual would actually originate from Yahweh."[41] To disobey or impersonate these human authorities, or to speak for another god as if that god possessed the authority of Yahweh, was to defy the Lord, to dishonor him.

We also see in these two sections that judges and prophets are to be held accountable to Torah standards. Note that this corresponds to the standard we have deduced about kings: the people are charged to establish a sort of kingship which honors God, which implies the accountability of the king to the people as well as to the Lord, as we will now develop.

Surprisingly, the prescriptions about the king (unit B) are worded to make the people responsible for the sort of king they authorize. The idea seems to be that if Israel *expects* the king to honor the Lord and conduct himself as a faithful servant of the Lord from the beginning (17:14–15), the king will be encouraged to obey the rules established for him in this Torah section (17:16–20). The payoff for the nation will be that he will not rule them harshly (17:20a), and that he and his descendants will enjoy long reigns (17:20b—because God blesses him with such, surely, but perhaps it is also implied that it is because the people will follow him loyally and submit to his godly kingship).

---

41. Nelson, *Deuteronomy*, 222.

Commandment 5: "Honor Your Father and Your Mother"

The qualification "impartially" for unit C is derived from the exhortation in 18:6–8. It is given since worshippers might naturally be inclined to support their neighbors who serve them but might be less inclined to do so for one who comes from far away whom they do not know.

The positive, comprehensive statement of commandment 5 can be articulated as, *we show our love for God and our neighbors by honoring those who extend God's authority over us by (1) obeying their directives, by (2) encouraging them to do their jobs well, and by (3) supplying what is due to them to sustain their service to us.*

Now that we have stated the positive principle, we must ask why God would begin his commandments about humans here, and why he frames it as an imperative about honoring others. We have already argued that this lays the foundation for respecting all others and minimizes the tendency to dishonor others by the actions forbidden in commandments 6–10. But we can go further.

Earlier in the book we examined the meaning of "love." We noted the definition of Jonathan Edwards, who defined love, whether God's love or human love, as the disposition to do good to others, to be concerned to promote their welfare.[42] Surely, honoring your father and your mother is an expression of love so defined. So, commandment 5 introduces the neighbor- commandments by calling for love: doing good to and promoting the well-being of the first "others" we encounter in life. Starting here establishes doing good to others and promoting their well-being as the basic obligation to others, the most foundational aspects of which are spelled out in commandments 6–10. So, when Jesus several times used "Love your neighbor as yourself" as a summary of the neighbor-oriented commandments, he was expressing their deepest meaning. Jesus, in fact, borrowed this expression from Lev 19:18, which is a summary statement of several of the neighbor obligations listed in Lev 19:9–18. Combined with what we have already seen about the commandments related to God, we can now say that *the Torah itself understood the Ten Commandments as being about loving God and loving neighbor.*

We may go still further. We have seen that commandment 5 bears special significance because it is stated in the positive, it is called a "commandment," it is the longest of the neighbor commandments, and it is longer here than in Exodus 20. Above we posed the questions, why would God begin his commandments about humans here, and why would he frame it as an

---

42. Edwards, *The End for Which God Created the World*, 439.

imperative about honoring others? We propose that the reason is that commandment 5, the first one about our responsibilities to our neighbors, is obviously a particular, concrete expression of love. Commandments 6–10 are not so obviously expressions of love. In fact, they constitute "negative minimum" expressions of love, but that is not at first obvious. So, commandment 5 is framed in the positive to show that a positive obligation to love others is the key impulse of the commandments about our neighbors. Once this is understood, it is easier to detect that commandments 6–10 are also expressions of love of neighbor. This also explains why Lev 19:18 and Jesus himself framed commandments 5–10 in this way: "Love your neighbor as yourself."

Finally, how does commandment 5's exposition in Deut 16:18–18:22 contribute to our practice of love? We have stated that honoring authorities beyond the family in the social order contributes to their well-being and that of society. Let us unpack this. Since the authorities addressed in Deut 16–18 are public authorities, it is apparent that the love we show to our neighbors is not to be limited to private expressions of love. That is, when we *honor those who are legitimate authorities over us—who extend God's authority over us—by (1) obeying their directives, by (2) encouraging them to do their jobs well, and by (3) supplying what is due to them to sustain their service to us*, we move into the realm of how honoring God's authority taught in commandment 5 benefits our neighbors as participants in the social order.

Scripture, from the Torah forward, maintains a lively interest in both the personal and social aspects of human life. While Christians often emphasize one at the expense of the other, commandment 5 addresses both since people are both individuals and are also deeply involved with others from the family to the national and international levels.[43] Deuteronomy's exposition of commandment 5 shows that when we *obey the directives* of the legitimate authorities God has placed over us, we show love to them by complying with their decisions. This also demonstrates love to our neighbors by advancing their well-being by contributing to a stable social order and by, we trust, sustaining policies which benefit the common good. Ben Franklin is sometimes credited as saying, "We must, indeed, all hang together or, most assuredly, we shall all hang separately." What he spoke regarding patriots in the American Revolution applies equally to all societies,

---

43. For a substantive approach to Christian faith and public life see VanDrunen, *Politics after Christendom* or the more accessible version in *Living in God's Two Kingdoms*.

Commandment 5: "Honor Your Father and Your Mother"

which cohere through pursuit of neighbor love and the common good or fall into violence and chaos.

When we *encourage our leaders to do their jobs well*, we show love to them by respecting their attempts to advance the common good, and helping hold them accountable to do good, which is good for them and sustains their time in office. It also shows love for our neighbors because good leaders advance justice, respect for the rule of law, public order, and defense of the innocent, the weak, and the vulnerable, such as minorities. These are essential for all of us to lead a peaceful and quiet life, going about our business, enjoying our families and our labors, and sharing our faith with others (see 1 Tim 2:2). Martin Luther King Jr. said it beautifully: "Injustice anywhere is a threat to justice everywhere. We are caught in an inescapable network of mutuality, tied in a single garment of destiny. Whatever affects one directly, affects all indirectly."[44]

Finally, when we *supply our leaders with what is due to them to sustain their service to us*, we show them love by providing for them. We also show love to our neighbors by enabling our leaders to do for us all what we cannot do nearly so well for ourselves, such as providing law enforcement, emergency services, national defense, etc.

In summary, when we respect God's authority which he has delegated to human authorities, we promote a stable, well-functioning social order which benefits our neighbors by supplying the conditions necessary for all to seek life, liberty, and the pursuit of happiness. Notice that the Bible's commandment is motivated not out of self-interest but out of community interest—and pleasing God. "This is good, and it is pleasing in the sight of God our Savior, who desires all people to be saved and to come to the knowledge of the truth" (1 Tim 2:3–4), the conditions for which are secured when leaders do their jobs well (1 Tim 2:1–2). It also pleases the God who loves all people and shows his love even to those who hate him by being good to them. "But I say to you, love your enemies and pray for those who persecute you, so that you may be sons of your Father who is in heaven. For he makes his sun rise on the evil and on the good and sends rain on the just and on the unjust" (Matt 5:44–45).

Martin Luther King Jr. once wrote, "Darkness cannot drive out darkness; only light can do that. Hate cannot drive out hate; only love can do that."[45] The contemporary world needs, as it always does, the reminder that

---

44. King Jr., *Letter from Birmingham Jail*.
45. King Jr., *Strength to Love*, 47.

love of neighbor is the best way to make the world a better place. But Jesus knew it before Dr. King, and Deuteronomy taught it long before either of them.

WHAT THE COMMANDMENT MEANS FOR CHRISTIANS

Jesus quotes and expands upon commandment 5, applying it to his contemporaries, in Matt 15:4–9.[46] He first explains not honoring father and mother as "reviling" them (Matt 15:4), but he then says of the teaching of the Jewish elders, "But you say, 'If anyone tells his father or his mother, "What you would have gained from me is given to God," he need not honor his father.' So for the sake of your tradition you have made void the word of God." Here, refusing to provide appropriately for one's parents is considered dishonoring them. Jesus's application is fully in line with the commandment in Deuteronomy and also reflects Prov 28:24.[47]

The NT applies this commandment in numerous ways: we should acknowledge that human authority was instituted by God (Rom 13:1–2); obey the law (Rom 13:5); pay our taxes (see Rom 13:6–7; Matt 22:21); and give respect to our leaders (Rom 13:7; 1 Pet 2:17). We are, however, authorized to disobey human authorities when their directives require us to disobey God (Acts 5:29).

But we have yet to consider a critical text, Rom 13:8–10, which must be cited in full:

> Owe no one anything, except to love each other, for the one who loves another has fulfilled the law. For the commandments, "You shall not commit adultery, You shall not murder, You shall not steal, You shall not covet," and any other commandment, are summed up in this word: "You shall love your neighbor as yourself." Love does no wrong to a neighbor; therefore love is the fulfilling of the law.

First, notice that the conclusions we have reached from Deuteronomy itself about the centrality of love to commandments 5–10 are reiterated here by Paul: he read the Ten Commandments just as we have, and as Jesus did. He cites commandments 7, 6, 8 and 10, but adds "and any other

---

46. Weinfeld, *Deuteronomy 1–11*, 309, points out the parallel.
47. Pointed out by Lundbom, *Deuteronomy*, 287.

Commandment 5: "Honor Your Father and Your Mother"

commandment" to include all the neighbor-oriented commandments, declaring that love of neighbor is the essence of them all, just as we have argued.

Second, he affirms that Jesus's use of "You shall love your neighbor as yourself" is indeed a summary of the neighbor commandments in the Decalogue.[48]

Third, Dunn writes, "the whole is summed up in a chiastic definition of love in negative terms as avoiding doing wrong to the neighbor and in positive terms as fulfilling the law (v 10)."[49] "Avoiding doing wrong" is the obverse of Jonathan Edwards's definition of love.

Romans 13:10 adds a fourth useful conclusion: "Love does no wrong to a neighbor." The "wrongs" Paul has in mind are obviously the neighbor commandments he has just cited in 13:9. So Paul's words are a negatively stated summary statement of commandments 6–10: love does not harm a neighbor by adultery, murder, stealing, lying, or coveting. Thus, we see that Paul reads Deuteronomy exactly as we have: the negatively stated neighbor commandments are the last things one would do if one loves their neighbor (the negative minimum). But the ultimate goal is the positive maximums.

Love is the core and essence of biblical faith. That's why it is the subject of the Ten Commandments, the most famous summary of Jewish faith, summarized by Jesus in two eternal principles: "You shall love the Lord your God . . . You shall love your neighbor as yourself. On these two commandments depend all the Law and the Prophets" (Matt 22:37–40).

The Torah says, "Every one of you shall revere his mother and his father . . . You shall not steal . . . You shall not lie . . . You shall not oppress your neighbor or rob him . . . You shall not hate your brother in your heart . . . but you shall love your neighbor as yourself" (Lev 19:3, 11, 13, 17, 18). So, it is undeniable: Deuteronomy is one of the important Bible books—one of the most rich, extensive, and detailed biblical treatments—of loving God and loving neighbor.

HEIDELBERG CATECHISM:

104. Q. What is God's will for us in the fifth commandment?

---

48. This is sometimes denied, but this text seems to end any debate.
49. Dunn, *Romans*, 781.

A. That I show honor, love, and loyalty to my father and mother and all those in authority over me; that I submit myself with proper obedience to all their good teaching and correction; and also that I be patient with their failings, for through them God chooses to rule us.

QUESTIONS FOR PERSONAL DEVOTIONS:

1. What does it mean for you to honor?
2. What barriers do you face to honoring father and mother?
3. Not all people have a mother and father. How could the fifth commandment still be instructive if you do not have a father and a mother?
4. What are some tangible ways that you could follow the commandment to honor father and mother?
5. How could you "honor father and mother" in your current life stage?
6. Are there any cultural considerations in your life that may affect what it means to honor father and mother?
7. Can commandment 5 inform your relationship with any other person in your life besides biological father and mother?
8. What else might God be saying to you through this commandment?

QUESTIONS FOR TEACHING AND PREACHING:

1. What do other verses of Scripture which use the word "honor" (Hebrew *kābed*) teach us about its meaning in the commandment?
2. Can you think of any stories in Scripture that might give a deeper understanding of what it means to honor father and mother and others placed in authority over us?
3. Discuss the ways in which following commandment 5 will lead to adherence to commandments 6–10.
4. Think about the promise associated with commandment 5 and Paul's teaching in Ephesians 6. How could this impact your teaching and preaching of the fifth commandment?
5. How does the positive framing of commandment 5 help us to understand the positive implications of negative commandments 6–10?

Commandment 5: "Honor Your Father and Your Mother"

6. The chapter demonstrates that Deuteronomy applies commandment 5 to other sources of authority. How can we follow the fifth commandment relating to other authorities, especially when those authorities do not always act justly?

7. How could you preach or teach the commandment to honor father and mother to someone who had a negative example of father and/or mother?

8. How could you teach or preach the commandment to honor father and mother to someone whose father and/or mother may not be living or otherwise present in their life?

Chapter 9

Commandment 6: "Don't Murder"

Text of commandment 6 in Deuteronomy 5: "Don't murder" (5:17).

Commandment 6 expounded in Deuteronomy: 19:1–22:8.

Positive principle summary: We love our neighbors by protecting their lives.

Full positive principle: Loving our neighbor honors them by encouraging respect for and protection of life, by discouraging attitudes and actions which might harm life, and by holding people accountable for their actions which harm life.

A QUESTION TO CONSIDER

Let us ask you a question. Have you murdered anyone today? The answer might be more complicated than you think.

WHAT THE COMMANDMENT MEANS IN DEUTERONOMY 5

We argued in the last chapter that commandments 6–10 are extensions of the basic demand of commandment 5 to honor others, beginning with our first authority figures, our parents. We also saw that commandment 5 is

Commandment 6: "Don't Murder"

a particular expression of loving our neighbor—in this case, our parents. Commandment 6 is also an expression of love, but it is stated as a negative minimum: the last thing one should ever do to a neighbor is to murder him or her. The other side of the coin is that we should care about the life and well-being of our neighbors, as will become clearer below.[1]

Since commandment 6 contains only two words, only the term "murder" requires examination. The Hebrew word (*rātsakh*) here is properly translated "murder" rather than "kill" as the King James translation (1611 CE) and some others have done. Of its forty-seven uses in the Hebrew Bible,[2] twenty-eight occur in the Torah, which defines it as homicide, killing of a human being. Every use of it in the Torah is about intentional killing ("murder") or unintentional killing ("manslaughter"), and every case but one is intended to help define the difference between the two (i.e., Deut 22:16).[3] Within the Torah, twice it is used as a prohibition in the Ten Commandments (Exod 20:13; Deut 5:17), obviously forbidding intentional, unjustified killing.[4] Once it is used of a "murderer" (Deut 22:26). The other twenty-five uses (20x in Numbers 35; Deut 4:42 (2x); 19:3, 4, 6) are all about distinguishing intentional from accidental killings and establishing "cities of refuge" where someone who kills unintentionally can flee to get a hearing for their case and be protected from vengeance if they are innocent.[5] In fact, Num 35:15-16 *defines* the term directly: "These six cities shall be for refuge for the people of Israel, and for the stranger and for the sojourner among them, that anyone who kills any person without intent may flee there. But if he struck him down with an iron object, so that he died, he is a murderer" (Hebrew *rātsakh*).[6]

---

1. So McConville, *Deuteronomy*, 129.

2. As both noun and verb.

3. The term "manslaughter" is a modern term, but it is properly used in our Bible translations to communicate the meaning intended in the Hebrew Bible.

4. Lundbom, *Deuteronomy*, 289; see also McConville, *Deuteronomy*, 129.

5. *rātsakh* is used 8x in Joshua regarding cities of refuge (20:3, 5, 6; 21:13, 21, 27, 32, 38); it is used meaning "murder" (Judge 20:4; 2 Kgs 6:32; Job 24:14; PSs 62:4; 94:6; Isa 1:21; Jer 7:9, repeating commandment 6; Hos 4:2, also referring to commandment 6; Hos 6:9) or "kill" (unjustly: 1 Kgs 21:19; Prov 22:13);

6. Numbers 35:17-21 gives several other instances which qualify as "murder" since Hebrew law is casuistry, which provides examples rather than abstract definitions: "if he struck him down with a stone tool" (35:17), "with a wooden tool" (35:18), etc., "he is a murderer" (35:17, 18, etc.).

We know that *rātsakh* implies unjustified killing because other forms of killing are authorized in the Hebrew Bible which are not described by the term *rātsakh*. These include killing an animal for food (Gen 9:3), self-defense when killing a nighttime intruder in one's home (Exod 22:2), judicial capital punishment, and killing in combat.[7] While Christians may disagree theologically about each of the examples just mentioned, our intent is only to distinguish the way in which this Hebrew word is used in the sixth commandment and throughout the Hebrew Bible.

While the OT is often thought of as barbaric for its invocation of capital punishment, it is worth noting that while other ANE law codes such as the Code of Hammurabi legislated death penalty for property crimes, the OT never does so; for the Bible, life is sacred, not property.[8] Further, the Code of Hammurabi and the Hittite Law Code have no statutes against murder, "probably because relatives of the deceased took care of avenging the crime."[9] In other words, they left it to individuals and families to secure justice. The OT, in contrast, not only forbids murder but institutes a system for punishing the guilty and protecting those falsely accused of intentional murder, thus institutionalizing protection of the innocent from homicide, and protecting those who kill accidentally from revenge killings.

Why is murder out of bounds? The Torah argues that it is because humans are made in the image of God (Gen 1:26; 9:5–6).[10] Kaiser well says, "It was because humans are made in the image of God that capital punishment for first degree murder became a perpetual obligation. To kill a person was tantamount to killing God in effigy. That murderer's life was owed to God; not to society, not to the grieving loved ones, and not even as a preventative measure for more crimes of a similar nature."[11] Wright concludes, "Human life is a gift from God and belongs to God, and no human has the right to destroy the gift or steal what belongs to God . . . The prohibition on murder, therefore, is a matter not merely of horizontal human rights, but of our accountability to God for the lives of our fellow human beings."[12] Murder, Merrill affirms, is "an affront to the sovereignty

---

7. Kaiser, *Ethics*, 90–91. Lundbom, *Deuteronomy*, 289, specifies war and capital punishment as excluded.

8. Kaiser. *Ethics*, 92.

9. Lundbom, *Deuteronomy*, 290.

10. Wright, *Deuteronomy*, 79.

11. Kaiser, *Ethics*, 91.

12. Wright, *Deuteronomy*, 79. On the validity of "human rights" when based upon a

of God, an assault upon his earthly representative."[13] Block adds, "Unlike Babylonian laws, this command draws no distinctions in value of life based on status, race, or gender. The life of all human beings is equally sacred."[14] In contrast to other ANE law codes, the Old Testament in general and the sixth commandment in particular teach that all human life is precious to God, regardless of a person's race, gender, wealth or any other distinction that people use as a basis for separation and division. All human beings are made in the image of God, which means that we are all equal before God and precious to him.

WHAT THE COMMAND MEANS IN DEUTERONOMY

Commandment 6 is elaborated in Deut 19:1–22:8, the longest of the commandment expositions in Deuteronomy. It is carefully structured in 9 sections:[15]

A 19:1–13: Cities of refuge to protect accidental killers
  B 19:14: don't move boundary markers— to preserve life
    C 19:15–21: rules for witnesses to crimes
      D 20:1–20: rules for killing in warfare
        E 21:1–9: atoning for murder by an unknown assailant
      D' 21:10–17 rules about wives from warfare
    C' 21:18–23 examples of crimes and capital punishment
  B' 22:1–7: various ways of preserving life
A' 22:8: parapets on rooftops to prevent accidental death

We will explain the logic of the corresponding parts of the structure section by section, showing how each contributes to an elaboration of commandment 6, "Don't murder." As before, we will see both negative and positive maximums expounded here, filling out the full meaning of commandment 6 and demonstrating how it explains loving one's neighbor.

The first paired unit in the chiastic structure is A and A', 19:1–13 and 22:8. Note first that there is a verbal *inclusio* with the word "bloodguilt" in

---

biblical rationale, see Wolterstorff, *Justice*.
  13. Merrill, *Deuteronomy*, 154.
  14. Block, *Deuteronomy*, 166.
  15. The structure adopted here is ours. It is, however, quite similar to Lundbom and Merrill. We believe this division of the material best demonstrates the chiastic parallels.

19:10 and 22:8,[16] demonstrating that 19:1–22:8 is a self-contained unit and also showing that 19:1–13 and 22:8 are matching units. These two sections frame the entire unit by treating different kinds of accidental killing. Deuteronomy 19:1–13 is about cities of refuge for those who kill accidentally. Deuteronomy 22:8 seeks to minimize accidental deaths by mandating a retaining wall around the flat rooftops, which were used regularly for many purposes, to minimize the chance someone would fall off and be killed. The first section establishes a system for distinguishing intentional murder from accidental manslaughter and for punishing the intentional perpetrator and protecting the one who committed an unintentional killing. The second establishes a due-diligence procedure that will protect people on one's property from accidents that are likely to happen if due diligence steps are not taken. The overall point of both is to institute procedures which minimize unnecessary death by advanced planning. The principle behind both is that the commandment forbidding "murder" also entails an obligation to avoid deaths through negligence, the first dealing with the corporate or social level and the second with the individual level. Further, as is usual in casuistic law (i.e., law which gives examples), the examples given are suggestive, or representative of the sorts of things that satisfy the requirement, rather than an exhaustive list, or a comprehensive catalogue, of what should be done. These are the *sorts* of things that one should do, but other similar obligations are also implied.

The next section (B and B') includes two units which are aimed at positive maximums that derive from "Don't murder!" like A and A'. As Merrill says, "The reverse side of taking life is preserving it."[17] Both sections (B and B') seem to deal with preserving life. The first (19:14) forbids moving someone's land-boundary markers. This disallows something which will predictably lead to conflict and possible violence or even death. The second unit (22:1–7) lists three circumstances which involve death in some way. They are:

1. 22:1–4 Lost animals   How *animals* are treated
2. 22:5   Rules about garments   How *humans* are treated
3. 22:6–7 A birds' nest   How *animals* are treated

---

16. Lundbom, *Deuteronomy*, 612.
17. Merrill, *Deuteronomy*, 296.

Note first the alternation between human and animal sections. This chiastic structure suggests that these three paragraphs are a related unit. It also shows that commandment 6 involves implications about death that extend beyond humans! The integrating factor in these paragraphs seems to be preservation of life.[18]

Unit 1 in 22:1–7 (21:1–4) is devoted to preserving the lives of animals. Merrill clarifies that when an animal is lost, "The implication is that animals left to roam would eventually become prey to harm or death by the elements or at the hand of unscrupulous thieves. Besides this, the animals in question were a valuable resource whose loss would bring hardship and even impoverishment to the man who lost them." Further, "A related case had to do with a neighbor's work animal that had fallen on the road … Love for one's neighbor alone should dictate that the fallen creature be assisted, but in the context here the focus is on the animal's well-being. If allowed to remain in that condition, it could well have suffered loss of life."[19] Thus, it appears that while animal life is less valuable than human life, it is nonetheless valuable as a creation of God and ought to be respected and preserved.

The third unit in 22:1–7 (22:6–7) likewise deals with preserving animal life, specifically the life of a bird. Again, Merrill, explains:

> Preservation of life, mixed, ironically, with permission to take it, is the subject of the stipulation concerning the mother bird and its young … there were to be wise policies in the procurement of life's necessities, for they were finite and conceivably could be depleted to the point of nonexistence. Therefore in the case of game birds one could take the eggs or even chicks for food but not the mother. Her life was to be preserved so that she could continue to produce offspring for human consumption.[20]

So, while biblical theology does not value animal or plant life on the same level as human life, and while it does not forbid killing and eating animals or using plants, e.g., trees, for fuel of for construction, it does encourage respect for all life in attitude and action.

The second unit (22:5) has been left for last because it is more difficult. It is difficult enough that some have concluded that 22:5 is unrelated to what comes before or after it. But Lundbom shows there are clear connections, for example, "garment" occurs in 22:3 and 22:5, binding the

---

18. Wright, *Deuteronomy*, 240; Mayes, *Deuteronomy*, 305–9.
19. Merrill, *Deuteronomy*, 297.
20. Merrill, *Deuteronomy*, 298.

sections together by keywords, a common feature of Deuteronomy.[21] There is no agreement about the exact meaning of 22:5, so we will not attempt to speculate.

The third section elaborating commandment 6 (C and C') deals with crime and death. The first unit, 19:15–21, addresses how to properly use witnesses to crimes. It makes two points. First, a single witness is not sufficient to convict someone of a crime because that would be easily abused by malicious people willing to lie. The second is that if someone does lie as a witness, that malicious witness is to receive the punishment that they attempted to inflict upon their victim. Deterrence is clearly the goal of this provision.

The other unit, 21:18–23, also deals with crimes, but in the context of capital punishment. Again, two different scenarios are addressed. The first is about a son who is irredeemably rebellious. In this case, "Don't murder" does not spare him from capital punishment: commandment 6 does not eliminate the need for capital punishment in some cases. In cases where someone stirs up trouble for others, as here, or when they resort to violence, punishing that person is an act of love (seeking their well-being) toward their victims because it protects them from someone who will not conform to respecting the life and well-being of others.

The second scenario is about the proper treatment of someone put to death for a crime and then hung on a tree for public display, a common ANE practice.[22] Why is leaving him there too long so undesirable? Merrill is helpful here: "The answer lies, perhaps, in the Hebrew abhorrence of death and the desire to provide for burial as quickly and unobtrusively as possible, especially where the wicked were concerned. To expose the body, therefore, would be to hold it up to public shame and ridicule. A greater curse than this could hardly be imagined."[23] So, the idea may be simply that death is alien to God and thus defiles the good land God gave to Israel.[24] But it likely also communicates that a long display of the victim is to degrade the victim, which is contrary to the respect he deserves as an image-bearer. This attitude is not only consistent with this text but is stated regarding a criminal in Deut 25:3: "Forty stripes may be given him, but not more, lest, if one should go on to beat him with more stripes than these,

---

21. Lundbom, *Deuteronomy*, 613–14.
22. Merrill, *Deuteronomy*, 296.
23. Merrill, *Deuteronomy*, 297.
24. Leviticus develops this idea. See also Deut 21:1–9.

Commandment 6: "Don't Murder"

your brother be degraded in your sight." Either way, punishment of crimes which result in execution requires specific treatment of dead human bodies. Finally, McConville comments, "The image of the land defiled by a dead body brings the chapter full circle to the opening image of the land defiled by the body of a murder victim [i.e., 22:1–9]."[25]

Section four (D and D') deals with issues related to war. It expounds commandment 6 by saying that killing in warfare is not prohibited by commandment 6, but the commandment still has implications for legitimate warfare. Wright writes that while war is more a concession to the reality of a world where violence is common, "the provisions of 20:5ff. and 21:10–14 are an exercise of neighbor love within the constraints of the grim reality of warfare."[26]

Deuteronomy 20:1–20 treats several issues related to the conduct of warfare. Sections treat exempting certain categories from the obligation to fight (20:1–9), the duty to seek peace before going to war and distinction in how to make war against near and far cities (20:10–18), and the environmental duty to spare trees except those which will assist the war effort (20:19–20). While war will sometimes be necessary, it is not considered "murder," yet must be conducted according to God's rules.

The corresponding section (21:10–17) has two parts which treat issues which arise because of warfare. The first (21:10–14) sets out rules for the fair treatment of women taken as captives who might be taken as wives, while the second paragraph (21:15–17) provides a procedure for avoiding favoritism that might naturally arise from a man taking a second wife as a result of warfare. The thrust is to treat these people with respect and fairness. Warfare in these and like circumstances does not eliminate the need to "love your neighbor as yourself."

The central section of the chiastic structure (E) is 21:1–9, the procedure for handling a homicide by an unknown assailant. The idea is that murder is so serious that it requires atonement to be made so that the nation is not guilty for such a heinous act. The section elaborates commandment 6 by reinforcing the gravity of murder and its effects: satisfaction must be made, even when no one knows who is responsible.

So, Deuteronomy 19:1–22:8 defines "murder" and expounds "Don't murder" by explaining numerous negative and positive maximums about how we are to love our neighbor.

---

25. McConville, *Deuteronomy*, 332.
26. Wright, *Deuteronomy*, 228.

There is one further observation to be made about the structure of this unit. Deuteronomy 22:1–8 also serves as a hinge between this and the following section. As Merrill points out, there is a chiastic structure here which overlaps the two sections:

  A Dress (22:5)
    B Animals (22:6–7)
      C House (22:8)
      C' Field (22:9)
    B' Animals (22:10)
  A' Dress (22:11–12)[27]

"This has the effect of linking *death* (sixth commandment) with *mixtures* (seventh commandment)."[28] As we have seen before, biblical texts often have multiple, overlapping structures. In this case, the effect is to show a connection between the expositions of commandments 6 and 7, and to provide a bit of light on Deut 22:5 by, at least, showing that Scripture's expectations can, in some cases, have an effect even on something as seemingly mundane as clothing (A and A' above).

WHAT THE COMMANDMENT MEANS AS A POSITIVE PRINCIPLE

In summary, Deut 19:1–22:8 elaborates commandment 6 in a series of ways. It puts in place procedures for inculcating in the population an attitude that takes murder with the utmost seriousness; for attempting to prevent violence by forbidding things which might lead to it; for teaching people to seek to preserve life, even animal and plant life; for protecting the innocent from being harmed unjustly; for treating non-combatant war survivors with respect and fairness; for treating even the bodies of executed criminals with respect (21:22–23); and yet, for establishing procedures for sanctioning those guilty of intentional murder with the ultimate punishment based on due process.

Taking all Deuteronomy says about this commandment into account, and remembering that commandment 5 establishes honor as the key principle in the commandments about our neighbor, we can state the positive principle in commandment 6 as: *Love of neighbor honors them by*

---

27. Merrill, *Deuteronomy*, 298.
28. Woods, *Deuteronomy*, 238.

encouraging respect for and protection of life, by discouraging attitudes and actions which might harm life, and by holding people accountable for their actions which harm life.

WHAT THE COMMANDMENT MEANS FOR CHRISTIANS

The prohibition of murder is repeated numerous times in the NT (e.g., Matt 5:21; 19:18; Mark 7:21; 10:19; Luke 18:20; Rom 13:9; Jas 2:11), and Jesus warned against the passions which could lead to murder (Matt 5:21–26).[29] But Jesus's declaration has a background in the OT, as Wright recognizes:

> The dangers of all that leads up to acts of violence and murder were also recognized in the stories of Cain's jealousy (Gen. 4), David's lust (2 Sam. 11), or his vengeful rage (1 Sam. 25), in Wisdom's portrait of murderous greed (Prov. 1: 10– 19), and in the penetrating law of Leviticus 19: 17f., "Do not hate your brother in your heart . . . Do not seek revenge or bear a grudge against one of your people, but love your neighbor as yourself." It was an authentic extension of this OT perception that led Jesus to condemn anger as the moral root of murder (Matt. 5: 21f.).[30]

Ben Franklin recognized that, generally, "Whate'er is begun in anger, ends in shame."[31] Paul had better advice: "Be angry and do not sin" (Eph 4:26). Jesus's words go the deepest: be careful with anger lest it lead to harm to your neighbor. But Jesus, in Matt 5:23–26, also drew the conclusion that pursuing reconciliation is entailed in commandment 6, thus drawing a positive maximum from the negative minimum.[32]

Finally, Paul cites Deut 21:22–23 and applies it to Christ in Gal 3:13. Paul means here that Christ's death on a "tree" ended the Sinai covenant which excluded Gentiles "so that in Christ Jesus the blessing of Abraham might come to the gentiles" (Gal 3:14).[33]

Further, based upon our positive statement of the principle embedded in commandment 6, we would urge that meditating on the positive principle will yield numerous other implications: we love our neighbor by

---

29. Lundbom, *Deuteronomy*, 290.
30. Wright, *Deuteronomy*, 79–80.
31. Franklin, *Poor Richard's Almanack*, p. 46.
32. Miller, *Deuteronomy*, 87.
33. See the exposition of this passage in Gordon, *Promise, Law, Faith*, 125–29.

encouraging respect for and protection of life, by discouraging attitudes and actions which might harm life, and by holding people accountable for actions which harm life.

In summary, Paul declared "For the commandments . . . you shall not murder . . . are summed up in this word: 'You shall love your neighbor as yourself.' Love does no wrong to a neighbor; therefore love is the fulfilling of the law" (Rom 13:9–10).

So, again, that it is undeniable: Deuteronomy is an important Bible book—one of the most rich, extensive, and detailed biblical treatments—of loving God and neighbor.

HEIDELBERG CATECHISM:

105. Q. What is God's will for you in the sixth commandment?

A. I am not to belittle, hate, insult, or kill my neighbor— not by my thoughts, my words, my look or gesture, and certainly not by actual deeds— and I am not to be party to this in others; rather, I am to put away all desire for revenge. I am not to harm or recklessly endanger myself either. Prevention of murder is also why government is armed with the sword.

106. Q. Does this commandment refer only to murder?

A. By forbidding murder God teaches us that he hates the root of murder: envy, hatred, anger, vindictiveness. In God's sight all such are disguised forms of murder.

107. Q. Is it enough then that we do not murder our neighbor in any such way?

A. No. By condemning envy, hatred, and anger God wants us to love our neighbors as ourselves, to be patient, peace-loving, gentle, merciful, and friendly toward them, to protect them from harm as much as we can, and to do good even to our enemies."

QUESTIONS FOR PERSONAL DEVOTIONS:

1. How does commandment 6 speak to the equality of all human life?
2. How does commandment 6 affirm the value and worth of each person?

Commandment 6: "Don't Murder"

3. What can you learn about commandment 6 from your value, worth and purpose?
4. What are some ways you are tempted to violate commandment 6?
5. What attitudes of your heart does commandment 6 speak to?
6. How could you live out the positive principle of commandment 6?
7. What else might God be saying to you through this commandment?

QUESTIONS FOR TEACHING AND PREACHING:

1. Why is the distinction between "do not kill" and "do not murder" important?
2. Discuss the implications of the claim that life and not property is regarded as sacred in the Hebrew Bible. Why is this important?
3. Discuss Matthew 21 in relation to the idea that "murder is an assault upon God's earthly representative."
4. Read Matt 5:21–26. How does Jesus's teaching on the sixth commandment inform your teaching and preaching?
5. Discuss the relationship between humans being made in God's image and the prohibition of murder.
6. What heart attitudes could this commandment speak to in your community of faith through your preaching and teaching?
7. How could the sixth commandment apply to those in your community of faith who are contemplating self-harm?
8. In Matthew 5, Jesus teaches about reconciliation as one way of living out this commandment. How could you teach or preach on reconciliation based on this commandment?

Chapter 10

Commandment 7: "Don't Commit Adultery"

Text of commandment 7 in Deuteronomy 5: "And don't commit adultery" (5:17).

Commandment 7 expounded in Deuteronomy: 22:9–23:18.

Positive principle summary: We love our neighbors by respecting the boundaries God has established.

Full positive principle: Loving our neighbor honors them when we practice purity in sexual behavior, avoid cultural practices God forbids, and respect the boundaries God has established.

WHAT THE COMMANDMENT MEANS IN DEUTERONOMY 5

In the ANE adultery was called the "great sin."[1] While sexual behavior did not conform to "traditional" standards and sometimes was wild even by modern standards (such as prostitution as part of worship in some ANE religions!), ANE people held that marriage was a sacred commitment and that adultery destroyed a home and the lives of those in it, and they scorned it as a serious evil. The Ten Commandments also value marriage and forbid

---

1. Lundbom, *Deuteronomy*, 291. See this phraseology in Gen 20:9.

Commandment 7: "Don't Commit Adultery"

sexual infidelity. Commandment 7 of the Ten Commandments articulates this stance. In two Hebrew words, it intones, "No adultery!" (Deut 5:18).

We have argued that commandments 6–10 are extensions of the positively stated demand of commandment 5 to honor others, each connected to commandment 7 by beginning with the word "and." We have also shown that commandments 5–10 are particular expressions of loving our neighbor. Finally, we have seen that the Ten Commandments are arranged in descending order of importance. So, by following "Don't murder," "Don't commit adultery" is signaled as just below murder in its seriousness.

Loving one's neighbor means respecting their marriage and considering one's neighbor's spouse off limits. Merrill articulates the foundational issues in this brief word:

> If murder is a violation of life itself, adultery is a violation of its most important and sacred human relationship, that of marriage. The seventh commandment deals with this matter rather specifically in that it addresses adultery and not sexual impropriety in general as the precise verb *nāā' 'ap* makes clear. Elsewhere such matters as fornication (Num 25:1), prostitution (Deut 22:21), and homosexuality (Judg 19:22; Lev 18:22; Deut 23:17–18) receive attention and are soundly condemned. Adultery, however, implies unfaithfulness, covenant breaking, and so is an apt analogue to covenant infidelity on a higher plane—the divine-human.[2]

But why is adultery such a great sin in the Hebrew Bible? Fornication was not subject to capital punishment there, but adultery was. Why? Wright helps us: "The answer to this lies in the nature of the Decalogue, in which fundamental covenant law is combined with the central importance of the family in Israel's social realization of the covenant."[3]

It has sometimes been argued that the prohibition of adultery had little to do with sexuality but rather was an assertion of the property rights of the husband, wives allegedly being considered chattel property, making commandment 7 simply a specific application of commandment 8, "Don't steal."[4] Levinson's discussion is fatal to this "chattel" view: "The

---

2. Merrill, *Deuteronomy*, 154.

3. Wright continues, "Adultery was a crime against God inasmuch as it was a crime against the relationship between God and his people, Israel; and it was a crime against that relationship inasmuch as it was an attack upon the social basis on which it rested." Wright, *Deuteronomy*, 80–81.

4. This view is problematic for several reasons. First, it would mean that the Ten Commandments, the most famous statement of Israel's religion, is really only the Nine

prohibition against adultery in the Decalogue is absolute. The Decalogue has transformed the ancient Near Eastern breach of the contractual rights of the woman's husband (see laws of Hammurabi #129) into an offense against both God and the larger community. Biblical law here removes the wife from the disposal of the husband and grants her the status of a legal person."[5] He comments further on Deut 22:22, which says, of male and female adulterers, "both of them shall die," as follows: "This stipulation makes a sharp contrast with ancient Near Eastern legal norms, which required the adulterer's death but left the fate of the adulterous wife to the disposition of the husband. That the wife is here removed from the authority of the husband defines her as a legal person who is accountable for her actions."[6] Levinson also comments perceptively on commandment 10, "Do not covet":

> Contrast order 'house . . . wife' in the Exodus Decalogue (Exod. 20.14). There this sequence suggests that 'house' is the inclusive term, with the following list (wife, slave, ox, or ass) serving to itemize its contents. Consistent with their view elsewhere, the authors of Deuteronomy here completely separate family law from property law. They invert the earlier sequence placing the wife first. By removing her altogether from the list of chattels, they established that the law does not regard the woman as merely one commodity among others comprising a house . . . This is consistent with Deuteronomy's general view of women.[7]

Mayes makes another significant observation about the place of commandment 7 in the Ten Commandments, "This general concern with the family connects the commandment with the fifth rather than the sixth

---

Commandments, with one commandment stated twice in two forms. Second, and more importantly, if everyone in the original context knew that wives were mere chattel, it would be unnecessary to have a separate commandment affirming that *a particular form of stealing* was prohibited, when commandment 8 prohibited stealing. Commandment 7 in this view is redundant and is belaboring the obvious! Third, on this view, were both stated, commandment 8 should have preceded commandment 7 as the logically prior principle. Fourth, the exposition of commandment 7 in Deut 22:9–23:18 (esp. 22:13–30) does not treat this as a property issue. See further Kaiser, *Ethics*, 92, 94.

5. Levinson, *Jewish Study Bible*, 377.

6. Levinson, *Jewish Study Bible*, 417.

7. Levinson, *Jewish Study Bible*, 377–78. One need not agree with Levinson's view of Deuteronomy's authorship to appreciate the perceptiveness of his comments. On further reasons against seeing a wife as chattel, see Kaiser, *Ethics*, 122–23, discussing Lev 19:20 and Wenham, *Leviticus*, 270, on the same text.

Commandment 7: "Don't Commit Adultery"

[commandment]."[8] His comment reinforces our earlier conclusion that the connection of commandments 7–10 by "and" binds them together as a unit which elaborates commandment 5.

Notice, finally, that the aim of commandment 7 is not primarily to restrict the behavior of the perpetrator but to protect the victim, the neighbor whose marriage and family will be destroyed by an act of adultery. This is evident when we notice the fact that commandments 5, 6, 8, 9, and even 10, are all so motivated. This is an important theme throughout the second table of the Ten Commandments. The commandments are given in order to protect the weak and the vulnerable from exploitation by their more powerful and wealthy neighbors. God clearly has a concern to protect those in the covenant community who are at risk from the commandments being violated.

WHAT THE COMMANDMENT MEANS IN DEUTERONOMY

Commandment 7 is expounded in Deut 22:9–23:18. Merrill argues persuasively that the organizing principle in this section is "purity."[9] Commandment 7 forbids adultery as a symbol of purity because

> adultery epitomizes all that impurity means, whether in family, social, political, or religious life . . . Israel's idolatry and covenant violation is frequently described as adultery, for the covenant between the Lord and Israel was akin to a marriage relationship . . . If adultery is the metaphor for illicit relationships in general, the antithesis is separation from such mixed behavior.[10]

The section elaborates purity in three broad categories: (1) purity in daily life (22:9–12); (2) purity in sexual relationships (22:13–30), and (3) purity in the community (23:1–18), as outlined below.

1. 22:9–12: Purity in daily life: do not mix unlike things; make tassels

2. 22:13–30: Purity in sexual matters, which is structures as a chiasm

   A 22:13–21: *When a man takes a wife,* when a bride is accused of not being a virgin

---

8. Mayes, *Deuteronomy*, 170. See also McConville, *Deuteronomy*, 129.
9. So, Merrill, *Deuteronomy*, 299.
10. Merrill, *Deuteronomy*, 299.

B 22:22: *when a man shall be found;* in the case of adultery
    C 22:23-24: *woman betrothed, man finds;* the case of premarital sex for a betrothed woman

    C' 22:25-27: *man finds betrothed woman;* the case of premarital sex for a betrothed woman

   B' 22:28-29: *When a man shall find;* in the case of rape of an unbetrothed woman

A' 22:30: *a man shall not take the wife;* marrying your father's wife forbidden[11]

3. 23:1-18: Purity in community life

A. 23:1-8: those who are separated from the assembly

B. 23:9-14: separation from impurity in a military camp

C. 23:15-16: separation from the pagan practice of repatriating slaves

D. 23:17-18: separation from cultic sexuality

Purity is first expounded by giving four examples from daily life (22:9-12). The purity here is very concrete: not putting together, or mixing, things that are different and thus ought to be kept distinct. Merrill explains these four: "To drive home the importance of separation from sexual (and, indeed, covenant) impurity, the passage provides a number of instances in which separation must be practiced for its pedagogical value alone."[12] The first three are parallel:[13]

you shall not	sow (22:9)
you shall not	plow (22:10)
you shall not	wear (22:11)

By practicing such mundane, daily forms of separating unlike things, the people were to learn that some things are not to be mixed but are to remain apart. The rest of the section then elaborates more important things that must be kept apart.

The fourth section, 22:12, requires more comment. At first glance, "you shall make yourself tassels...." seems unrelated to its context. But this is not the case. Note that this one alone is stated as a positive command.

---

11. This chiasm is from Lundbom, *Deuteronomy*, 628.

12. Merrill, *Deuteronomy*, 299.

13. Lundbom, *Deuteronomy*, 621.

Commandment 7: "Don't Commit Adultery"

That's because it states an exception to this rule of separation based on earlier Torah instruction,[14] affirming that the former rule still holds. Numbers 15:37-41 instructs Israel to make tassels on their garments to remind them to obey God's commands so that they remain "holy." The instructions required a blue cord on each tassel. It seems certain that the tassels mandated in Numbers 15 included mixed threads that 22:11 prohibits.[15] So, this positive command reaffirms that this previous instruction is not prohibited. But even if this were not the case, the purpose stated for the tassels in Numbers 15 is that remembering God's laws would encourage obedience which would make the people holy, (Num 15:41), and holiness (separation from sin) is the goal aimed at in these purity instructions.

The next, and longest section, 22:13-30, addresses purity in sexual matters. The point is to respect the boundaries God has established regarding sexual practice, i.e., keeping sexual intercourse within marriage and not mixing that activity with someone who is not one's spouse. Detailed comments on the section are not necessary, as the standard commentaries treat the specifics. But we must show how the sections elaborate the principle stated above: sex belongs in marriage and sexual activity is not to be mixed with others outside the marriage. Each section raises a specific circumstance and states how to handle it.

A 22:13-21: when a bride is accused of not being a virgin (either not guilty or guilty)
B 22:22: when a man commits adultery with another man's wife
C 22:23-24: when a man commits consensual adultery with a betrothed woman
C' 22:25-27: when a man rapes a betrothed woman
B' 22:28-29: when a man rapes an unbetrothed woman
A' 22:30: when a man desires to marry his father's wife

Some, not recognizing that Deuteronomy expounds the Ten Commandments, have mistakenly argued that in commandment 7, "we have a very generally stated prohibition, with no definition given and no distinctions

---

14. Lundbom, *Deuteronomy*, 621.

15. Tigay explains (*Deuteronomy*, 203): "According to early rabbinic sources, the blue cord is made of wool while the other cords are linen. In other words, the tassels are made of *sha-atnez*, the combination of fabrics forbidden in verse 11. This interpretation most likely stems from biblical times, since it is highly unlikely that the rabbis would have initiated a practice contradicting a biblical prohibition."

drawn."¹⁶ Our exposition shows that is untrue. In Deut 22:9–23:18, we see numerous distinctions and numerous examples given with instructions which provide insight into how to handle the many sexual infractions which could occur over the course of time.

The final section of this commandment exposition is 23:1–18, which treats purity in community life. Four situations are raised:

A. 23:1–8: those who are separated from the worship assembly

B. 23:9–14: separation from impurity in a military camp

C. 23:15–16: separation from the pagan practice of repatriating slaves

D. 23:17–18: separation from cultic sexuality

Brief comments will clarify what is unclear. Unit 1 (23:1) excludes from the assembly of the Lord those who are emasculated. The connotations of unholiness here may be because of its association with Canaanite religion or for the same reason it rendered a priest unworthy to officiate at religious ceremonies and made animals so damaged not acceptable as sacrifices.¹⁷ But the association with impurity is clear.

Merrill points out that the third unit (22:15–16) is connected to the previous provision in that the military campaigns alluded to there were likely to give rise to slaves escaping from the enemy. But further, since repatriating escaped slaves to their owners was common ANE practice, Israel demonstrated its separation from the pagan nations by refusing this practice. He continues, "Israel, after all, had been a slave nation whom the Lord had delivered from bondage never to be returned to their Egyptian overlord. How appropriate that slaves of enemy nations be allowed free access to and refuge among the Lord's covenant people."¹⁸

So, once again, elaborate comment is not necessary to conclude that purity is the central theme and that these laws expound positive maximums entailed by commandment 7. Merrill observes that obeying these regulations "would impress indelibly upon God's people the need to be separated from the contaminating influences of Canaanite social and religious life."¹⁹ Purity is protection in family, social, political, and religious life. This is the reason for the repetition of "So you shall purge the evil" in 22:21, 22, 24.

---

16. Harrelson, *Ten Commandments*, 124.

17. Tigay, *Deuteronomy*, 210–11.

18. Merrill, *Deuteronomy*, 312.

19. Merrill, *Deuteronomy*, 299.

Commandment 7: "Don't Commit Adultery"

We also see that large portions of the exposition of commandment 7, especially those about sexual infractions and liberating escaped slaves, are obviously elaborations of positive implications of what love of neighbor entails.

WHAT THE COMMAND MEANS AS A POSITIVE PRINCIPLE

Taking all of Deuteronomy into account, and remembering that commandment 5 establishes honor as the key principle in the neighbor commandments, we can state the positive principle in commandment 7 as *Loving our neighbor honors them when we practice purity in sexual behavior, avoid cultural practices God forbids, and respect the boundaries God has established.*

WHAT THE COMMANDMENT MEANS FOR CHRISTIANS

The prohibition of adultery is repeated many times in the NT (see Matt 5:27; 19:18; Mark 10:19, Rom 13:9, 1 Cor 6:9, etc.). As with commandment 6, Jesus goes further and condemns the passion which leads to adultery as a violation of the spirit of commandment 7 in Matt 5:27–30.[20] As Wright observes, "Wisdom also offers the first step toward Jesus' radical view of the roots of the sin of adultery in lustful looks (cf. Prov 6: 25; Job 31: 1, 9ff.)."[21]

In summary, Paul declared "For the commandments, you shall not commit adultery . . . are summed up in this word: 'You shall love your neighbor as yourself.' Love does no wrong to a neighbor; therefore love is the fulfilling of the law" (Rom 13:9–10).

So, we see—again—that it is undeniable: Deuteronomy is one of the important Bible books—one of the most rich, extensive, and detailed biblical treatments—of loving God and loving neighbor.

HEIDELBERG CATECHISM:

108. Q. What is God's will for us in the seventh commandment?

---

20. Lundbom, *Deuteronomy*, 292.
21. Wright, *Deuteronomy*, 81.

A. God condemns all unchastity. We should therefore thoroughly detest it and, married or single, live chaste and decent lives.

109. Q. Does God, in this commandment, forbid only such scandalous sins as adultery?

A. We are temples of the Holy Spirit, body and soul, and God wants both to be kept clean and holy. That is why God forbids everything which incites unchastity, whether it be actions, looks, talks, thoughts, or desires.

QUESTIONS FOR PERSONAL DEVOTIONS:

1. What kind of examples of marriage have you had in your life and how do they shape your thoughts about this commandment?
2. What can be learned from the broader understanding of this commandment if you are not currently married?
3. What positive habits and practices might this commandment suggest for how we live our lives?
4. What does this commandment's exposition later in Deuteronomy teach us about our daily life?
5. How do the other places in the New Testament where this is quoted help you understand and live this commandment?
6. What else might God be saying to you through this commandment?

QUESTIONS FOR TEACHING AND PREACHING:

1. What are some of the different ways in which this commandment encourages love of God and love of neighbor?
2. Why is it significant that the Hebrew word used in this command is specific to adultery and not another sexual sin?
3. How does this commandment affirm the dignity and rights of women and seek to protect them from abuse?
4. How does Jesus's teaching on this commandment in Matt 5:27–30 demonstrate the three-fold nature of the commandments (negative minimums, negative maximums, and positive maximums) discussed earlier in this book?

Commandment 7: "Don't Commit Adultery"

5. Think about the relationship between this commandment and Paul's teaching in Rom 13:9–10.

6. What stories in Scripture might be useful for the purposes of illustrating this commandment?

7. In what ways can this commandment be seen as an extension of and related to the fifth commandment?

Chapter 11

Commandment 8: "Don't Steal"

Text of commandment 8 in Deuteronomy 5: "And don't steal" (5:19).

Commandment 8 expounded in Deuteronomy: 23:19–24:7.

Positive principle summary: We love our neighbors by treating them with generosity.

Full positive principle: Instead of taking from others, loving our neighbor honors them by seeking ways to be generous to them, as you would like others to treat you.

STEALING DAMAGES OUR NEIGHBORS

A friend from India told me, Van, the story of a man he knew who needed to raise money. The man approached a number of people in his village and invited them to invest money in a business that he was convinced would give them good returns on their investment. Though his clients were poor, he was persuasive, and a number of people did invest, and the man collected a sizeable amount of cash. But when time passed and no profits were returned, the investors investigated. It turned out that the business was a scam. The man who collected the money had pocketed and spent it and so there was no hope of restoration of the stolen funds. In a wealthier country such a loss might be chalked up to learning a painful lesson, but in a poor country, such a loss can be devastating. It might take food from the mouths

Commandment 8: "Don't Steal"

of one's children or mean the loss of one's home for failure to pay the rent. Those who had lost money in the scheme were seriously damaged financially and they were angry.

Worse still, perhaps, was that the man who had stolen the money claimed to be a Christian. In a country where Christians stand out because they are a tiny minority, the plundering of neighbors would not only ravage the well-being of the victims but would also desecrate the reputation of the Christian community. People would say, "That's a Christian for you."

The man who told me the story was also a Christian. He too was poor. But seeing the wreckage that had been done, and caring for the suffering of the victims, he came up with a plan. He approached several businesspeople that he knew, explained the dire consequences to the defrauded people, and asked if they would donate funds to help make a partial restoration to those who had been robbed. His reputation was such that a number did contribute. He took those donated funds and purchased clothing and other items and presented them as gifts to all those from whom the Christian has stolen. It was not a full restitution. But it was a gesture he could make which acknowledged the injustice done to them, which apologized to those who had been swindled, and which proclaimed that there were Christians who cared to bless rather than to cheat their neighbors. Stealing damages our neighbors. Christians ought to be concerned to honor and bless their neighbors. That's the spirit of the eighth commandment, "Don't steal."

WHAT THE COMMANDMENT MEANS IN DEUTERONOMY 5

To review, we have seen that commandments 6–10 form a unit, connected by beginning with the word "and," and extending of the demand of commandment 5 to honor others. We have also seen that commandments 5–10 are each specific expressions of loving our neighbor.

Beyond these considerations, Craigie reminds us of the proper starting-point for discussion of the meaning of "Don't steal:" "The commandment, unlike the more general legislation on theft, is concerned specifically with relationships between persons within the covenant community, rather than with property." In this, it is like commandments 5–10, as we have seen: the subordinate goal is that people not steal, but the ultimate goal, stated negatively, is to avoid harm to neighbor; stated positively, love of neighbor (seeking their well-being) is the ultimate goal.

The Hebrew term used here means "to take something that does not belong to you, usually in a secretive fashion."[1] McConville reminds us of something we moderns easily forget because we are so wealthy compared to ancient peoples. "The seriousness of the offence of theft must be understood in the context of a poor society, where property is both limited and a necessary means to survival."[2] To steal might well endanger someone's life and certainly could threaten their well-being. These things are the antithesis of "love" of neighbor. Block notes the interrelated nature of commandments 8 and 10, observing that examples of the sorts of things one should not steal are listed in commandment 10.[3] This suggests that the act of stealing begins in the heart with illicit desires, which is why commandment 10 is added to augment what is stated in commandment 8.

While theft was prohibited in other ancient law codes, Israel's law differs dramatically from ANE law. While murder and adultery are capital crimes in the Torah, theft is not.[4] Wright explains, "This feature of Israelite law stands in sharp contrast to the laws of theft in other ancient Near Eastern law codes, where there was a wide range of penalties, including mutilations and death, for different kinds of theft, as well as a gradation of penalties according to the social rank of the victim. In the OT, theft was penalized and remedied by restitution . . . but never punished by death."[5] People are sacred, made as God's image; property is not sacred in the same sense.

Merrill contributes these thoughtful comments:

> The sixth commandment, then, speaks of the theft of life, the seventh the theft of the purity and sanctity of the marriage relationship, and the eighth the theft of goods and possessions. There obviously is an inherent evil in the illegitimate appropriation of another's property, but on an even higher covenantal and theological level theft betrays an essential dissatisfaction with one's lot in life and an acquisitive desire to obtain more than the Lord,

---

1. Lundbom, *Deuteronomy*, 293.
2. McConville, *Deuteronomy*, 129–30.
3. Block, *Deuteronomy*, 166.
4. An early example, Acahan's theft, did result in death, but that was exceptional in that it was in time of war and involved a direct disobedience to a divine command (Josh 7:20–27). Kidnapping is also an exception to this rule, which will be discussed below.
5. Wright, *Deuteronomy*, 81–82.

the Sovereign who dispenses to his vassals what seems best, has granted already.[6]

So, commandment 8 is fundamentally about loving our neighbor by avoiding what will compromise their well-being. This deduction is well-justified in light of how Deuteronomy expounds commandment 8.

WHAT THE COMMANDMENT MEANS IN DEUTERONOMY

Commandment 8 is expounded in Deut 23:19–24:7, in the following sections.

1. 23:19–20: charging interest on loans
2. 23:21–23: failing to fulfill a vow to the Lord
3. 23:24–25: taking food to which you are not entitled
4. 24:1–5: two issues regarding marriage and sexuality
5. 24:6: taking a millstone in pledge
6. 24:7: kidnapping

It is obvious that all of these sections deal with stealing except perhaps section 4 (24:1–5). This section is best seen as one unit with two parts, both introduced with exactly the same words, "When a man takes a wife" (24:1, 5), and dealing with sexuality and marriage.

The more important issue is how each section forbids stealing, and the answers are not hard to find. Each section is devoted to preventing some type of stealing, i.e., taking something that is not rightfully yours. The words "steal" and "thief" occur only twice in the passage (24:7; cf. 5:19), but that confirms that this unit is indeed elaborating commandment 8. The chart below shows how each section elaborates a kind of stealing.

  A 23:19–20: stealing from your "brother" by charging interest on loans
    B 23:21–23: stealing from God by failing to fulfill a vow to the Lord
      C 23:24–25: stealing food from your neighbor
      C' 24:1–5 sexual stealing from your neighbor
    B' 24:6 stealing from God by "taking a life" by taking a millstone in pledge

6. Merrill, *Deuteronomy*, 155.

A' 24:7 "stealing" by kidnapping a "brother"

The first and last sections (A and A') are about stealing—taking something not your own—from a "brother" (23:19; 24:7). The first forbids charging a fellow Israelite interest. The rationale is profiting from the poverty of a brother Israelite who needs a loan is to abuse him, to steal from him.[7] Wright elaborates, "Once again we find that Israel's law stands in marked contrast to surrounding ancient Near Eastern countries, where the charging of interest, often at very high rates, was common. In Israel, it was among the defining marks of righteousness that a person did not lend at interest; conversely, the charging of interest was morally and socially condemned (cf. Ps 15: 5; Prov 28: 8; Ezek 18: 8, 13, 17)."[8] Lending at interest is apparently allowed for foreigners because they were merchants who were not in poverty.[9]

Section A' (24:7) is also about a brother Israelite, but the prohibition is against kidnapping and using or selling them as a slave. Here, in perhaps the least expected context in this section of Deuteronomy, the text calls this "stealing," rather than "kidnapping," in order to make its correlation with commandment 8 clear. Craigie draws an important conclusion: "the law assumes the inviolable freedom of man under God."[10] This is in fundamental agreement with the American Declaration of Independence, which states, "We hold these truths to be self-evident, that all men are created equal, that they are endowed by their Creator with certain unalienable Rights, that among these are Life, Liberty and the pursuit of Happiness." Further implications of this will be spelled out below.

The following two sections (B and B') also develop implications of stealing.[11] Deuteronomy 23:21–23 forbid stealing from God by failing to fulfill a vow to the Lord, i.e., promising then reneging on the voluntary commitment to give something to God. The other section, 24:6, also describes a form of stealing from God: "taking a life" by taking in pledge (as collateral) something upon which a person's livelihood depended.

The inner sections (C and C') complete the discussion by elaborating other forms of stealing. Deuteronomy 23:24–25 allows eating from your

---

7. Merrill, *Deuteronomy*, 315.
8. Wright, *Deuteronomy*, 251.
9. Wright, *Deuteronomy*, 251.
10. Craigie, *Deuteronomy*, 161.
11. Merrill, *Deuteronomy*, 319.

"neighbor's" vineyard or field as you pass through, but disallows taking too much, which means taking more than what you can eat as you pass through. Taking too much is defined here as stealing.

The other text, Deut 24:1–5, is also about stealing, but is a bit more complex. It has often been read as the great OT permission for divorce, largely because the King James Version (1611) mistranslated verses 1–4. The proper translation is, "*If a man takes a wife* . . . and he puts a certificate of divorce in her hand . . . and her second husband puts a certificate of divorce in her hand, *her first husband may not* take her again to be his wife" (emphasis added). The point of the passage is not to explain when divorce is permitted, but to forbid the first husband remarrying her after her divorce from a second husband. The question is "Why"? The best answer is that such a marriage is tantamount to incest.[12] So, Deut 24:1–4 prevents taking sexually what is inappropriate: stealing sexual privileges that are out of bounds.

The last verse of C,' 24:5, also forbids an inappropriate taking away of a sexual privilege: denying a husband and wife the pleasure and companionship of each other by calling him to war or some other public duty within the first year of their marriage. In this case, the provision prevents the inappropriate denying of someone that which they are due. To do so would be a form of stealing.[13]

WHAT THE COMMANDMENT MEANS AS A POSITIVE PRINCIPLE

Taking all of Deuteronomy into account and remembering that commandment 5 establishes honor as the key principle in the neighbor commandments, we can state the positive principle in commandment 8, "Don't steal," as *Instead of taking from others, loving our neighbor honors them by seeking ways to be generous to them, as you would like others to treat you.*

Here is why we think this positive statement captures the essence of Deuteronomy's exposition of commandment 8. We frame this as loving our

---

12. Wenham ("Restoration of Marriage Reconsidered," 36–40) points out that in the OT view of marriage, marriage makes a man and a woman as closely related as parents and children; they become "one flesh" (Gen 2:24). Thus, such a remarriage after the wife's marriage to another man is tantamount to marrying one's sister or another close relative, which was forbidden in the Torah. Cited by Kaiser, *Ethics*, 202–03, which see for more detailed analysis and verbal parallels with incest passages in Leviticus 18 and 20.

13. Merrill, *Deuteronomy*, 319.

neighbor because, as we have seen already, commandments 5–10 are about love of neighbor. We also include a negative prelude with the positive main statement because Deut 23:19–24:7 itself handles it this way, as the figure below shows:

> A 23:19–20: *don't* steal from your "brother" by charging interest; you *may* to a foreigner
> > B 23:21–23: *do* fulfill your vows to God; failing is to steal from God; you *may* refrain
> > > C 23:24–25: you *may* eat [but] *don't* steal food from your neighbor
> > > > C' 24:1–5 man *may not* take former wife back; newly-wed *man not* to be called
> > > B' 24:6 you *shall not* steal from God by "taking a life" by taking a millstone in pledge
> > A' 24:7 If a man is found "stealing" by kidnapping a "brother" he *shall be* put to death

If we label the positive statements "A" and the prohibitions "B," we see this pattern:

A B, A

B A, A

C A, B

C' B, B

B' B

A' A

Notice that the passage balances the prohibitions and positive obligations it elaborates, giving five examples each of negative and positive maximums. Note also that A and C are opposites (B, A; A, B) and that B and C' are also opposites but in a different pattern (A, A; B, B). The A and B elements are so arranged to provide attractive symmetry, and perhaps easier memorization, for an audience that heard them read aloud.

Our positive principle states that love of neighbor is shown by "seeking ways to be generous." We see this in A above (Deut 23:19–20) in that a brother Israelite is not charged interest, but is treated as family, seeking to meet his need with a loan, but foregoing any profit out of a generous spirit. We see generosity in B in the emphasis that vowing to the Lord is entirely voluntary, i.e., it is out of love for God and a giving, generous spirit toward him that one would vow. We also see generosity in C' (i.e., 24:5) in granting newlyweds a reprieve from public service for the sake of their marital happiness. In most cultures, this would be considered "unnecessary" because public duty would be seen as trumping personal issues. Yet here, a couple's early marriage is granted priority even over national defense! That is a generous spirit.

Our positive principle ends with "generous, as you would like others to treat you." We see this in several places and believe this is a necessary addition to the mere statement of generosity. We can see this in A, in that all of us would like to be offered no-interest loans. We see it in C, where we would all like the privilege of eating while we walk through someone else's farm; we also see it in that sort of generosity that is expected from a landowner. We see this principle in C', in which it is obvious that all of us would like the opportunity to focus on our marriage in the first year and be free from external obligations: this is how we would like to be treated, and it is how God expects Israel to treat their neighbors. We see it in A' (24:7) because we would all desire to be liberated from someone who took advantage of us and to see them face justice.

Once again, it is our sense that Paul states commandment 8 in a positive way which reflects our positive statement. In fact, we suspect that Paul's statement is intended to show us exactly what commandment 8 always meant. Paul says in Eph 4:28, "Let the thief no longer steal, but rather let him labor, doing honest work with his own hands, so that he may have something to share with anyone in need." After restating commandment 8, he draws the positive lesson that we should seek ways to be generous (for example, by working hard and accumulating surplus) and he then explains that that generosity is expressed by giving freely to people in need, which is exactly how all of us would wish to be treated.

WHAT THE COMMANDMENT MEANS FOR CHRISTIANS

Commandment 8 is repeated four times in the NT (Matt 19:18; Mark 10:19; Luke 18:20; Rom 13:9), besides other NT echoes such as Eph 4:28.[14] As we have already seen, the grand positive maximum is articulated by Paul in Eph 4:28, a maximum which is clear from Deuteronomy's exposition of commandment 8. Christians should be looking for ways to be generous,

14. Lundbom, *Deuteronomy*, 293.

a central test being to think of what we would enjoy others doing for us. Calvin recognized all we have been saying long ago:

> We must bear in mind also, that an affirmative precept, as it is called, is connected with the prohibition; because, even if we abstain from all wrong-doing, we do not therefore satisfy God, who has laid mankind under mutual obligation to each other, that they may seek to benefit, care for, and succor their neighbors. Wherefore He undoubtedly inculcates liberality and kindness, and the other duties, whereby human society is maintained; and hence, in order that we may not be condemned as thieves by God, we must endeavor, as far as possible, that every one should safely keep what he possesses, and that our neighbor's advantage should be promoted no less than our own.[15]

Wright concurs:

> It is clear, then, that the prohibition was treated seriously and applied to a wide range of antisocial behavior, alongside other forms of economic exploitation and injustice. Calvin's instinct was valid, then, in seeing the eighth commandment as concerned not only with the precise crime of burglary or robbery but with all forms of unjust gain at the expense of others.[16]

Deuteronomy's exposition of commandment 8 and the broader biblical teaching about property and wealth have been nicely summarized by Kaiser:

> Property was viewed in the Old Testament as a gift and stewardship from God; the Lord owned everything in heaven and earth (Pss. 24:1; 115:16), and he it was who entrusted it to others. Hence, no one could despotically enslave another by kidnapping him or usurp his claim to goods over that of its rightful owner. Wealth and goods were, on the other hand, to be shared with the poor and weaker members of society ... Thus the distribution and unnatural accumulation of wealth is kept in fairly balanced check since the land, with its means of producing food and surplus, was the baseline for the whole economy and this was shared equally.[17]

The generosity taught in commandment 8 is evident in 2 Cor 8–9, esp. 9:6–13.

---

15. Calvin, *Commentaries*, Deut 5:19, Olive Tree e-book edition.
16. Wright, *Deuteronomy*, 82.
17. Kaiser, *Ethics*, 94–95.

Commandment 8: "Don't Steal"

But the key NT text is 1 Tim 6:17–19. It merits stating in full:

> As for the rich in this present age, charge them not to be haughty, nor to set their hopes on the uncertainty of riches, but on God, who richly provides us with everything to enjoy. They are to do good, to be rich in good works, to be generous and ready to share, thus storing up treasure for themselves as a good foundation for the future, so that they may take hold of that which is truly life.

In this, perhaps the NT's most comprehensive overview of wealth and Christian responsibility with it, Paul teaches principles thoroughly in line with Deuteronomy's commandment 8. First, he says that wealth is a gift of God, not a source of guilt (6:17) unless it makes us proud and becomes an idol. But he moves on to pile up expressions explaining our duty of generosity: we are to do good, be rich in good deeds, to be generous and ready to share. Commandment 8 comes through powerfully in Paul's exhortations to NT Christians about generosity.

In sum, Paul clearly summarized the meaning of commandment 8: "For the commandments . . . you shall not steal . . . are summed up in this word: 'You shall love your neighbor as yourself.' Love does no wrong to a neighbor; therefore love is the fulfilling of the law" (Rom 13:9–10).

So, we see a fourth time that it is undeniable: Deuteronomy is one of the important Bible books—one of the most rich, extensive, and detailed biblical treatments—of loving God and loving neighbor.

The Heidelberg Catechism expounds commandment 8 profitably. Note again that in Answer 111 the positive side of the commandment's meaning is elaborated.

HEIDELBERG CATECHISM:

110. Q. What does God forbid in the eighth commandment?

A. God forbids not only the theft and robbery which civil authorities punish, but God also labels as theft all wicked tricks and schemes by which we seek to get for ourselves our neighbor's goods, whether by force or under the pretext of right, such as false weights and measures, deceptive advertising or merchandising, counterfeit money, exorbitant interest, or any other means forbidden by God. In addition God forbids all greed and pointless squandering of his gifts.

111. Q. What does God require of us in this commandment?

A. That I do whatever I can for my neighbor's good, that I treat others as I would like them to treat me, and that I work faithfully so that I may share with those in need.

QUESTIONS FOR PERSONAL DEVOTIONS:

1. How does following commandment 8 demonstrate God's love to your neighbor?
2. How does commandment 8 teach us about trust?
3. What specific attitudes of the heart does God speak against in commandment 8?
4. How does this commandment speak to you in ways other than physical theft?
5. What would it look like to live in generosity instead of theft?
6. What are a few specific ways that you could cultivate a heart of generosity?
7. How could Jesus's instructions in Matt 7:12 be viewed as an exposition of commandment 8?
8. What else might God be saying to you through this commandment?

QUESTIONS FOR TEACHING AND PREACHING:

1. Discuss the difference between the Old Testament consequence of theft (restitution) vs. other ANE codes of law (death) and why this is important.
2. What are some of the ways in which we are tempted to violate this commandment today?
3. Think about how the positive principle of generosity found in this commandment is taught elsewhere in Scripture. How could this inform your teaching and preaching?
4. Discuss how love of neighbor is the basis of not stealing and of being generous instead.
5. What are some ways that your community of faith could live out the positive implications of the eighth commandment?

Commandment 8: "Don't Steal"

6. How does Paul's argument in Ephesians chapter 4 demonstrate the positive implication of this commandment?

7. How does the eighth commandment deal with relationships between people, not just the taking of physical property?

8. What does the exposition of commandment 8 in Deuteronomy teach us about how stealing affects the one who steals?

9. What lessons could you draw regarding the atoning death of Christ from the punishment for theft being restitution instead of death?

Chapter 12

Commandment 9: "Do Not Bear False Witness"

Text of commandment 9 in Deuteronomy 5: "And you shall not bear false witness against your neighbor" (5:29).

Commandment 9 expounded in Deuteronomy: 24:8–25:4

Positive principle summary: We love our neighbors by treating them fairly and with respect.

Full positive principle: Loving our neighbor honors them by treating them fairly, which means treating them with dignity, respect, and honesty and not taking advantage of them.

POTIPHAR'S WIFE

Perhaps one of the most instructive stories in all of Scripture as relates to the ninth commandment comes from the story of Joseph in the book of Genesis. Joseph is sold into slavery in Egypt by his brothers. The Scriptures tell us that God is with Joseph and his situation begins to improve. Eventually, he is second in command in the house of a powerful Egyptian man named Potiphar. Everything seems to be going in the right direction in the story, until Potiphar's wife wants to have an affair with Joseph. When Joseph refuses, Potiphar's wife breaks the ninth commandment. She gives false testimony against Joseph. That false testimony stands in stark contrast with the character of Joseph who has been nothing but truthful. Potiphar's wife is not only telling a lie. She is using her powerful position to bring harm to Joseph. She is deliberately abusing her power, the power that she has over someone in a less powerful position than herself. She is not only telling a lie and abusing a power-differential. Potiphar's wife also is breaking the covenant relationship that she has with her husband. She is stealing the truth from him. She is not treating him with dignity and respect. The story of Joseph and Potiphar's wife gives us a powerful example of what can happen and how lives can be torn apart when we give false testimony against our neighbor.

The story of Joseph and Potiphar's wife points us forward to Jesus. Jesus also suffered at the hands of those who gave false testimony about him. The religious leaders and the witnesses at his trial broke the ninth commandment. They gave false testimony. In doing so they, like Potiphar's wife, misused a position of power in order to deliberately harm someone else. They, like Potiphar's wife, broke their covenant relationship with God and with their neighbor. The false witnesses at Jesus's trial not only brought suffering to Jesus. They also stole the truth from others who had seen Jesus preach, teach, and heal. They tore apart the bonds that bound an entire community together.

Sadly, we still see this all too often in our world today. Truth is treated lightly and lies seem to be an accepted way to get ahead. When we are tempted, like Potiphar's wife and the witnesses at Jesus's trial, to participate in deception, we are being tempted to turn our back on who God proclaims us to be. When someone gives false testimony, it not only brings harm to that person, but it also breaks a covenant relationship with God, with themselves, with their neighbors, and with an entire community.

WHAT THE COMMANDMENT MEANS IN DEUTERONOMY 5

Commandment 9, like the other neighbor commandments after commandment 5, is a (negatively-stated) example of what it means to honor others, i.e., to love one's neighbor, beginning with the word "and." It addresses testimony in court, and reads in the Hebrew, "You shall not respond (i.e., when giving witness in court) against your neighbor with worthless testimony."[1]

---

1. Wright, *Deuteronomy*, 83. Craigie agrees that court is the context of the witness here, *Deuteronomy*, 162, as does Lundbom, *Deuteronomy*, 294. Mayes notes that the verb here "is used as a technical term 'to testify, give testimony in a court' in Num. 35:30; Dt.

"What we have then," Lundbom correctly notes, "is not a general prohibition of lying, as bad as lying might be, but against lying testimony regarding another person."[2] Again we see, as we saw earlier, that the concern is primarily to prevent harm to a neighbor.

Craigie notes the larger context: "The principle involved, once again, was that the breach of the commandment undermined a basic characteristic of the covenant, namely, faithfulness—of God to man, of man to God, and of man to fellow man."[3] He adds, importantly, "Though the immediate context of the commandment was in the sphere of legal process, the implications applied to the activities of daily life."[4] Merrill elaborates, "The ninth commandment forbids false testimony against another. Such testimony is tantamount to character assassination and so is another form of killing or theft."[5]

McConville calls our attention to the social importance of this commandment, consistent with what we have seen in the neighbor commands. He writes, "The ninth commandment illustrates clearly that the Decalogue aims at sustaining the life of the community. It . . . concerns false charges brought against one's 'neighbor,' that is, another member of the covenant community . . . Its standards imply . . . the means of investigation and enforcement (best illustrated in 19:4–13)."[6] Wright comments on Deut 19: the Torah "established a remarkably retributive law on perjury: anyone discovered to have given false testimony was to be punished with the same punishment that the victim of his accusation would have received if the verdict had gone against him (Deut 19: 16– 21)."[7] Wright adds, "The OT, especially in the Psalms and Wisdom literature, has a passionate interest in truth, partly as a reflection of an essential characteristic of Yahweh himself,

---

19:16, 18 so indicating that the concern of this prohibition is with a witness at law, not with lying generally (see the longer treatment of the subject in Dt. 19:15ff.)" (*Deuteronomy*, 171).

2. Lundbom, *Deuteronomy*, 294.
3. Craigie, *Deuteronomy*, 162.
4. Craigie, *Deuteronomy*, 163.
5. Merrill, *Deuteronomy*, 155.
6. McConville, *Deuteronomy*, 130.
7. Wright, *Deuteronomy*, 84, where he continues, "One wonders what a salutary effect such a law might have in the modern world, which is plagued with miscarriages of justice notoriously caused by false testimony and conspiracy."

Commandment 9: "Do Not Bear False Witness"

and partly out of a thoroughly practical and consequential awareness of the cost to individuals and society as a whole when lying becomes endemic."[8]

We may conclude by observing that loving our neighbor is expressed by honoring them by refusing to damage them by false testimony.

WHAT THE COMMANDMENT MEANS IN DEUTERONOMY

Commandment 9 is expounded in Deut 24:8–25:4. Kaufman crystallizes the essence of commandment 9: "A single motif—firmly grounded in the Ninth commandment—runs through the laws of Command IX: fairness to one's fellow as regards both his substance and his dignity. Even the criminal is not to be belittled (25:3)."[9] The chiastic exposition follows:

A Moses and Miriam (24:8–9)				Do not show disrespect
	B Debtor (24:10–13)			Show respect
		C Poor workers (24:14–15)		Do not take advantage
			D Fathers & children (24:16)	Be fair
			D' Helpless & justice (24:17–18)	Be fair
		C' Helpless gleaning (24:19–22)		Do opposite of taking advantage
	B' Criminals (25:1–3)			Show respect
A' Animals (25:4)				Do not show disrespect

---

8. Wright, *Deuteronomy*, 84–5. Obeying God's commands are indeed good for us; for a social science demonstration that honesty and the trust that results from it in a society promote human well-being and wealth, see Fukuyama, Trust, 1995).

9. Kaufman, "Structure of Deuteronomic Law," 141. Kaiser agrees: "Fairness is the hallmark of the ninth commandment and of these laws in Deuteronomy 24:8–25:4." (*Ethics*, 136).

The left side of the figure summaries the content of each passage and the right side the principle behind it. Note that A and A,' B and B,' C and C,' and D and D,' correspond. As is often the case in a chiastic structure, the center (D, D') states the main principle: fairness. The other pairs provide elaboration: fairness is expressed by showing respect, refusing to display disrespect, and by refusing to take advantage of our neighbor. Note that A, A,' B, and B,' all stress respect, which is a synonym for the "honor" which commandment 5 enunciated as the core principle of commandments 5–10. Merrill titles Deut 24:8–25:4, "respect for the dignity of others."[10] This reinforces our conclusion that "honor" is the key principle of how loving our neighbor is expressed in commandments 5–10.

Kaufman "sees a descending order of hierarchy in the list of offended parties with Moses, as paradigmatic leader, listed first (24:8–9), followed by the nonpoor debtor (24:10–13), the poor debtor (24:14–15), the indigent (24:17–22), the criminal (25:1–3), and even the animal (25:4)."[11]

The first unit of the section, A (24:8–9), at first seems unrelated, but it only appears this way at first glance. Kaufman helps here: "Fortunately, our writer provides the clue himself, lest we fail to catch his train of thought: 'Remember Miriam.' Miriam was afflicted with leprosy for speaking unjustifiably against Moses and his wife. Was there ever a more serious case of libel?"[12] By speaking disrespectfully of God's leader, Miriam crossed a bridge too far and broke commandment 9: she brashly bore false witness against Moses.

Section B (24:10–13) is also about fairness, this time to a debtor, then a poor debtor. Two acts of fairness are given as examples of how to be fair to someone who owes a person money. One says that one who is owed a debt is to stand outside; that is, not to barge into a man's house, which would be to treat him disrespectfully. The second warns against keeping a poor man's cloak overnight, since it is his means of warmth; again, not treating him with disrespect. Both of these reflect the respect we would want another to show to us in like circumstances. The appropriate actions honor the debtor.

Farness is again the principle elaborated in section C (24:14–15). The specific point is that an employer should not take advantage of a worker by

---

10. Merrill, *Deuteronomy*, 320.

11. Merrill, *Deuteronomy*, 321. Merrill's summary is quoted here because it is succinct; Kaufman's list is in "Structure of Deuteronomic Law," 141.

12. Kaufman, "Structure of Deuteronomic Law," 141. The text also provides general instruction about how to handle leprosy, which was occasioned by Miriam's breaching commandment 9.

Commandment 9: "Do Not Bear False Witness"

withholding the wages which are needed to put food on the table for his family. To do so is to "oppress" him and is the "sin" of dishonoring a needy person.

Deuteronomy 24:16-18 (D, D') is the center of the chiasm. Merrill writes, "Verse 16 serves as both the focal point of the whole section and as the introduction to the legislation regarding justice in punishment (24:17-25:3)."[13] Two examples here illustrate prohibited unfairness. No one should be punished for something they did not do; it's unfair! Further, "perverting justice" to the most vulnerable is particularly offensive: it's unfair!

Section C' (24:19-22) balances C above ("do not take advantage") by its opposite: be generous to the needy: it's fair and expresses God's generosity in liberating you from the poverty and oppression of Egypt, where you learned the pain of not being fairly and generously treated.

The next section is about how to treat a criminal (B', 25:1-3). Two ideas contained in the text are expressions of fairness. First, the convicted criminal is punished only as appropriate for his offense. Second, and more telling, is that a limit is placed upon how much punishment any noncapital offense may occasion. The motive clause is revealing: "lest your brother be degraded in your eyes" (25:3). That is, the criminal is still "your brother," and he must not be degraded beyond appropriate chastisement. A criminal is still a person made in (or as) the image of God and he deserves the respect that is due to him, in spite of his offense. He is not worthless but must be granted the dignity he still deserves.

The final section which expounds commandment 9 is Deut 25:4 (A'): "you shall not muzzle the ox when it is treading out the grain." The lowest human in the socioeconomic ranking in Deut 24:8-25:3 is the criminal. But below him in the honor due to them is an animal. Mirroring the first unit about Moses (24:8-9, A above), this text says, "do not show disrespect!"— even to an animal! Merrill captures the thought expertly:

> Finally, the very lowest creatures on the "social" scale, the animals themselves, fell under the protection of the Lord and the covenant. Man had been created to have dominion over all things (Gen 1:26-28; Ps 8), but even after his fall and the consequent alienation that had developed between him and all creation, including the animal world (Gen 9:2), he was not to exploit nature but live in harmony with it (Gen 9:3-10). The prohibition here (Deut 25:4) about muzzling the working ox reflects the spirit of mercy

---

13. Merrill, *Deuteronomy*, 321.

that pervades all of God's dealings with his creation, human or otherwise. The purpose clearly was not only to provide for the ox itself but to make the point by *a fortiori* argument that if a mere animal was worthy of humane treatment, how much more so was a human being created as the image of God. Paul, in fact, cited this very text twice in making a plea for the support of those involved in Christian ministry (1 Cor 9:9–14; 1 Tim 5:17–18).[14]

So, we see that Deut 24:8–25:4 applies one principle, fairness, to all these instances in order to communicate that commandment 9's positive meaning is that treating people and even animals unfairly is to "bear false witness against them." It is to treat them contrary to their God-given status and thus lie about who they are. Showing disrespect and taking advantage of people (A, B, C, C,' B,' A') are forbidden as expressions of bearing false witness to the honor that people, and even animals, deserve. Such actions dishonor them, as commandment 5 exhorted us not to do. In other words, to do such things is to fail to love our neighbor.

Lies are damaging to the perpetrator and to the target, to the community and to the individual. Commandment 9 is a wide-ranging exhortation to avoid such devastation by swearing off bearing false witness.

WHAT THE COMMANDMENT MEANS AS A POSITIVE PRINCIPLE

Kaufmann, cited above, came close to stating the positive principle of commandment 9 when he summarized it as "fairness to one's fellow."[15] Besides "Do not bear false witness," here are the principles we deduced in Deuteronomy about commandment 9.

  A Do not show disrespect
    B Show respect
      C Do not take advantage
        D Be fair

        D' Be fair
      C' Do opposite of taking advantage
    B' Show respect

---

14. Merrill, *Deuteronomy*, 325–26.
15. Kaufman, "Structure of Deuteronomic Law," 141.

Commandment 9: "Do Not Bear False Witness"

A' Do not show disrespect

Taking all that Deuteronomy says into account, and remembering that commandment 5 establishes honor as the key principle in the neighbor commandments, we can state the positive principle in commandment 9 as *Loving our neighbor honors them by treating them fairly, which means treating them with dignity, respect, and honesty, and going of your way to not take advantage of others, especially those less powerful than yourself.*

The psalmist lauded this truth when he sang, "I hate and abhor falsehood, but I love your law" (Ps 119:163), for when "Princes persecute me without cause," "my heart stands in awe of your words" (Ps 119:161).

WHAT THE COMMANDMENT MEANS FOR CHRISTIANS

The New Testament reiterates this commandment several times (Matt 19:18; Mark 10:19; Luke 18:20).[16] Paul also cites Deut 25:4, "Do not muzzle the ox when it is treading out the grain," in 1 Cor 9:9 and 1 Tim 5:18. His use of it is consistent with how we have expounded it.

In summary, Paul declared "For the commandments . . . are summed up in this word: 'You shall love your neighbor as yourself.' Love does no wrong to a neighbor; therefore love is the fulfilling of the law" (Rom 13:9–10).

So, we see for a fifth time that Deuteronomy is an important Bible book—one of the most rich, extensive, and detailed biblical treatments—of loving God and loving neighbor. The Heidelberg Catechism expounds negative and positive implications of commandment 9.[17]

HEIDELBERG CATECHISM:

112. Q. What is God's will for us in the ninth commandment?

A. That I do not give false testimony against anyone, twist anyone's words, or gossip or slander, or join in condemning anyone without a hearing or without just cause. Rather, in court and everywhere else, I should avoid lying and deceit of every kind; these are devices the devil uses, and they

---

16. Lundbom, *Deuteronomy*, 293.
17. Heidelberg Catechism (1563).

would call down on me God's intense wrath. I should love the truth, speak it candidly, and openly acknowledge it. And I should do what I can to defend and advance my neighbor's good name.

QUESTIONS FOR PERSONAL DEVOTIONS:

1. How does the prohibition on bearing false witness show love for God and for neighbor?
2. How does this commandment and its concern for truth reveal the heart of God?
3. How does lying do damage to your own soul in addition to that of your neighbor?
4. Why are we tempted to lie and what might this reveal about where our hope is?
5. How does Paul's command to love in Romans 13 show the heart of God's commandments (including forbidding false witness) in Deuteronomy?
6. What are some practical ways that you could show this kind of love?
7. What else might God be saying to you through this commandment?

QUESTIONS FOR TEACHING AND PREACHING:

1. What is the significance of the fact that the commandment applies to foreigners as well as to Israelites?
2. What does the specific meaning of the commandment as giving false testimony in court show us about the damage lying does to our neighbor?
3. What can we learn about the fuller meaning of the commandment from its exposition in Deuteronomy 24 and 25?
4. How is Miriam an example of violating this commandment? (See Deut 24:8–9)
5. Discuss how fairness is the positive implication of this negative commandment.

Commandment 9: "Do Not Bear False Witness"

6. What can be learned from Paul's use of this commandment in 1 Cor 9:9–14 and 1 Tim 5:17–18?
7. How might this commandment inform your preaching of the trial of Jesus in the Gospels?
8. How do other stories in Scripture where this commandment is violated show us the damage that lying can do?
9. How does violating this commandment also violate the rest? (For example, murder or theft?)
10. How does your answer to the last question impact your understanding of the gospel? (See Jas 2:1–13)
11. What does the application of this commandment to criminals, the poor and foreigners teach us about how God views all human life?
12. How does the use of this commandment in the New Testament enrich your understanding and preaching of it?

Chapter 13

Commandment 10: "Don't Covet"

Text of commandment 10 in Deuteronomy 5: "And you shall not covet your neighbor's wife. And you shall not desire your neighbor's house, his field, or his male servant, or his female servant, his ox, or his donkey, or anything that is your neighbor's" (5:21).

Commandment 10 expounded in Deuteronomy: 25:5–19.

Positive principle summary: We love our neighbors by attitudes which place their well-being above our own.

Full positive principle: Loving our neighbor honors them by entertaining and endorsing only attitudes which safeguard our neighbor's well-being above our own, especially for the weak and vulnerable.

ARE WE THANKFUL FOR OUR BLESSINGS—AND ALSO DEVOTED TO OUR NEIGHBOR'S BLESSING?

As we come to the final one of the Ten Commandments, it seems that the commandments end by going back to the beginning. The commandment, "you shall not covet" calls to mind the story of Eve being tempted in the Garden of Eden by the serpent. The serpent tempts Eve by getting her to believe that God has not given her everything that she needs for life and happiness. The serpent makes Eve believe that God is holding out on her. The serpent, in other words, tempts Eve to covet, to covet the fruit of the

Commandment 10: "Don't Covet"

tree and the knowledge and beauty which it brings. The question of what that first temptation entailed has been asked since the story of Adam and Eve was recorded. Many people throughout the history of the church have viewed the first sin as an act of pride. Many say that the sin of Adam and Eve was the sin of being prideful and thinking that they did not need God.

It is a widely held view that the first sin of humanity was pride. However, I must admit that this never seemed very persuasive to me, Derek, personally. There have been times in my life when I have been discouraged, even discouraged greatly. There have been times in my life that I have dealt with grief and pain and loss. There have been times in my life where I did not feel much pride. There have been times in my life when I did not feel much pride in myself, or in who I was or in how I had handled certain things. There have been times in my life where I did not have a strong sense of self-worth. So, when I hear that the first sin of the human race was pride, sometimes I find that hard to identify with and it does not speak deeply to my faith in Christ.

Now, while it has been widely held that the first sin of Adam and Eve was pride, this is not the only view. Others throughout the history of the church, especially in the early Eastern church, have viewed this story differently. They have taught that the original sin of humanity was not an act of pride, but rather that it was an act of unthankfulness. Adam and Eve's greatest sin is that they are not thankful for all of the incredible and beautiful gifts that God has provided. They were not thankful, and when we are unthankful, then we can become rebellious and hardhearted. The apostle Paul would seem to agree with this view. In one of his most famous passages on sin, he lists a lack of thankfulness as a primary motivating factor. Romans 1:21 says, "For although they knew God, they neither glorified him as God *nor gave thanks to him*, but their thinking became futile and their foolish hearts were darkened" (emphasis added). According to Paul, one of humanity's primary problems is that we are not thankful. We are not thankful to God, and we are not thankful to our neighbor. Now, this is certainly something that I can identify with. Even in my lowest moments, when I did not feel any pride, I can still recognize ways that I have not been thankful. I can still recognize ways that I was not thankful for the blessings that God had provided and ways that I was not thankful for the kindness of my neighbors. So, what does it really mean to not covet? Well, are we thankful to God and our neighbors for their generosity to us? Are we as thankful for our neighbor's well-being as for our own? Or, like Adam and

Eve, are we so unthankful for the blessings God has given us that we covet those of our neighbor?

WHAT THE COMMANDMENT MEANS IN DEUTERONOMY 5

Commandment 10 is the final particular expression of honoring neighbor which began with commandment 5, "honor your father and your mother." Beginning "and," it extends commandment 5 by providing the most unique commandment about how to love one's neighbor, unique because it deals not with actions but with attitudes.

The word "covet" strikes modern ears as old-fashioned since it is no longer a commonly used term. It means to desire something, but the nature of all the desires mentioned here is inordinate, since all the forbidden things belong to someone else.[1] Lundbom clarifies, "reference is not to a . . . lighthearted wish, which would be harmless."[2] Tigay adds that the mental state here forbidden goes "beyond simple, or passive, desire," to include "maneuvering to acquire," and could be paraphrased, "do not scheme to acquire"[3] from one's neighbor. Thus, the text does not forbid desiring to possess more for oneself, but rather desiring to take from one's neighbor in order to have more for oneself. A contemporary equivalent translation might be "crave," or "lust after" anything which is one's neighbors. As in all the neighbor commandments, the point is less about what I do and more about what I must not do *to harm my neighbor*. Hence, "you shall not covet *your neighbor's* wife. And you shall not desire *your neighbor's* house, *his* field, or *his* male servant, or *his* female servant, *his* ox, or *his* donkey, *or anything that is your neighbor's*." (Emphasis added.) That is, Commandment 10 is about loving neighbor, formulated in the negative, stating things incompatible with loving him or her. Merrill draws out the significance:

> What is less frequently observed is that this is in line with the progression of violence or disruption in a descending spiral from the shedding of blood to the ruin of personal reputation. What has been manifest empirically in acts and words is now hidden

---

1. Driver, *Deuteronomy*, 86: the term covet, "expressing in itself a perfectly lawful affection (Is. 53:2 Ps. 68:16), acquires from the context the sense of sinful coveting (cf. Mic. 2:2 Ex. 34:24)."

2. Lundbom, *Deuteronomy*, 295.

3. Tigay, *Deuteronomy*, 72.

Commandment 10: "Don't Covet"

in thoughts and cravings. Also of interest is the fact that this last commandment appears to be a summary of at least the previous three. To covet another's wife is tantamount to adultery, to covet another's properties is akin to theft, and to covet anything else would certainly cover such matters as a person's good standing in the community.[4]

Merrill adds that, compared to Exodus, in the statement of the commandment in Deuteronomy "house and wife are reversed and land is added . . . [likely reflecting] a theological development in which women's rights come increasingly into the foreground in view of the social situations envisioned by Moses on the eve of the conquest and occupation of Canaan."[5] As we saw discussing commandment 7, women are not chattel property in the OT.[6]

Deuteronomy 5:21 contains two synonymous words for "covet,"[7] which serve an important function, as repetition often does in the Torah.[8] The two words repeat two terms used to describe Eve's temptation in the Garden,[9] showing that the author is alluding to Eve's experience as the "showcase example"[10] of coveting.[11] Genesis 3:6 reads (the repeated words are in italics), "So when the woman saw that the tree was good for food, and that it was a *delight* to the eyes, and that the tree was to be *desired* to make one wise, she took of its fruit and ate." Note that the sin was not in desiring food, beauty ("delight to the eyes"), or wisdom, all of which are God-given desires, but in desiring them inordinately, such that she was willing to disobey God's instructions to acquire them. In addition, just as Deuteronomy sees Gen 3:6 as a prime example of coveting, so John uses the same text to define loving the world: "Do not love the world . . . For all that is in the world—the *desires* of the flesh and the *desires* of the eyes and pride of life—is not from the Father but is from the world" (1 John 2:15–16). The three things John specifies here parallel the three things Eve craved, in the same

---

4. Merrill, *Deuteronomy*, 156.
5. Merrill, *Deuteronomy*, 156–57.
6. Levinson, *Jewish Study Bible*, 377, 417. Weinfeld, *Deuteronomy*, 318, says, "Deuteronomy gives special attention to women's rights," citing Deut 15:12–18 and 22:28–29.
7. Lundbom, *Deuteronomy*, 295; Merrill, *Deuteronomy*, 156.
8. On repetition as a literary device, see Alter, *Art of Biblical Narrative*.
9. Wenham, *Genesis 1–15*, 75.
10. Lundbom, *Deuteronomy*, 296.
11. See the discussion of repetition in Turner, "Broad Reference."

order.¹² Further, the same Greek word used in the Septuagint (the Greek translation of the Hebrew Bible) for "covet" in Deut 5:21 is used twice by John in 2:16 (italicized above; Greek *epithumia*). So, the classic OT and NT passages forbidding inordinate craving take Genesis 3 as their paradigm.

We have seen that the last commandment is the least serious of the Ten Commandments, listed as they are in descending order of importance.¹³ But it is also true, in another sense, that commandment 10 is perhaps the most important, bringing the Ten Commandments full circle. Merrill is spot-on when he explains, "coveting, though last on the list of commandments, may after all encapsulate them all. At the same time that it is the least overtly violent and injurious, it is the commandment most at the root of covenant disobedience in that it logically precedes the rest."¹⁴ Further, Craigie calls Commandment 10 "an effective summary of the spirit of commands 6–9."¹⁵ He concludes, "Thus all the last five commandments prohibit a wrong attitude to neighbors; commandments 6–9 prohibit wrong acts toward them and commandment 10 is comprehensive in prohibiting desire leading to any such act."

Block reminds us of the community emphasis implicit in commandments 5–10, affirming:¹⁶

> The aim of these last two commandments is to create a climate of trust and security within the covenant community. By concluding the Decalogue on this note Yahweh recognizes that actions arise from within, and that neither proper behavior by the individual nor the security of the community can be legislated. These are achieved only as all the members purpose within their hearts to place the interests of others ahead of themselves.¹⁷

That is, commandments 5–10 mean love your neighbor as yourself. While this wording first occurs in Lev 19:18, it is undeniably this sentiment that animates commandments 5–10.

---

12. Ross, *Creation and Blessing*, 136. Commentators on 1 John often deny this connection, e.g., Marshall, *The Epistles of John*, 146. But the three-fold description in both, the parallel in ideas and the repetition of *epithumia* ("desire, lust") seem to justify the conclusion.

13. Tigay, *Deuteronomy*, 72.

14. Merrill, *Deuteronomy*, 157.

15. Craigie, *Deuteronomy*, 163.

16. Block, *Deuteronomy*, 167–8.

17. Craigie, *Deuteronomy*, 164.

Commandment 10: "Don't Covet"

WHAT THE COMMANDMENT MEANS IN DEUTERONOMY

Commandment 10 is elaborated in Deut 25:5–19. It contains four sections which address the motives hidden in the heart, as commandment 10 itself does. These are the sections:

1. 25:5–10   Levirate marriage
2. 25:11–12   Inappropriate fighting
3. 25:13–16   Unjust weights
4. 25:17–19   Remember Amalek

The first section treats levirate marriage,[18] a common ANE custom treated in the Mosaic law only here, though stories about it are recorded in Genesis 38 and in the book of Ruth. The passage first provides instructions (25:5–6) for the case of a widowed woman with no sons. Her dead husband's brother, if he lives in the family unit, is to marry her so that the first son of that marriage will assume his dead father's name, which would also mean that he would inherit the dead man's property and carry on his family name in Israel. This first section serves three functions. First, it institutionalizes levirate marriage for Israel as a provision to care for a widow with no sons. Such widows would otherwise be destitute after the husband's death, since women did not normally inherit property. Second, it provides an exception to the rule that a man should not covet another's wife.[19] But third, this shorter section introduces the longer section, 25:7–10.

The bulk of the passage (25:7–10) is nearly twice as long as its introduction and deals with the case in which the brother refuses his duty of levirate marriage. The length of the two sections shows that the emphasis of the text is not on the levirate marriage as such, but on the potential of refusal by some men to provide for their sisters-in-law in this way. It is here that we must seek the primary relation to coveting in the passage. Lundbom supplies the insight we need: "The most likely reason for his refusal would be that a son born for his deceased brother would gain the brother's share of the family estate, whereas by not begetting a son the share of the

---

18. "Levirate" comes from Latin *levir*, "husband's brother:" Lundbom, *Deuteronomy*, 705.

19. Kaufman, "Structure," 143; Merrill, *Deuteronomy*, 327. This text also provides an exception to the Levitical prohibition of marrying one's sister-in-law after the death of one's brother (Lev 18:16; see Wenham, *Leviticus*, 254).

estate belonging to the deceased will be added to his share and after his death his own son will inherit everything. The brother's widow will also be left without anything."[20] So the major point for this entire section seems to be to provide an example of one way coveting might occur in family life: a man might covet the inheritance of his dead brother and thus refuse to care for the needs of his neighbor's (brother's) widow. He would be loving himself and not his unfortunate sister-in-law. That is, the passage discourages a bad interior motive: coveting an inheritance over the immediate needs of relatives, and thus also robbing his relative of her livelihood. Millar agrees: "The main point is the prohibition of setting one's own desires above responsibilities to the immediate family and the community."[21] This fits the nature of casuistic law: to give representative examples.

The second section of the passage, Deut 25:11–12, at first seems harder to understand as a reflection of coveting. It is about a woman defending her husband by grabbing his assailant's "private parts." Wright is perceptive: "Like the previous law, this law is concerned with actions that threaten family continuity. There, the unwilling brother-in-law threatens the survival of his deceased brother's name, since he will remain childless. This woman's action threatens the assailant's ability to have children, if serious damage is inflicted on his genitals."[22] Craigie explains, "Though the end (rescuing her husband) was honorable, the particular means could not be tolerated."[23] That is, the focus here seems to be on *the way* she acts in his defense. Lundbom again is helpful: her harsh[24] punishment (cutting off her hand) "is likely for injuring or possibly injuring the man's testicles, which could end his reproductive capacity."[25] This way of stopping him allows the possibility to injure him permanently and so deny him a future family. Such a means is disproportionate for the situation, offending the biblical proportionality mandate that the punishment should fit the crime. This

---

20. Lundbom, *Deuteronomy*, 709. So also, Craigie, *Deuteronomy*, 315; Wright, *Deuteronomy*, 268.
21. Millar, *Choose Life*, 142.
22. Wright, *Deuteronomy*, 266.
23. Craigie, *Deuteronomy*, 316.
24. This is the only place where bodily mutilation is prescribed in the OT, even though it was common in the ANE, apart from "an eye for an eye."
25. Lundbom, *Deuteronomy*, 712. Cragie agrees (*Deuteronomy*, 316): "More probably, it may be implied that the woman's action would cause permanent injury to the male . . . [and] could result in the inability of the man to father children." So also, McConville, *Deuteronomy*, 371; Merrill, *Deuteronomy*, 329; Wright, *Deuteronomy*, 266.

Commandment 10: "Don't Covet"

provides another representative example of offending the intent of commandment 10 by coveting to take away from a neighbor something which would naturally belong to him, as the last phrase of Deut 5:21 mentions, "or anything else that is your neighbor's."

We can now see that 25:5–10 and 25:11–12 function as a unit. The two are parallel in that both deal with "brothers" living in the same extended family (25:5; 25:11 in Hebrew says "when two fight together, a man and his brother").[26] They are parallel in that the offending man and the offending woman in the respective passages both do something shameful.[27] Finally, they are also opposites: the first section aimed to protect a sister-in-law from her covetous brother-in-law while the second aimed to protect a brother-in-law from a covetous sister-in-law.[28]

The third section, 25:13–16, is easier to relate to coveting. Ancient people bought and sold by using a balance. Wright concisely explains: "Two differing sets of measures are of course for the dishonest purpose of obtaining more than standard measure when purchasing and giving less when selling. Fair trade is one of the essential hallmarks of any human society seeking to protect everybody's interests in a civilized way."[29] Kaufman gets to the heart of the matter of how this law relates to coveting with this penetrating observation: the text prohibits "not the use of false weights and measures—that would be theft—but rather their possession!"[30] That is, the spotlight of the text falls not on stealing, but on *the intent to steal*, which is the only reason one would carry around such weights in one's bag. Again, we are provided an example of bad motives in the arena of commerce. The act of stealing begins in the heart, and that is what this law forbids.

Deuteronomy 25:17–19 is not usually included as part of the exposition of commandment 10,[31] but Lundbom makes a persuasive case that it is connected. He points out that verbal repetition, so often used to connect passages in Deuteronomy, and used to connect sections 1 and 2, occurs here also, when "blot out" is repeated in 25:6 and 25:19, serving as in

---

26. Lundbom, *Deuteronomy*, 704.

27. Block, *Deuteronomy*, 584. Block also comments (585), "Whereas verses 5–10 had involved a man who had wrongfully withheld his genitals from a woman, this case involves a man whose genitals have been shamelessly grabbed, perhaps with the intent of injury so he cannot have children."

28. McConville, *Deuteronomy*, 371.

29. Wright, *Deuteronomy*, 267.

30. Kaufman, "Structure," 144.

31. For example, Kaufman, "Structure," 144; Merrill, *Deuteronomy*, 330.

inclusio around these four sections.³² This suggests that this unit belongs with the three in Deut 25:6–16, and that it completes the exposition of commandment 10.

But how would it expound commandment 10? The common feature of 25:5–10 and 25:17–19 is that both display a bad inner motive: lack of concern for the vulnerable. Deuteronomy 25:6 explains that levirate marriage is instituted lest the dead brother's name "be blotted out of Israel." That is, his death leaves his family, and his name, defenseless and vulnerable, and the brother who refuses to care about that is shamed for the bad attitude behind his action in 25:7–10, i.e., his lack of concern for a vulnerable neighbor. Likewise, Deut 25:17–19 zeroes in on the shamefulness of the same attitude. To the Exodus account of the encounter with the Amalekites, Deuteronomy adds that Amalek attacked Israel "when you were faint and weary, and cut off your tail, those who were lagging behind you, and he did not fear God" (25:18). Wright clarifies that "Those lagging behind would have been the elderly and the very young, the sick, pregnant women, etc. To attack such defenseless people is a sign of extreme human callousness, which in turn is evidence of no fear of God." He adds, "They were *merciless to the weak*. They showed total lack of compassion in attacking Israel in their extreme vulnerability immediately after the exodus." He concludes, "The Amalekites are to be judged, then, not just because they had been *anti-Israel*, but because they had been *anti-human* by disregarding basic human obligations instilled by the creator God."³³

Thus, the opening and closing sections of the exposition of commandment 10 provide two examples of people who do not care about their neighbors' well-being, which resulted in both cases in actions which displayed that callousness toward the vulnerable. For this reason, God commands Israel to fulfill the promise he made to "blot out the memory of Amalek from under heaven" (Exod 17:14). So, the positive correlation of the attitude of "not coveting" is to concern ourselves with the plight of the weak and vulnerable.

---

32. Lundbom, *Deuteronomy*, 704.
33. Wright, *Deuteronomy*, 267–68, emphasis in the original.

Commandment 10: "Don't Covet"

WHAT THE COMMANDMENT MEANS AS A POSITIVE PRINCIPLE

Taking all of Deuteronomy into account and remembering that commandment 5 establishes honor as the key principle in the neighbor commands, we can state the positive principle in command 10 as *Loving our neighbor honors them by entertaining and endorsing only attitudes which safeguard your neighbor's well-being above your own, especially toward the weak and vulnerable.*

Most of this statement is straightforward, but the term "endorse" is added because sections 2 and 4 (unfair fighting and punishing Amalek) go beyond the attitudes one entertains within oneself to the attitudes one countenances in others. In a theocracy, public punishment (for inappropriate fighting) and even national action (destroying Amalek) in such circumstances were appropriate. But in contemporary life, which is not under a theocratic government, the principle would suggest at least not endorsing or encouraging attitudes in others which place a neighbor's well-being below one's own, especially toward the weak and vulnerable.

WHAT THE COMMANDMENT MEANS FOR CHRISTIANS

Jesus's discussion of commandment 10 in Matt 5:21–48 shows that God is concerned with our attitudes, not just our actions. Holiness is far deeper than the externals. Jesus agreed with our conclusion: "For *out of the heart come evil thoughts, murder, adultery, sexual immorality, theft, false witness, slander*" (Matt 15:19, emphasis added).[34] "The truth taught here is the same as Paul taught Timothy: 'Godliness with contentment is great gain' (1 Tim 6:6)."[35] We began this chapter with a discussion of the fall of Adam and Eve. The first sin has been seen by many as pride but has also been seen by others as a lack of thankfulness. Now, having seen how the commandment against coveting leads us to put the needs of our neighbors above our own, we can see how a lack of thankfulness and coveting go hand in hand. Paul teaches that "Godliness with contentment is great gain." If I am thankful, thankful for God and for my neighbor, then I will not as easily

---

34. So, Kaiser, *Ethics*, 95.
35. Kaiser, *Ethics*, 95.

fall into patterns of coveting. A heart of thankfulness prevents us from falling prey to a heart of covetousness.

So again, we can say in summary what Paul declared: "For the commandments . . . you shall not covet . . . are summed up in this word: 'You shall love your neighbor as yourself.' Love does no wrong to a neighbor; therefore, love is the fulfilling of the law" (Rom 13:9–10). We see for a sixth time that it is undeniable: Deuteronomy is an important Bible book—one of the most rich, extensive, and detailed biblical treatments—of loving God and loving neighbor.

The Heidelberg Catechism has long seen positive and negative meaning in commandment 10.

HEIDELBERG CATECHISM:

113. Q. What is God's will for us in the tenth commandment?

A. That not even the slightest thought or desire contrary to any one of God's commandments should ever arise in our hearts. Rather, with all our heart we should always hate sin and take pleasure in whatever is right.

QUESTIONS FOR PERSONAL DEVOTIONS:

1. Why is it important that this commandment refers not simply to desiring something, but to desiring that which is your neighbor's?
2. How does commandment 10 summarize the heart of commandments 5 through 9?
3. How does the discussion of Levirate marriage in Deuteronomy 25 help us understand the meaning of commandment 10 in our closest family relationships?
4. What might tempt you to violate this command?
5. How does the positive principle stated in this chapter inform how you could love your neighbor?
6. What else might God be saying to you through this commandment?

Commandment 10: "Don't Covet"

QUESTIONS FOR TEACHING AND PREACHING:

1. What are the implications of the term "covet" meaning not simply "passive desire," but "maneuvering to acquire"?
2. What does this commandment say to us about our relationship with our neighbor?
3. How would you restate this commandment in your own words?
4. How does the possession of "dishonest weights" discussed in Deuteronomy reveal a heart of covetousness?
5. How should we teach and preach this commandment knowing that it deals with attitudes and not only with actions?
6. How does it change the way you teach and preach this commandment to know that it refers not to all desires, but to inordinate desires?
7. How could the allusion to Adam and Eve help you to expound the meaning of this commandment?
8. How does the positive principle of this commandment help us to understand what it means to live lives which reflect the gospel? (Compare the positive principle mentioned in the chapter with Paul's teaching in Philippians 2.)
9. How does Jesus's teaching in Matt 5:21–48 inform your teaching of this commandment?

Chapter 14

The Beginning and the End of Deuteronomy

WE HAVE NOW DEALT with commandments 1–10. We have argued that the bulk of Deuteronomy is an exposition of the Ten Commandments, one by one and in order. We have tried to show that an examination of the book in detail confirms that thesis. We have shown that commandments 1–4 are particular examples of what it means to love God while commandments 5–10 explain how to love one's neighbor. Finally, we have contended that this demonstrates that Deuteronomy is *the* biblical exposition of love of God and love of neighbor. All of this explains why Jesus said that "the most important" of God's commandments was to love the Lord and to love our neighbor as ourselves, that "There is no other commandment greater than these" (Mark 12:28, 31), and that "On these two commandments depend all the Law and the Prophets" (Matt 22:40). We believe that Jesus was not declaring new revelation here, but that he was telling us what Deuteronomy itself had always argued. He was confirming what we have argued: that the Torah established the key elements of the spiritual life for God's people of all times, and that the Shema (Deut 6:4–5) is the paramount summary of that life, a relationship of love with God, as the Jewish community has always maintained.

What this chapter will add is to show why an introduction and a conclusion to the book, Deuteronomy 1–4 and 27–34, are included and how they strengthen the argument we have made to this point. After all, Deuteronomy 5–26 could have stood alone to "explain this law" (Deut 1:5). Instead, the author framed that explanation with chapters 1–4 and 27–34. One reason, we have contended, is that he desired to present Deuteronomy as a suzerain-vassal treaty, and the elements in those framing sections are necessary for that purpose. Further, parts of Deuteronomy 27–34, such as the material about Joshua's succession of Moses, also serve as a conclusion to the Torah, of which Deuteronomy is the final installment. But is that all? We believe there is more to it.

THE SPIRITUAL LIFE IS A JOURNEY OF CHOICES

Many scholars have long felt that the chapters 1–3 were so different from the central part of the book that that section must have been a later addition.[1] Millar observes sagely: "But there has always been one major problem with this view. It could never adequately explain how the book reached its final form."[2] Besides, such thinking assumes that the author was incompetent, which short-circuits the search for a reason why the book may have been arranged as it stands.

Such a search yields a fruitful result. Millar instead argues that, in point of fact, "there are strong conceptual and rhetorical links between chapters 1–3 and the rest of the book . . . It is here, in these chapters, that the basic theological and ethical message categories of the book are introduced."[3] He then argues persuasively that the major theme of Deuteronomy's frame is that the spiritual life is a journey, an emphasis begun by chapters 1–3 but also continued in 27–34.[4] Most of Deuteronomy expounds the Ten Commandments as loving God and loving neighbor, but in the framework, Israel is "on the move," which pictures her as journeying.[5]

Unlike most of Deuteronomy 6–26, 1–3 is full of stories. Millar shows that "old stories are retold to make theological points . . . The account of the journey to the land in chapters 1–3 is dominated by *places of failure* and *the road to success*."[6] The failure theme is introduced in Deut 1:1–3, where we are reminded that the "journey" from Mount Horeb (Sinai) to Kadesh Barnea was only eleven days, though it took Israel forty years (1:2–3). The reason for this forty-year delay is quickly explained in excruciating detail in a section framed by "Kadesh" (1:19, 46): Israel's refusal to enter the land at

1. Millar, *Choose Life*, 67, cites Wellhausen, Steuernagel and Noth.
2. Millar, *Choose Life*, 67. I rely heavily on Millar in this entire section.
3. Millar, *Choose Life*, 68.
4. Millar, *Choose Life*, 67–98.
5. Millar, *Choose Life*, 67.
6. Millar, *Choose Life*, 68–9. His inspiration was Norbert Lohfink.

Kadesh out of fear, the root of which is "you did not believe the Lord your God" (1:32). A journey characterized by failure.

But the theme of the road to success is also introduced in the book's introduction. The author reminds us in 1:4 that Israel defeated Sihon and Og after they arrived near the border of the promised land. That story is told in 2:26–3:29. By introducing the book (1:1–4) with reminders of both failure and success as they journeyed and then spending the bulk of chapters 1–3 detailing those experiences, we learn that a journey with both possibilities was Israel's story.

Chapters 27–34 continue the journey theme but looking toward the future.[7] Chapter 4 compared Horeb (the past) to Moab (the present).[8] Chapters 27–28 begin a focus on the future possibilities for Israel: blessing or curse. Chapters 29–30 promise both a future exile and a still-later restoration of Israel to her land. Finally, chapters 31–34 look to the future with Moses's succession by Joshua and Moses's swansong regarding Israel's future. The aim of this portion of the frame is to teach us that the future spiritual life is a journey which offers success or failure, just as the journeys of the past did, and to call God's people to "choose wisely"![9]

The primary lesson of the entire frame is stated in the frame and frames the book: "And now, O Israel, listen to the statutes and the rules that I am teaching you, and do them, that you may live, and go in and take possession of the land that the LORD, the God of your fathers, is giving you (Deut 4:1). Or summarized differently, "Therefore choose life, that you and your offspring may live, loving the LORD your God, obeying his voice and holding fast to him, for he is your life and length of days, that you may dwell in the land that the LORD swore to your fathers, to Abraham, to Isaac, and to Jacob, to give them" (Deut 30:19–20).

Then and now, the spiritual life is a journey which requires daily choices: to believe and obey or to fear, disbelieve, and disobey.

ISRAEL WAS INCAPABLE OF OBEDIENCE

Millar has made a compelling case that a major function of the frame of the book is to present Israel as both called to obedience and unable to actually

---

7. See Millar, *Choose Life*, 88–97.
8. Developed in Millar, *Choose Life*, 74–80.
9. See McGrath, *Point of Theology*, 79.

The Beginning and the End of Deuteronomy

accomplish it.[10] One point of framing the exposition of the Ten Commandments, God's good instruction presented in Deuteronomy 6–26, with chapters 1–4 and 27–34, is to communicate that while obedience to God is the route to abundant life, people are incapable of obedience without divine help. In other words, "no one will be declared righteous in God's sight by the works of the law; rather, *through the law we become conscious of our sin*" (Romans 3:20, NIV, emphasis added). In doing this, we witness another method by which the author of the Torah points the audience beyond the Torah, and beyond the entire Tanak (the Hebrew Bible), to the distant future, to a new covenant that will eventually replace the Mosaic covenant. This both highlights the temporary nature of the Mosaic covenant and points believers to the future in hope. All of this we must now demonstrate.

The strange paradox of Israel called to obedience yet seemingly incapable of it is presented in both Deuteronomy 1–4 and 27–34, as well as elsewhere in the book. In fact, Millar claims, "Chapter 30 has much in common with chapter 4 (see, e.g., 30:1–3 and 4:29–31), and if chapter 4 acts as an overture to the book, then chapter 30 is the finale. Here many of the themes introduced in chapter 4 reach their *denouement*."[11] In essence, themes introduced in chapter 4 are placed on pause while chapters 5–26 expound the Ten Commandments. Then they are taken up again in 27–34 to close the book.

In Deuteronomy 1–4 the paradox is stressed in the repeated treatment of Israel's failures. Extensive treatment is devoted to the failure at Kadesh Barnea (Deut 1:2, 19–46; 2:14) which resulted from fear of the people living in Canaan (Deut 1:28). It is also evident in the rebuke implied every time it is mentioned that those Israel feared in the land were dispatched by others to whom God had given land in Canaan (Deut 2:12, 21, 22). Perhaps the capstone of this pessimistic view of Israel's prospects for obedience is that "Chapter 3 concludes with the rejection of Moses' appeal to be allowed to enter Canaan."[12] If Moses, the leader, cannot obey, what are Israel's prospects? Because Moses himself was unable to obey the law, he ended his life excluded from the land of promise due to disobedience (Num 20:1–12). But the reason behind his disobedience was a stunted faith which

---

10. Millar, *Now Choose Life*, 161–80. We depend upon his argument in much of what follows here. McConville had argued this earlier in *Grace in the End*, 134–39. Millar, however, is more extensive.

11. Millar, *Choose Life*, 95.

12. Millar, *Choose Life*, 163.

resulted from living under the law (Num 20:12).[13] Thus the opening frame stresses Israel's seeming inability to obey, except at particular points (Deut 2:26–3:22).

Israel's sorry record of obedience is also highlighted in the central portion of the book. The dismal failure of the golden calf which began Israel's journey with her God is rehearsed in Deut 9:16–21. This perhaps hints that this incident foreshadows Israel's defining characteristic. Then the characterization of Israel in Exodus as a "stubborn" (or "stiff-necked") people is repeated in Deut 9:6, 13; 10:16; and finally in 31:27.

But the high-point of this theme occurs in Deuteronomy 27–34.[14] Israel's eventual scattering among the nations, treated as a possible outcome for disobedience early in the book (Deut 4:25–27), is declared to be a certainty in the outer frame (esp. 30:1–10). Blessing in the land they were about to inherit depended upon obedience, and Israel is commanded to obey: "Circumcise therefore the foreskin of your heart, and be no longer stubborn" (Deut 10:16). But Deuteronomy seems to be arguing that obedience is unlikely. In fact, the root issue is pinpointed in a cryptic text, Deut 29:4 which declares, "But to this day the LORD has not given you a heart to understand or eyes to see or ears to hear." This seems to imply that Israel, while commanded to and expected to obey if she desires God's blessing, is actually not capable of doing so very well, at least not without divine help. Then Deut 30:6 provides an answer to the implied indictment: in the future "the LORD your God will circumcise your heart and the heart of your offspring, so that you will love the LORD your God with all your heart and with all your soul, that you may live."

McConville calls this "the central problem posed by Deuteronomy," arguing, "In 10:16 we read a simple exhortation to Israel: 'Circumcise your hearts . . . ' In 30:6, however, a shift occurs, so that now Yahweh himself declares that *he* will take an initiative in this respect."[15] Thus, Deuteronomy realistically portrays Israel as needing divine help to deal with their stubborn heart, "the enduring problem of human nature."[16] Millar is spot-on in concluding, "Both the Horeb and Moab covenants are fatally flawed,

---

13. See the development of this argument in Campbell and Campbell, *Invitation to the Torah*, 131–37; Sailhamer, *Pentateuch as Narrative*, 59–78.

14. See McConville, *Grace in the End*, 134–39, and Millar, *Choose Life*, 172–76, for more extensive analysis in defense of the views expressed in this paragraph.

15. McConville, *Grace in the End*, 136.

16. Millar, *Choose Life*, 174.

because they can do nothing about the problem of human nature." They constitute "an admission that laws do not change people."[17] So, how and when will this occur?

WE NEED A NEW COVENANT

Deuteronomy 29–30 constitutes a very interesting portion of the book. We will briefly address three issues here: (1) the "secret things" in Deut 29:29; (2) whether Deut 29:1–29 is a renewal of the Sinai covenant or a new covenant; and (3) the relation of Deut 30:1–10 to the new covenant treated in Jeremiah and Ezekiel. While the argument here does not depend upon our conclusions on these matters, it is appropriate that we state our understanding of them.

Benjamin Franklin said that three people can keep a secret—if two of them are dead![18] Secrets are indeed hard for people to keep. But God reveals in Deut 29:29 that he has a secret. Can we determine what it is? Regarding this issue, we cite Millar:

> The chapter closes with a cryptic allusion to the secret things and the revealed things in verse 28 [verse 29 in English Bibles]. This refers most naturally to the content of chapter 29 . . . I would suggest that 'the revealed things' refer to the insights of this 'Moab covenant'—in other words, the understanding that this revelation is contingent and will one day be superseded. The 'secret things', then, look to a new covenant, which will not simply call Israel to obey, but will enable them to do so by dealing with the enduring problem of the human heart. In the meantime—which is clearly expected to be a substantial period—Israel must do all that she can to obey.[19]

So, we take this rather mysterious text to point the reader forward to a time when God will enable people to obey by supernatural means, though the call to obedience, and the promise of blessing for obedience, remains in place. When this will occur we will address below.

On the second question, we hold that Deuteronomy 29–30 is establishing a new covenant with Israel rather than simply renewing the Sinai covenant with the generation that has now survived the wilderness

---

17. Millar, *Choose Life*, 174.
18. Franklin, *Poor Richard's Almanack*, 53.
19. Millar, *Choose Life*, 174.

wanderings. Once again, commentators are divided, but we state our reasons for our position that this "Moab covenant" is a distinct covenant.[20] First, Deut 29:1 most naturally reads as a new covenant: "These are the words of the covenant that the LORD commanded Moses to make with the people of Israel in the land of Moab, besides the covenant that he had made with them at Horeb." Second, perfectly consistently with this, the term "covenant" is repeated in chapter 29 (29:1, 9, 12, 14, 19, 21, 25), and is associated throughout with the command "today" (29:10, 12, 13, 15, 18). Especially significant is 29:10–12: "You are standing here today . . . so that you may enter into the sworn covenant of the Lord your God, which the Lord your God is making with you today." It is only because a new covenant has not been regularly seen here that the language is assumed to be a renewal of the former covenant. Third, and perhaps most significantly, the covenant here is not a repetition of the Sinai covenant. It adds the significant provision of a return to the land after the future exile. Explains Lundbom, "Both covenants, and the laws that accompany them, Israel is under obligation to keep."[21] While Israel will fail to keep the Sinai covenant all is not lost because a future restoration after that failure is promised.[22]

On the third question, the relation of Deut 30:1–10 to Jeremiah's new covenant, these are our conclusions. To quote Millar, "If the covenant at Moab reveals the need for something to be done about human nature, then the new covenant promised in chapter 30 meets that need. One day, the 'secret things' will be revealed and God will act to change his people."[23] This promise is stated in Deut 30:6, "The LORD your God will circumcise your heart and the heart of your offspring, so that you will love the LORD

---

20. Millar calls this the "Moab covenant" (due to Deut 29:1): *Choose Life*, 173; see 172–74. Sailhamer agrees: *Meaning of the Pentateuch*, 400–410. It has also been called the "Palestinian covenant," e.g., Walvoord, *Millennial Kingdom*, 174–77. One need not agree with the dispensational theology of Walvoord to see why he distinguishes this covenant from the Sinai covenant, as do many others.

21. Lundbom, *Deuteronomy*, 799.

22. Millar, *Choose Life*, 173. Lundbom, *Deuteronomy*, 799, sees it as a separate covenant, as do Driver, *Deuteronomy*, 319, von Rad, *Deuteronomy*, 178–79, and Mayes, *Deuteronomy*, 360–61. Others see it as new, yet not exactly new: Thompson, *Deuteronomy*, 278, says that while distinct, it can also be interpreted as "a covenant renewal which both extended and adapted the Sinai covenant." Woods, *Deuteronomy*, 282, agrees, but states "the words *in addition* not only separate Moab from Horeb in terms of time and space, but express the idea of a new embodiment or renewal of the Horeb covenant, rather than its complete replacement" (emphasis in the original).

23. Millar, *Choose Life*, 174.

your God with all your heart and with all your soul, that you may live." This alludes to the Shema in Deut 6:4–5, where Israel is called to "love the LORD your God with all your heart and with all your soul and with all your might," and anticipates the day when this will finally come true. It is the center of the chiastic structure.[24]

> A When you and your children return (v. 2a)
>   B and obey . . . with all your heart and soul (v. 2b)
>   C you will be restored to the land and be more prosperous than the fathers (vv. 3– 5)
>   D God will circumcise your hearts to love him with heart and soul (v. 6)
>   C' you will have prosperity in the land, like the fathers (vv. 8– 9)
>   B' if you obey the LORD your God (v. 10a)
> A' and turn to the LORD . . . with all your heart and soul (v. 10b)

Millar elaborates,

> this is basically a prototype of the new covenant thought which we see in Jeremiah and Ezekiel. One day Yahweh will solve the problem of the human heart. Until Yahweh's climactic (eschatological) action, the only satisfactory option open to Israel is to strive to obey the law which they had been given in the preceding chapters.[25]

McConville elaborates further,

> The particular terms of 30:6 can hardly be accidental. They propose an answer to the problem of Israel's infidelity to the covenant that finds echoes elsewhere in the OT, notably in Hosea (Hos 14:4) and especially in the new covenant theology of Jeremiah (Jer 31:33; 32:39–40). These places affirm that the answer to Israel's infidelity lies in God himself. He will somehow enable his people ultimately to do what they cannot do in their strength, namely, to obey him out of the conviction and devotion of their own hearts.[26]

So, we see that Deut 29–30 affirms that love of God is the critical element in obedience to the Lord, that sinful humans do not have the natural capacity to obey well because they do not love well, and that God will someday act

---

24. Wright, *Deuteronomy*, 289, slightly adapted.
25. Millar, *Choose Life*, 175.
26. McConville, *Grace in the End*, 137.

to resolve that issue. It remains only to conclude how and when that will happen.

The answer, as suggested above, is in the new covenant promised in Jeremiah and elsewhere. It is clear from the NT that Jesus inaugurated that new covenant (Luke 22:20; 1 Cor 11:25; Col 3:6; Heb 8:8, 13; 9:15; 12:24). Christians do not all agree, however, regarding exactly how this works out. Some believe that the church has replaced Israel and that the new covenant is fulfilled in the church in the present age. Others see Jesus's inauguration of the new covenant as its beginning but not its complete fulfillment, as with other aspects of the "already and not yet" which begin in the present but await an eschatological completion.[27] However, all agree that present-day Christian believers are experiencing the new covenant reality of supernatural endowment, by the Spirit, for a deeper ability to love the Lord and to obey him than Israel had in OT times under the Sinai and Moab covenants.

GRACE IN THE END

With McConville, we affirm that a major purpose of Deuteronomy's frame is to shine a spotlight on the grace of God.[28] While many Christians have long assumed that the Old Testament is about law and the New Testament finally adds grace, in reality the OT, and especially Deuteronomy, is rich with grace. The reality is that the grace of God—his unmerited goodness and steadfast devotion to his people—is abundantly displayed throughout the Torah. For example, in Exodus, at the birth of Israel as God's people, eight instances of complaining or rebellion by the newborn people are recorded, culminating in the infamous golden calf fiasco in Exodus 32. It's almost like the "terrible twos"—except the nation is not yet that old! Further, in Numbers, about ten additional ones are enumerated, the most egregious

---

27. Christians are divided about whether the new covenant promised in Deut 30:1–10, Jer 31:3–34, Ezek 36:25–27, etc., promises a future for ethnic Israel. Traditionally, premillennialists said "yes" while amillennialists said "no." But things have been changing here. Reformed and amillennial theologian Waltke affirms a future for ethnic Israel in fulfillment of the new covenant, which "finds fulfillment in believers today (Rom. 2:29), and will be consummated in ethnic Israel before the Parousia (Rom. 11:26)" (*OT Theology*, 495). He elaborates, "Before the establishment of the State of Israel in 1947, most Christians held to the doctrine of supersession (i.e., the church replaced or superseded Israel). Since then, many Christian theologians have supported the notion that ethnic Israel still has a role to play in salvation history," which he terms "the new consensus" (*OT Theology*, 331–32, note 33).

28. See McConville, *Grace in the End*.

being Kadesh Barnea, where Israel refuses to enter the promised land.[29] Yet God did not abandon his people.

But the major showcase of God's grace is Deuteronomy. In Deuteronomy, the Torah's psychoanalysis of Israel's character reaches its crescendo. There are climactic statements of Israel's relentless moral turpitude in the body of the book, such as 9:23-29. But the grand exemplar is in the book's frame. It is fair to argue that Deuteronomy 1-4 develops God's grace in Israel's past while Deuteronomy 27-34 develops God's grace for Israel's future. But let's be more detailed.

Deuteronomy's frame contains the most devastating announcement of Israel's depravity in the Torah. Here it is revealed that Israel will eventually be scattered among the nations because they abandoned God's covenant (Deut 29:25). Here it is revealed that Israel would never love and obey her God until a new covenant dawns (Deut 29:4; 30:6). Here it is made known that the most important thing—love of God—will never be displayed by the nation until she has suffered a devastating exile (Deut 30:1-3). Yet in the face of these shattering pronouncements, God promises to restore Israel's fortunes and to give them the heart he requires (Deut 30:1-10). Deuteronomy's frame paints the most dismal portrait of the nation in the Torah, then follows it with the most stunning display of the grace of God to this point in Holy Scripture. This is akin to Jesus's story of the prodigal son, who despised his father and yet was lovingly and lavishly welcomed back home, a parable inspired by the story of Jacob and Esau in Genesis, yet which reveals the heart of God in the face of a rebellious nation even more fully.[30] So Deuteronomy is *the* Torah paradigm of the grace of God. So McConville is justified to conclude that while Deuteronomy displays Israel's drastic failure, it is fundamentally about God's "grace in the end."[31]

WE MUST OBEY TODAY: DEUT 30:11–20

Millar rightly concludes, "Verses 11-20 stand in many ways as a conclusion to the Deuteronomic preaching. After the explicit statement of Israel's need to be transformed comes one of the most powerful calls to decision

---

29. Exod 5:21; 14:11-12; 15:24; 16:2; 16:20; 16:27; 17:3; 32:1-35; Num 11:1; 11:4; 12:1; 14:1, 27, 29; 14:36; 16:1-11; 16:41; 17:5; 20:3, 13; 21:5; 25:1-18.

30. On Jesus's prodigal son story retelling the Jacob and Esau story, see Bailey, *Jacob and the Prodigal*.

31. McConville, *Grace in the End*, 138 and 134-38.

in the whole of the Bible."[32] But after all we have seen in Deut 29:1–30:10, this passage comes as a shock. Having announced that Israel cannot obey, 30:11–20 now calls Israel to do exactly that! How can we make sense of this?

This issue is perplexing, but its placement immediately after 30:1–10 makes clear that it was intended to be striking! Some find it so surprising that they see 30:11–14 as a statement of the possibility of obedience *after* God has circumcised Israel's heart (30:6),[33] with 30:15–20 returning to address the generation at Moab. Yet 30:11–14 and 15–20 seem to form a unit, both beginning with the term "today," and there do not seem to be adequate clues in the text to warrant such a distinction. Deuteronomy 30:11–20 seems to clearly affirm that "both the supreme command and the detailed body of instructions that flow from it are, in fact, doable."[34] But either way, Deut 30:15–20 is agreed by all to say this, so the disposition of Deut 30:11–14 does not resolve the perplexing question. Block seems to get it right: "In calling for wholehearted obedience, Yahweh does not demand what is unknowable, impossible, or unreasonable. If Israel fails—and they will (31:16–18)—it will not be because the people *cannot* keep the law because the bar is impossibly high, but that they *will not* keep it."[35] It is not that God has established an impossible standard; it is a practical matter: Israel is unwilling to obey. Why? Because they do not love the Lord. That love in the heart is a work of Yahweh, then and now.

Wright elaborates on Deut 30:11–14:

> [This text] reassures Israel that God's law *can* be kept... The idea that God deliberately made the law so exacting that nobody would ever be able to live by it belongs to a distorted theology... The frequent claims by various psalmists to have lived according to God's law are neither exaggerated nor exceptional. They arise from the natural assumption that ordinary people can indeed live in a way that is broadly pleasing to God and faithful to God's law, and that they can do so as a matter of joy and delight.[36]

---

32. Millar, *Choose Life*, 175–76.
33. So, Millar, *Choose Life*, 93–96; 176.
34. Block, *Deuteronomy*, 709.
35. Block, *Deuteronomy*, 709.
36. Wright, *Deuteronomy*, 290.

As Block explains, "While every generation will produce individuals who are righteous and loyal to Yahweh (i.e., true Israelites), here the concern is spiritual recidivism of the nation as a whole."[37]

All of this can be explained clearly using NT parlance. Individuals who believe come into a relationship with God and receive his aid in loving and obeying him. This was true in the OT, as the psalmists attest, and in the NT, as we have already argued. The problem is that Israel as a corporate entity was not regenerate, though individuals in the nation were. As Paul understood, "For not all who are descended from Israel belong to Israel" (Rom 9:6). Rather, the nation as a whole would need to look forward to the day when God regenerated them as a whole.

Millar draws a significant conclusion: "This relativizes not simply Horeb ... but Moab as well. Both are only transitional moments in Israel's journey to transformation."[38] That is, the Mosaic law was always a temporary administration. While it did reveal God's heart, character, and good expectations for human behavior—for the time it was in effect—it could not regenerate people. That was never its purpose. Its purpose was to show Israel, and the world, that humans are less capable of doing good than they like to believe. Paul stated this clearly: "Now we know that whatever the law says it speaks to those who are under the law, so that every mouth may be stopped, and the whole world may be held accountable to God. For by works of the law no human being will be justified in his sight, since through the law comes knowledge of sin" (Rom 3:19–20). So, the final point related to this section is this: believers are called to obey God's word as the route to real life.

BELIEVERS MUST CHOOSE LIFE: DEUT 30:15–20

There is final emphasis in Deuteronomy's frame. Deuteronomy 1:8's, "See, I have set the land before you" is a conscious parallel to 30:15's, "See, I have set before you today life and good, death and evil." God's great promise to Israel is life in the land, so to "Go in and take possession of the land that the LORD swore to your fathers" (Deut 1:8), is essentially the same thing as "Therefore choose life, that you and your offspring may live, loving the LORD your God, obeying his voice and holding fast to him, for he is your life and length of days, that you may dwell in the land that the LORD swore

37. Block, *Deuteronomy*, 709.
38. Millar, *Choose Life*, 175.

to your fathers" (Deut 30:19–20). That is, Deuteronomy frames the explanation of the Ten Commandments, which occupies the body of the book, with exhortations to take the land (1:8) and to choose life in the land by loving and obeying the Lord (30:15–20), i.e., by obeying Deuteronomy's Ten Commandments. In other words, a final function of the frame is to stress—and stress again—that understanding what the Ten Commandments mean is critical, but only the first step. The *real* issue at stake, the vital matter, is *choosing to obey* because we love the Lord.

Deuteronomy 30:15–20 is widely acknowledged as the crux of the book.[39] Millar calls it, "probably the most eloquent exposition of the Deuteronomic theology of daily life in the entire book."[40] Mayes is correct: "the verses do clearly function as a conclusion. They bring together the covenant themes of the whole book: commandments, blessing and curse, witnesses, and end with an appeal for obedience so that the ancient promises to the patriarchs might be fulfilled.[41] The frame here reaches its apex: people must choose life by loving and obeying the Lord; any other choice is to choose death.

The framework of Deuteronomy, then, advances the argument of the book about love of God and love of neighbor. While Deut 5–26 "explain" the law (1:5) as loving God (commandments 1–4) and loving neighbor (commandments 5–10), chapters 1–4 and 27–34 augment that by teaching that understanding the law is not enough. Believers must recognize that the spiritual life is a daily journey of choosing to believe and obey, that humans are not capable of obeying God very well because our natural state is not to love God. We need a change of heart ("circumcise your hearts") to enable us to love and obey him better than we do naturally. In the end, God's grace is stronger than our weakness, and while contemporary believers have divine enablement through the Holy Spirit under the new covenant, we must still struggle to obey and thus choose life day by day.

So, we see once again in the framework of Deuteronomy, that it is undeniable: Deuteronomy is an important book—one of the most rich, extensive, and detailed biblical treatments—of loving God and loving neighbor.

---

39. Woods refers to it as, "the rhetorical climax of Deuteronomy" (Woods, *Deuteronomy*, 296). Wright agrees: it is a "powerful summary of the whole book." (Wright, *Deuteronomy*, 291.)

40. Millar, *Choose Life*, 176.

41. Mayes, *Deuteronomy*, 370.

HEIDELBERG CATECHISM:

114. Q. Can those converted to God obey these commandments perfectly?

A. No. In this life even the holiest have only a small beginning of this obedience. Nevertheless, with all seriousness of purpose, they do begin to live according to all, not only some, of God's commandments.

115. Q. Why, then, does God have the Ten Commandments preached so strictly since no one can keep them in this life?

A. First, so that the longer we live the more we may come to know our sinfulness and the more we may eagerly look to Christ for forgiveness of sins and righteousness. Second, so that, while praying to God for the grace of the Holy Spirit, we may never stop striving to be renewed more and more after God's image, until after this life we reach our goal: perfection.

Chapter 15

Beyond Deuteronomy

BECAUSE OF GOD'S REVELATION in Holy Scripture, the future isn't what it used to be! What God has promised not only determines the future, but it provides a foundation for God's people to face the future, whatever it holds, with hope. Let's see how the future isn't what it used to be because of Deuteronomy.

We saw in the last chapter that Deuteronomy's framework (chapters 1–4, 27–34) pointed God's people to the future.[1] It framed the explanation of the Mosaic law (Deut 5–26), i.e., how to love God and our neighbors, with a call to decision, most memorably summarized in Deut 30:15–20. We developed the new covenant promise announced in Deut 30:1–10 and argued that since the new covenant has now been inaugurated, the message for contemporary believers is that we must choose, day by day, and with the help of God's Spirit, to believe and obey the Lord, for in that choice lies the measure of blessing—of "life"—that God's people experience. It is now time to finish our study of Deuteronomy by looking at other ways the book speaks to the future of God's people in every generation about loving God and neighbor.

A PROPHET LIKE MOSES

First, there is a promise in Deut 18:15–18 about a "prophet like Moses" to guide Israel after Moses died.[2] The promise, read in context, clearly

---

1. We argued in a previous book that the entire Torah/Pentateuch has a future orientation. See Campbell & Campbell, *Invitation to the Torah*, chapter 2, 10–17.

2. We develop this idea in Campbell & Campbell, *Invitation to the Torah*, 14–15.

refers to a line of prophets, and the Jewish community saw this as fulfilled in those who wrote Israel's history and prophetic literature, naming the next sections of Scripture after the Torah the Former and Latter Prophets. But it means more than that. Deuteronomy 34:10–12, the Torah's closing paragraph, appears to have been added by one of the last prophets as the gift of prophecy was ceasing, an event the Jews dated with Malachi about 400 BCE. The codicil seems to clearly state that none of the great prophets who came in Israel's history ever measured up to Moses, pushing the reader to look beyond the entire line of OT prophets for someone else after OT Scripture was complete. The NT sees Jesus as fulfilling that prophecy (John 1:21; 6:14; 7:40).

So, Christians see Jesus as the final fulfillment of God's promise to send someone on—indeed, above—Moses's level. Jesus is the great spokesperson for God who would succeed Moses and deliver a final commandment for God (see Heb 1:1–2). Christians see Jesus as the ultimate revelation of God, one who not only spoke infallibly for God, but incarnated him so people could see and hear and touch him. Thus, Deuteronomy's promise of a great future prophet is fulfilled in Jesus.

Further, Jesus claimed that the OT ultimately pointed to him (Luke 24:25–27, 44–45). So, Christians see Jesus as the highest revelation of God and all Scripture as pointing people to him. While we no longer see Jesus, we do have the OT and NT Scriptures which bear witness to him. The OT exhorted believers to "meditate on Torah day and night" (Josh 1:8–9; Ps 1:1–3). When one does that, one seeks the greater prophet to follow Moses and one finds Jesus revealed in the OT offices, institutions, and prophecies.[3] Further, the NT reveals more about him and the implications of following him than did the OT, constituting the final revelation of God. While there are Christians who affirm that God still speaks in dramatic ways today, just as he did through the OT prophets, all Christians agree that any such contemporary revelations must be weighed and evaluated by the written Scriptures of the Old and New Testaments and must be consistent with them.[4]

In summary, the promise in Deuteronomy of a prophet greater than Moses leads us to recognize that the entire Bible points people to Jesus,

---

3. See Campbell and Campbell, *Invitation to the Torah*, where the chapters on Genesis, Exodus, etc., end with discussing ways Christians see Jesus in each book, the Torah institutions, etc.

4. See Grudem, *Miraculous Gifts*.

who declared that the "greatest" commandments were to love God and love one's neighbor, just as the Torah did (Mark 12:28–32). Deuteronomy, we have argued, is *the* OT book on loving God and neighbor, and the NT, and especially the person of Jesus, brings that revelation to its highpoint. Deuteronomy points believers to Jesus and Jesus points us to how to love God and neighbor into the future.

WAITING IS THE NORMAL CHRISTIAN LIFE

Another way that Deuteronomy points contemporary believers toward the future is summarized in the title of Leder's study of the story line of the Pentateuch: "waiting for the land."[5] It is fascinating that the Torah, God's prime instruction manual in OT times, ended *before* Israel inherited the land God promised them. Throughout the Torah, God's people, from Abraham forward, were called upon to wait for God's promises. This is particularly true of Deuteronomy, where the narrative in the frame (1–4, 27–34) turns on Israel always heading toward the promised land and yet never arriving there. They are continually journeying toward Canaan in Deuteronomy 1–4, and then again in 27–34, never arriving. Highlights in chapters 27–34 include Moses excluded from the land—a foreshadowing of Israel's eventual fate—and the promise that even after inheriting the land, they will lose it again and have to wait through a long exile for God to restore them. Speaking of the book of Numbers, Olson declares, "the new generation in the second half of Numbers functions as a paradigm for every succeeding generation of God's people . . . The concern of the book is to establish a model or paradigm which will invite every generation to put itself in the place of the new generation,"[6] i.e., to heed to call to obey, as the generation that perished in the wilderness did not. Leder astutely draws this implication: "Thus all generations of God's people are called upon to await the promised inheritance by remembering the past of the first generation so that they comply with God's instructions, in his presence, 'today.'"[7]

This theme is abundantly repeated in the NT (e.g., Acts 1:14; Rom 8:23–25; 1 Cor 1:7; Gal 5:5; 1 Thess 1:10). While Christians often wait for many things, perhaps the grand example is our waiting for the full fruits of

---

5. Leder, *Waiting for the Land*. Campbell & Campbell, *Invitation to the Torah*, develops this, 104–6.

6. Olson, *Death*, 183.

7. Leder, *Waiting for the Land*, 164.

our redemption to come true (Rom 8:23; Gal 5:5). We now possess eternal life, but not the full implications of that, such as the removal of sin from our nature. We are already seated with Christ in the heavenly places (Eph 1:20), but we have not yet arrived in heaven for our final reward. Biblical scholars often refer to this as the "already and the not yet," or "inaugurated eschatology."[8] We already are promised many things that we have only tasted but not yet fully experienced, experiences for which we wait. Leder is correct: "As a whole, then, the Pentateuch declares to God's people of every generation that the presence of God *already* is, but that the land is *not yet*, a present reality. Until the exile is completely resolved by the coming again of Immanuel, God's people will have no place to call home."[9]

How does this relate to love of God and neighbor? Contemporary believers are indeed empowered by the Spirit under the new covenant to love the Lord and obey him better than was ancient Israel as a whole. But we still live between the already and the not yet. We already have greater ability, but we have not yet arrived at the place where obedience is perfect, or easy. In other words, the stakes are still high and the outcome for every successive generation of believers is not yet determined. We must strive diligently to obey by loving God and our neighbors, for we can still fail badly as have previous generations of Christians. And if we, caught up in the spirit of our times and swept up in the winds of current beliefs and practices (Eph 4:14), fail to love our God and our neighbors well, the Lord is dishonored and our neighbors are deprived of the light of God which is to be shed upon them by us. Sometimes Christians are hated because we bear the cross with its unavoidable offence. But sometimes we are hated because we deserve it: we fail to love as we ought. May we strive for the former and strain to avoid the latter!

SEEING THE BIG PICTURE OF SCRIPTURE

People sometimes speak of ignoring the elephant in the room. Jesus warned against "straining out a gnat while swallowing a camel" (Matt 23:24). The most important thing is to focus on the most important thing. This is the final thought that will close our treatment of Deuteronomy.

We have already examined how to use the law, but we must emphasize one final point. Scripture has a big picture which matters more than

---

8. Bird, *Evangelical Theology*, 2nd ed., 306–11.
9. Leder *Waiting for the Land*, 196.

the specifics. The big picture is the great commandments of the Torah, to love God and to love one's neighbor, both taught in their greatest detail in Deuteronomy in its exposition of the Ten Commandments. We want to stress that the preeminence of those commandments remain unchanged, as is undeniably demonstrated by Jesus's repetition of these commandments (e.g., Mark 12:28–32). In other words, the Bible as a whole maintains a unified ethic: the greatest commandment and highest duty of believers is to love the Lord and to love their neighbor as themselves. *This is the big picture.* This will always be the big picture. "In other words, here are the primary values, the overriding priorities, that govern the rest of the detailed legislation."[10]

Paul related love to the future: "Owe no one anything, except to love each other, for the one who loves another has fulfilled the law" (Rom 13:8). That is, love is a debt believers owe to our neighbors, and the future demands that we keep practicing it, but we can never exhaust that obligation. It is a debt we can never fully pay; the best we can do is to move into the future practicing love. There are many rules in the OT, but love governs them all.[11] So, our focus is not the rules, but love of the God who has expressed in Scripture how we show our love for him, and others, and how we avoid offending the God we love.

The corollary to this is that we must keep the "prime directive" as the prime directive. We must not allow ourselves to fall into legalism or rule-keeping as our great priority. They are brought up so often in the NT because their pitfall is a perennial temptation. Christians have also sometimes been famous (or infamous) for rule-keeping, or for trying to force others to keep their rules. But Christians are not to be "rule people," but "love people."

So, the big picture of Scripture, beginning in the Torah, and especially in Deuteronomy, and continuing unabated throughout the OT and the NT, is loving God and loving neighbor. This is particularly applied in the Bible to the weak and the vulnerable, often denominated in Scripture as the orphan, the widow and foreigners, an emphasis which is paramount in Deuteronomy (1:16; 5:14–15; 10:18–19; 14:28–29; 16:11–12; 24:17–19; 24:19–22; 27:19; 31:12).[12]

---

10. Wright, *OT Ethics*, 305.
11. Wright, *OT Ethics*, 305.
12. This list is from Campbell & Campbell, *Invitation to the Torah*, 120–21.

Deuteronomy's *Shema* (Deut 6:4–5) is the big picture, what Jesus called "the most important" (Mark 12:29): "Hear, O Israel: The LORD our God, the LORD is one. You shall love the LORD your God with all your heart and with all your soul and with all your might." This is what commandments 1–4 explain. The rest of the big picture is clarified by Jesus (Mark 12:31), "The second is this: 'You shall love your neighbor as yourself.' There is no other commandment greater than these." This is what commandments 5–10 expound.

Deuteronomy is *the* Bible book that explains love of God and love of neighbor. May we who call ourselves "Christians" be famous for these two primary values and overriding priorities.

Martin Luther is reputed to have written,

> If I profess with loudest voice and clearest exposition every portion of the truth of God except that little point which the world and the Devil are at that moment attacking, I am not confessing Christ, however boldly I may be professing Christ. Where the battle rages, there the loyalty of the soldier is proved, and to be steady on all the battlefield besides, is mere flight and disgrace if he flinches at that point.[13]

We may conclude our study of Deuteronomy by acknowledging that while defending biblical truths that are currently besieged is important, surely the great battle for followers of Jesus Christ does not lie here. Defending the details is not the key battle. *The* battle is surely to keep the main thing as the main thing! It is to avoid what C. S. Lewis called, "Christianity And," a substituting for the faith itself a Christian coloring to whatever happens to be the cultural fashion of the moment.[14] Jesus told us what the main thing is. It is to love God and love our neighbor. Whatever else changes, that remains Jesus's, and the Bible's, greatest commandment for our lives of faith. May we embrace what Jane finally learned: "Lead me in the path of your commandments, for I delight in it" (Ps 119:35).

---

13. The quote's source is actually disputed. Whatever its origin, the sentiment is stimulating.

14. Lewis, *Screwtape Letters*, 126. For brilliant treatments of how Christians tend to be tempted into such substitutions see, besides *Screwtape Letters*, Guinness, *Gravedigger Files* and Guinness and Seel, *No God But God*.

Bibliography

Alter, Robert. *The Art of Biblical Narrative*. Rev. ed. New York: Basic, 2011.
Bailey, Kenneth E. *Jacob and the Prodigal: How Jesus Retold Israel's Story*. Downers Grove, IL: InterVarsity, 2003.
Bar-Efrat, Shimon. *Narrative Art in the Bible*. Oxford: T & T Clark, 2004.
Beale, G. K. "Sunday Sabbath Observance of the Church." In *A New Testament Biblical Theology: The Unfolding of the Old Testament in the New*, 775–801. Grand Rapids, MI: Baker Academic, 2011.
Bird, Michael F. *Evangelical Theology: A Biblical and Systematic Introduction*. 2nd ed. Grand Rapids, MI: Zondervan, 2020.
Blackman, Philip, ed. *The Mishnah*. 7 vols. New York: Judaica, 1977.
Block, Daniel I. *Deuteronomy*. The NIV Application Commentary (NIVAC). Grand Rapids, MI: Zondervan, 2012.
———. *The Gospel According to Moses: Theological and Ethical Reflections on the Book of Deuteronomy*. Eugene, OR: Cascade, 2012.
Braulik, Georg. "The Sequence of the Laws in Deuteronomy 12–26 and in the Decalogue." In Christensen, Duane L., ed. *A Song of Power and the Power of Song: Essays on the Book of Deuteronomy*, 313–35. Winona Lake, IN: Eisenbrauns, 1993.
Bruce, F. F. *The Epistles of John*. Old Tappan, NJ: Fleming H. Revell, 1970.
Brueggemann, Walter. *Deuteronomy*. The Abingdon Old Testament Commentaries. Nashville: Abingdon, 2001.
Burgess, John P. *After Baptism: Shaping the Christian Life*. Louisville, KY: Westminster John Knox, 2005.
Calvin, John. *Commentaries on the Bible*, 23 volumes, 500th Anniversary edition. Grand Rapids, MI: Baker, 2009. Olive Tree e-book.
Calvin, John. *Institutes of the Christian Religion*, 2 vols. Edited by John T. McNeill. Louisville: Westminster John Knox, 1960.
Campbell, George Van Pelt, and Derek Van Pelt Campbell. *Invitation to the Torah: A Guide to Reading, Teaching, and Preaching the Pentateuch*. Eugene, OR: Wipf & Stock, 2020.
Carson, D. A., ed. *From Sabbath to Lord's Day: A Biblical, Historical and Theological Investigation*. Grand Rapids, MI: Zondervan, 1982.
Charry, Ellen T. *By the Renewing of Your Minds: The Pastoral Function of Christian Doctrine*. New York: Oxford University Press, 1997.
Christensen, Duane L. *Deuteronomy*, 2 vols. The Word Biblical Commentary. Waco: Word, 2018.

Bibliography

———, ed. *A Song of Power and the Power of Song: Essays on the Book of Deuteronomy*. Winona Lake, IN: Eisenbrauns, 1993.

Churchill, Winston. *The Gathering Storm* New York: RosettaBooks, 2013.

Copan, Paul. *Is God a Moral Monster? Making Sense of the Old Testament God*. Grand Rapids, MI: Baker, 2011.

Craigie, P. C. *The Book of Deuteronomy*. The New International Commentary on the Old Testament (NICOT). Grand Rapids, MI: Eerdmans, 1976.

Cranfield, C. E. B. *A Critical and Exegetical Commentary on the Epistle to the Romans*, 2 vols. The International Critical Commentary (ICC). Edinburgh: T&T Clark, 1979.

———. "Love." In *Theological Word Book of the Bible (TWBB)*, edited by Alan Richardson. New York: Macmillan, 1951, 131–36.

DeRouchie, Jason S. *How to Understand and Apply the Old Testament: Twelve Steps from Exegesis to Theology*. Phillipsburg, NJ: P&R, 2017.

Driver, S. R. *A Critical and Exegetical Commentary on Deuteronomy*. 3rd ed. The International Critical Commentary (ICC). Edinburgh: T. & T. Clark, 1902.

Dunn, James D. G. *Romans*, 2 vols. The Word Biblical Commentary. Dallas: Word, 1988.

Edwards, James R. *The Gospel According to Mark*. The Pillar New Testament Commentary (PNTC). Grand Rapids, MI: Eerdmans, 2001. Olive Tree e-book.

Edwards, Jonathan. *The Works of Jonathan Edwards: Ethical Writings*, edited by Paul Ramsey. New York: Yale University Press, 1989.

France, R. T. *Mark*. New International Greek Testament Commentary (NIGTC). Grand Rapids, MI: Eerdmans, 2002. Olive Tree e-book.

Franklin, Benjamin. *Poor Richard's Almanack* Waterloo, Iowa: The U. S. C., 1914.

Fukuyama, Francis *Trust: The Social Virtues and the Creation of Prosperity*. New York: Free, 1995.

Gordon, T. David. *Promise, Law, Faith: Covenant-Historical Reasoning in Galatians*. Peabody, MA: Hendrickson, 2019.

Grudem, Wayne A., ed. *Are Miraculous Gifts for Today? Four Views*. Grand Rapids, MI: Zondervan, 1996.

Guinness, Os. *The Gravedigger Files: Papers on the Subversion of the Modern Church*. Downers Grove, IL: InterVarsity, 1983.

Guinness, Os, and John Seel, eds. *No God But God: Breaking with the Idols of our Age*. Chicago: Moody, 1992.

Gundry, Stanley N., series ed. *Show them No Mercy: Four Views on God and the Canaanite Genocide*, with contributions by C. S. Cowles, E. H. Merrill, Dainiel L. Gard, and Tremper Longman III. Grand Rapids, MI: Zondervan, 2003.

Harrelson, Walter. *The Ten Commandments and Human Rights*. Philadelphia: Fortress 1980.

Hebrew and Aramaic Lexicon of the Old Testament. Ludwig Koehler, Walter Baumgartner, and Johann J. Stamm. Translated and edited under the supervision of Mervyn E. J. Richardson. 4 vols. Leiden: Brill, 1994–1999.

Hooker, Morna D. *The Gospel According to Saint Mark*. Black's New Testament Commentary (BNTC). Peabody, MA: Hendrickson, 1992.

Hopkins, Ezekiel. "The Ten Commandments." In *Classical Evangelical Essays in Old Testament Interpretation*, Walter C. Kaiser Jr., ed. Eugene, OR: Wipf & Stock, 2008.

Imes, Carmen Joy. *Bearing God's Name: Why Sinai Still Matters*. Downers Grove, IL: InterVarsity, 2019.

Bibliography

———. *Bearing YHWH's Name at Sinai: A Reexamination of the Name Command of the Decalogue*. Bulletin for Biblical Research Supplements 19 (2018). Richard S. Hess and Craig L. Blomberg, eds. University Park, PA: Eisenbrauns, 2018.

Kaiser, Walter C. Jr. *Toward Old Testament Ethics*. Grand Rapids, MI: Zondervan, 1983.

Kitchen, Kenneth. *Ancient Orient and Old Testament*, Downers Grove, IL: InterVarsity, 1966.

———. *On the Reliability of the Old Testament*. Grand Rapids, MI: Eerdmans, 2006.

Kaufmann, Stephen A. "The Structure of the Deuteronomic Law." *Maarav* 1/2 (1978–79) 105–58.

Langworth, Richard. *Churchill by Himself*. New York: Public Affairs, 2011.

Last, Jonathan V. *What to Expect When No One's Expecting*. New York: Encounter, 2013.

King Jr., Martin Luther. *Letter from Birmingham Jail*. London: Penguin, UK, 2018.

King Jr., Martin Luther. *Strength to Love*. Minneapolis, MN: Fortress, 2010.

Leder, Arie C. *Waiting for the Land: The Story Line of the Pentateuch*. Phillipsburg, NJ: P&R, 2010.

Levinson, Bruce. *The Jewish Study Bible*, edited by Adele Berlin and Marc Zvi Brettler. Oxford: Oxford University Press. 2004.

Lewis, C. S. *The Screwtape Letters*. Uhrichsville, OH: Barbour and Company, 1940.

Lohfink, Norbert. "Distribution of the Functions of Power: The Laws Concerning Public Offices in Deuteronomy 16:18–18:22." In Duane L. Christensen, ed., *A Song of Power and the Power of Song: Essays on the Book of Deuteronomy*, 336–52. Winona Lake, IN: Eisenbrauns, 1993.

———. *Theology of the Pentateuch*. Translated by Linda M. Maloney. Minneapolis: Fortress, 1994.

Lundbom, Jack R. *Deuteronomy: A Commentary*. Grand Rapids, MI: Eerdmans, 2013.

Marshall, I. Howard. *The Epistles of John*. Grand Rapids, MI: Eerdmans, 1978.

Marx, Karl, and Friedrich Engels. *The Communist Manifesto*. Translated by Samuel Moore; edited by Joseph Katz. 1848; first English edition, 1888. Reprint. New York: Simon & Schuster, 1964.

Mayes, A. D. H. *Deuteronomy*. The New Century Bible. London: Marshall, Morgan & Scott, 1979.

McConville, J. Gordon, *Deuteronomy*. Downers Grove, IL: InterVarsity, 2002.

———. *Grace in the End: A Study in Deuteronomic Theology*. Grand Rapids, MI: Zondervan, 1993.

McGrath, Alister. *What's the Point of Theology? Wisdom, Wellbeing and Wonder*. London: SPCK, 2022.

Millar, Gary J. *Now Choose Life: Theology and Ethics in Deuteronomy*. Grane Rapids: Eerdmans, 1998.

Miller, Patrick D. *Deuteronomy*. Interpretation: A Bible Commentary for Teaching and Preaching. Louisville: Westminster John Knox, 1990.

Merrill, Eugene H. *Deuteronomy: An Exegetical and Theological Exposition of Holy Scripture, NIV Text*. The New American Commentary. Nashville: Broadman & Holman, 1994.

———. *Everlasting Dominion: A Theology of the Old Testament*. Nashville, Broadman & Holman, 2006.

Morris, Leon. *New Testament Theology*. Grand Rapids, MI: Zondervan, 1986.

———. *Testaments of Love: A Study of Love in the Bible*. Grand Rapids, MI: Eerdmans, 1981.

Bibliography

Nelson, Richard D. *Deuteronomy*. The Old Testament Library (OTL). Louisville, KY: Westminster John Knox, 2004.

Olson, Dennis T. *The Death of the Old and the Birth of the New: The Framework of the Book of Numbers and the Pentateuch*. Brown Judaic Studies 71. Chico, California: Scholars, 1985.

Passmore, John. *The Perfectibility of Man*. 3rd ed. Indianapolis: Liberty Fund, 2000. https://oll.libertyfund.org/titles/passmore-the-perfectibility-of-man .

Piper, John. *God's Passion for His Glory: Living the Vision of Jonathan Edwards*, with the complete text of *The End for Which God Created the World*. Wheaton, IL: Crossway, 1998.

Peter, Laurence J. *Peter's Quotations: Ideas for our Time*. New York: Bantam, 1977.

Rad, Gerhard von. *Deuteronomy*. The Old Testament Library (OTL). Louisville: Westminster John Knox, 1966.

Ramsey, Paul, ed. *The Works of Jonathan Edwards: Ethical Writings*. New York: Yale University Press, 1989.

Rosner, Brian S. *Paul and the Law: Keeping the Commandments of God*. Downers Grove, IL: InterVarsity, 2013.

Ross, Allen P. *Creation and Blessing: A Guide to the Study and Exposition of the Book of Genesis*. Grand Rapids, MI: Baker, 1988.

Sailhamer, John H. *The Meaning of the Pentateuch: Revelation, Composition, and Interpretation*. Downers Grove, IL: IVP Academic, 2009.

———. *The Pentateuch as Narrative: A Biblical-Theological Commentary*. Grand Rapids, MI: Zondervan, 1992.

Schorch, Stefan. " 'A Young Goat in its Mother's Milk'? Understanding an Ancient Prohibition." *Vetus Testamentum* 60 (2010) 116–30.

Spurgeon, Charles. *Strengthen My Spirit: Daily Devotional Insights*, compiled by Jennifer Hahn. Uhrichsville, OH: Barbour, 2004.

Stott, John. *The Epistles of John: An Introduction and Commentary*. Tyndale New Testament Commentary (TNTC). Grand Rapids, MI: Eerdmans, 1978.

Strauss, Mark L. *Mark*. Zondervan Exegetical Commentary on the New Testament (ZECNT). Grand Rapids, MI: Zondervan Academic, 2014.

Thompson, J. J. *Deuteronomy: An Introduction and Commentary*. Tyndale Old Testament Commentary (TOTC). Grand Rapids, MI: Eerdmans, 1974.

Tigay, Jeffrey H. *Deuteronomy*. The Jewish Publication Society Torah Commentary (JPS). Philadelphia: Jewish Publication Society, 1996.

Turner, Ian. "Going Beyond What is Written or Learning to Read? Discovering OT/NT Broad Reference." *Journal of the Evangelical Theological Society* 61 (2018) 577–94.

VanDrunen, David. *Politics After Christendom: Political Theology in a Fractured World*. Grand Rapids, MI: Zondervan Academic, 2020.

Waltke, Bruce K., with Charles Yu. *An Old Testament Theology: An Exegetical, Canonical, and Thematic Approach*. Grand Rapids, MI: Zondervan, 2007.

Walvoord, John F. *The Millennial Kingdom: A Basic Text in Pre-millennial Theology*. Grand Rapids, MI: Zondervan, 1959.

Weinfeld, Moshe. *Deuteronomy 1–11: A New Translation with Introduction and Commentary*. The Anchor Bible (AB) 5. New York: Doubleday, 1991.

Wenham, Gordon J. *The Book of Leviticus*. Grand Rapids, MI: Eerdmans, 1979.

———. "Deuteronomy and the Central Sanctuary." *Tyndale Bulletin* 22 (1971) 103–18.

———. *Genesis 1–15*. Dallas: Word, 1987.

———. "The Restoration of Marriage Reconsidered." *Journal of Jewish Studies* 17 (1966) 1–11.

Williamson, Lamar Jr. *Mark*. Interpretation: A Bible Commentary for Teaching and Preaching. Louisville: Westminster John Knox, 2009.

Woods, Ted. *Deuteronomy: An Introduction and Commentary*. Tyndale Old Testament Commentary (TOTC). Downers Grove, IL: InterVarsity, 2011.

Wolterstorff, Nicholas. *Justice: Rights and Wrongs*. Princeton: Princeton University Press, 2008.

Wright, Christopher J. H. *Deuteronomy*. Understanding the Bible Commentary. Grand Rapids, MI: Baker, 1996.

———. *Old Testament Ethics for the People of God*. Downers Grove, IL: InterVarsity, 2004.